REASONING

REASONING

Michael Scriven

McGRAW-HILL BOOK COMPANY

New York   St. Louis   San Francisco   Auckland   Bogotá   Düsseldorf
Johannesburg   London   Madrid   Mexico   Montreal   New Delhi   Panama   Paris
São Paulo   Singapore   Sydney   Tokyo   Toronto

REASONING

2 3 4 5 6 7 8 9 0   DODO   7 8 3 2 1 0 9 8 7

This book was set in Times Roman by Rocappi, Inc.
The editors were Jean Smith and James R. Belser;
the cover was designed by Albert M. Cetta;
the production supervisor was Charles Hess.
The drawings were done by Vantage Art, Inc.
R. R. Donnelley & Sons Company was printer and binder.

Library of Congress Cataloging in Publication Data

Scriven, Michael.
    Reasoning.

    Includes index.
    1. Reasoning.   I.   Title.
BC177.S37   160   76-49937
ISBN 0-07-055882-5

To Mary Anne Warren
whose inspiration and support
caused this book to be
and benefited what it became

Contents

The Aims of the Book

1 To improve your skill in *analyzing* and *evaluating arguments and presentations* of the kind you find in everyday discourse (news media, discussions, advertisements), textbooks, and lectures.

2 To improve your skill in *presenting arguments, reports and instructions* clearly and persuasively.

3 To improve your *critical instincts,* that is, your immediate judgments of your attitudes toward the communications and behavior of others and yourself, so that you consistently approach them with the standards of reason and the attitude of reasonableness.

4 To improve your *knowledge* about the facts and arguments relevant to a large number of important contemporary issues in politics, education, ethics, and several practical fields.

These are *practical* aims but not *narrow* practical aims: the third one, in particular, is very far-reaching and requires a whole shift of values for most of us. So this is intended to be a powerful, as well as a practical, book using practical, everyday examples of the kind that a citizen, especially a citizen-student, runs into all the time.

The text starts with a short discussion of reasoning itself, then explores the details of this approach, and then gets down to practical procedures for improving one's reasoning skills. The discussions and examples always begin at a rather elementary level, but they get into harder material fairly quickly. If you are, or are hoping to be, a teacher or a lawyer, a scientist or an executive, what you learn here will be professional skills for you—vital professional skills. But for *any* citizen, they are also essential skills.

To the Student

You've just read what this book tries to do. It does it in some unusual ways, which are discussed in Chapter 2, as soon as we've talked about the general nature of reasoning in Chapter 1. But two special features of the book need to be called to your attention immediately. The first is that there is a substantial prize fund for the best criticism and/or suggestions for improving the book—a minimum of $250 in the first year after publication and more if the book sells well. I believe that consumers not only should, but can, improve products at least as much as the experts. At least half, and quite likely all, the awards will go to student suggestions—and their originators will be acknowledged in later editions.

The second point to keep in mind from the beginning is that the book is set up to allow you to move fast through any material that seems too easy for you. Believe me, it's there only because someone appeared to need it; but it won't get in your way if you remember that the "A quizzes," at the end of each chapter, are self-testing devices. You can skim any chapter quickly and then test yourself on the A quiz. If you get all but one or two answers correct, and can see why you're wrong on the others (or can give good reasons for thinking *I'm* wrong—in which case, write and tell me), then spend a little time thinking about the C quiz questions and move on to the next chapter. If you do worse than this, read the chapter carefully and try the B quiz (the "basic assignment quiz"), which your instructor will grade. While doing this more careful reading, check your comprehension by writing titles for the numbered sections in the space to the right of the number. (If you look at the last couple of chapters in the text, you'll see that the sections already have titles. See if you can do a similar job for the sections in the early chapters; it's a good basis for summarizing or outlining them.)

The first chapter is a bit more philosophical than the rest of the book. The second is more pedagogical than the rest. Be sure to try the third before you feel you've got into the wrong meeting.

Michael Scriven

To the Instructor

This book provides a basic structure on which you can elaborate or from which you can diverge in many ways. It can be assigned entirely as background reading for all the members of a class, or for those having difficulty in basic argument analysis skills; or the first two chapters can be assigned for background reading and the rest used as a text; or the entire book, plus some extra reading, can make a very full semester's course.

   The simplest procedure for its use is outlined in the preceding section ("To the Student"). Students should be assigned one (or more) chapters and asked to do the basic checkup, self-grading quiz at the end (Quiz A) for their own information. If they pass this (with no more than one or two errors), they should then do the B quiz for you, and also one or more of the questions in the C quiz. If you give them a free choice in C, they can suit their own interests better, but you'll have to discuss in class, or make written comments on, a number of different questions. That's good if you want to spend substantial time on that chapter. If you want to move faster, assign a particular question from the C quiz, and you'll only have to talk about or grade a single question. For example, you may want to avoid getting deeply into questionable issues about the nature of reason (Chapter 1) before getting into skill training. You could assign just one (or no) question from Quiz 1-C. But it is important to have each student turn in either Quiz 1-B or Quiz 2-B, preferably both, because you need to know whether you're dealing with some students with real reading deficiencies, an increasingly serious problem. One reason why Chapters 1 and 2 are there is to enable you to diagnose that problem fast. The B quiz in each chapter is to provide feedback to you (and possibly also to your students). If you need to be sure they're not over their heads, ask them to do the quiz and turn it in. It is designed for either anonymous or signed use, fast grading, and for either handback or retention.

A number of novel teaching procedures that you may find worth adopting are suggested at various places throughout, but especially in Chapter 2. No doubt you'll find that some of them don't suit your style of teaching or are unsatisfactory in other ways, and you'll have ideas of your own. I'd appreciate hearing about both your reactions and your own ideas. In any case, a glance at Chapter 2 may interest you in the pedagogy of this approach, and Chapter 3 will give you a preview of the basic content. Different levels of student ability can be accommodated in the way described in the instructions to the student. Various interesting topics are raised in the "advanced" quiz on each chapter, enough to hold your better students' attention, in most cases. If those options are still not enough, you will probably have a dozen others occur to you—don't forget that I value your suggestions enough to have set up a prize fund for them. A proportion of the royalties from this book will always, as they should, go into that fund for rewarding those who help to improve the book, teachers as well as students.

I believe reasoning is the most worthwhile, though one of the hardest, subjects to teach. It would be absurd to suppose I alone can teach it half as well as we can together, with users (students and teachers) helping to do it better, and the author serving as a coordinator—and as a contributor, too. No other approach really makes sense. Future editions of the book will be steadily and, I expect, extensively redone in the light of our joint experience. No suggestion, however radical, will be dismissed without careful consideration and, when possible, a careful reply. Those adopted will of course be acknowledged, whether or not rewarded.

There are a number of fascinating technical issues involved in the problem of approaching the teaching of reasoning, whether as an introduction to other philosophy courses or science courses or composition or law school, or just as a general-purpose tool for the thinking person. At some point, it may seem worth discussing these issues at length in a separate teacher's guide, but for the moment let me make two points that seem crucial. The first is that the evidence from educational psychology seems entirely overwhelming with respect to one point, namely, that so-called "transfer of learning" or "generalization" always turns out to be less than educators had previously supposed. It is not so long ago that Latin was justified because it was supposed to make people think more clearly. Then the same was said of mathematics. Then of science. But the fact is that no significant transfer from the standard approaches to any of these subjects to the analysis of problems outside the subject matter they cover has ever (to my knowledge) been demonstrated, whereas the incredible *incompetence* of a brilliant mathematician in handling business affairs, of a physicist expounding on politics or psychology, has been too often authenticated to be treated as aberrant. (The extreme example of this was a study of teaching children how to tell time which revealed they couldn't transfer their mastery with clock faces with one design of numerals to even modest success when the numerals were changed.)

It follows that one has to view with great skepticism the very idea that formal logic is likely to help improve reasoning skill. What it improves is skill in doing formal logic. The syllogism was probably nearer to reality (though not to comprehensiveness) than the propositional calculus, but not near enough to make it useful in handling the average editorial or columnist today. It's not incidental that there are ferocious unresolved issues even within the theory of the syllogism and in interpreting the connectives of the propositional calculus.

But even if those issues were somehow settled to the satisfaction of the specialist, the difficulty of using the results surfaces in another way, which can be put as follows. The use of any calculus to handle problems that surface in reality (in natural language) involves three steps. *Encoding* the original problem into its formalized representation; computing or *transforming* it, using the formalized version of the problem; and *decoding* that, i.e., translating it back into the original language or real-world terms. This is what we do when we use math to solve problems of making change or designing planes; and this is what we have to do in applying formal logic. The attraction of the whole procedure lies in the reliability of the transformations made within the calculus. But unless the reliability of the encoding and decoding steps is at least as good as that of the transformation steps, we may gain nothing from the use of the calculus. And the problem with formal logic is that the encoding step, particularly, is just about as debatable (in anything but trivial arguments where there's no need to use the calculus) as the assessment of the original argument. A similar argument shows why the attempt to make a Newtonian science out of psychology has been such a dismal failure. And it shows why computerization often fails to solve applied problems.

It is for these reasons that I believe the only way to improve reasoning skills is by staying very close to real examples. One can use checklists; simple devices for display and abbreviation; paradigm examples; and handy labels.

But a calculus is a diversion one can't afford; it is a combine-harvester when we need a carving knife.

One might suppose that the preceding argument establishes a strong case for the "fallacies approach." It might, except that the fallacies generally turn out not to be fallacies—unless one builds into the identification process, and hence into the labels, all the skills needed for analysis without the taxonomy of fallacies. In that case one has made it a formal approach, and the encoding (i.e., diagnosing) step has become the tricky one. There are residual elements of the fallacies approach in what we do here—we do use some pejorative names for certain types of error, but only as a way to wind up, or put a seal on, the analysis. The hard work comes first.

I sometimes think one can best spotlight the gap between formal logic and real reasoning by pointing out that almost every real argument involves assumptions, but that, as far as I know, there has never been an even moderately successful attempt to analyze the concept of an assumption. (The enthymeme approach is not even moderately successful as a pragmatic device.) Without such an analysis, effective criticism of an argument, or an arguer, is hopelessly crippled. I am sure the analysis I give has faults (and I hope to hear of them from you), but at least it seems to help in handling most arguments.

There are a dozen other examples; the status of the "paradoxes of material (or strict, or formal) implication" is one. These have been called paradoxes, "paradoxes," and logical truths. In the context of practical reason, they are just symptoms of incorrect analysis, no more, no less. It is merely an error to suggest that a false (or necessary false) proposition implies every proposition; it's not paradoxical, quasi-paradoxical, or true. It's even false to say that a proposition implies itself. No better example of the lack of interest in reasoning, as opposed to interest in formal systems, can be given than the efforts to substitute formal simplicity for practical utility in the development and assessment of modern symbolic logic. Halfway (though hardworking) efforts ranging from those of C. I. Lewis to those of Anderson and Belnap simply do not tackle the need to distinguish between the relations (1) "guarantees the truth of," (2) "is a good reason for believing," and (3) "allows the derivation of." The truth of p guarantees the truth of p, but it sure isn't a good reason for believing it. The falsity of p allows the derivation of q (in the propositional calculus), but neither guarantees its truth nor provides a good reason for believing it. This book is about good reasons, not repetitions or transformations. It's just a start on what shouldn't be but is, almost an untouched subject.

I now turn to some particular issues, logical, terminological, and pedagogical.

On terminology, I have given up the fight on "valid," which I believe is now used in the scientific literature as well as in common parlance to cover the truth of the premises as well as the soundness of the inferences in an argument (as in "valid reason"). However, I do not support the broader usage: I simply put the weight on "sound inferences" versus "true premises." But I draw the line at "infers" used to mean "implies" and I spend some time teaching the distinction. I abandon efforts to be strict about symbolizing the use/mention distinction with quotation marks, since if Quine can't get it right in his text, I suspect it's not an exact distinction. Instead, I use quotes as they are normally used, for quotation for reference which is not otherwise obvious, or for "raised eyebrows." Although I distinguish "deductive" from "inductive" in the usual way, I do not argue for the distinction as being sharp, and nothing in the analytical procedures depends on deciding whether a raw argument is deductive or inductive, since most of them can be reconstructed either way. There's essentially no technical jargon in this text; the instructor will have to judge whether the loss is serious, and can always add some on a handout sheet or two.

Most of the pedagogical devices are discussed at length in Chapter 2, since I think students should understand and discuss them, and they make good subjects for arguments and analysis. Aids for the instructor will be added in an instructor's guide if there are later editions, including extra quizzes, tear-out answer sheets and templates for rapid correction, comments on the B and C quiz questions, and more references. Two procedures worth mentioning here are having the students correct one another's quizzes at the start of a class in order to get fast feedback to you and to them about progress; and having them give their quizzes anonymously, which reduces anxiety about a possible prejudice on your part originating with their poor early performance. To do this, you simply have them turn in the paper with a code number (any six-figure number they select) instead of a name, and you put the papers on the desk in numerical order at the next class, leaving five minutes early so they can recover their papers in your absence. If my students do well, I encourage them to start signing their papers so as to build up a buffer against an unluckly performance on the midterm and final exams (which have to be signed). And so on; many of you have more ingenious teaching procedures, I'm sure.

I believe in pretests on the first day of class, and the last example in Quiz 2-B will serve quite well for that purpose. There are several examples from the later chapter quizzes that will serve as posttests, and you can then compare performances to see if you think the course teaches something useful.

Question 4 on Quiz 2-B is the only one on which we have good, recent national data; the only (!) flaw is that the "official" answers—indeed, the alternatives offered—are not persuasive. This is the National Assessment of Education Progress question, and the official answers are: 4-1, *d;* 4-2, *c;* and 4-3, *e.* The percentages getting the "correct" answers, in the population of seventeen-year-olds, in 1970–1971, were 45, 24, 29. Young adults (ages twenty-six to thirty-five), scored about the same (46, 29, 31). The latter group chose "I don't know" 8 percent, 3 percent, and 30 percent of the time. On very simple comprehension tests, with obvious correct answers, these groups still failed about one-third of the time. Your students will virtually all do better than this, of course, but the baseline data is useful in counseling the weaker ones.

ACKNOWLEDGMENTS

Special thanks are due to Bob Ennis and Mary Anne Warren, who have shared the teaching of my extension course Speed Reasoning; to Bob Cunningham and Bob Struckman, who used a pilot version of this course at the University of San Francisco, as did Mary Anne Warren at Sonoma State; to Brian Holm and Larry Wright, who helped with the Analytical Reasoning course at the University of Indiana; and to Douglas Gasking, who taught the first course in logic I ever attended and never forgot. This edition incorporates many benefits from Alan Walworth's and Brian Holm's critical reading. On the production side, many thanks to Judy Simmons for an outstanding job in preparing the original typescript and to Sondra Harris for modifying it.

                                                          Michael Scriven

Chapter 1

The Nature of Reasoning

1-1

This first chapter is not intended to improve your skill in reasoning as such, but to give you some general understanding of what it is and what it isn't. Consequently, the basic tests on this chapter and the next, which lay out the special procedures of this text, are straight tests of your ability to comprehend what you read. And that's the prerequisite skill in reasoning, so it's extremely important that you test yourself on it. Very few people read carefully, and starting in on argument analysis when you haven't even got clear what the argument says is a waste of time. Moreover, there's no sharp line between reading and reasoning, because reading with understanding requires that you see at least "obvious" implications of what's being said, which means making inferences from what's being said, which is reasoning. If you look at reading tests, you'll see that some of the items are really tests of reasoning; and so they should be. So the tests on this chapter are not only tests of your straight reading care, but also tests of this very basic kind of reasoning. Here's an example. Suppose you read a long newspaper article which states that Prime Minister Gandhi has imposed press censorship in India. One question to test your reading skill might be: Does freedom of the press still exist in India (at the time of the article)? The obvious answer is, no. But notice that the question tests understanding and not mere rote memory, because freedom of the press is a technical phrase which does not occur in the original. You have had to do a bit of translating and comparing of the language in the question with the language in the original in order to answer the question. That process of transforming and comparing language is the most basic kind of reasoning process; and it's also part of what's referred to as understanding the original material. So even basic quizzes at the end of Chapters 2 and 3 are partially tests of reasoning itself as well as tests of a prerequisite for reasoning, namely, reading carefully. About one-third of the answers to questions that I use in a doctoral examination for school principals are incorrectly directed because the principal has not read the question carefully. You may find that a useful by-product of this text is an improved ability to read carefully—and when it comes to reading contracts of sale or descriptions of a referendum or motion on which you have to vote, careful reading is not an exercise in nit-picking, though it may strike you that way at times when you're doing the exercises.

So reasoning begins with a careful reading—reading with understanding. But it goes on to more complicated matters like giving and analyzing arguments. It is the process of systematically working toward the solution of a problem, toward the understanding of a phenomenon, toward the truth of the matter. And that's when it becomes, not quite the exclusive property, but the main power, of humanity.

1-2

Reasoning is the only ability that makes it possible for humans to rule the earth and to ruin it.

All the other alleged distinctions between us and the other life forms on the planet turn out to be illusory. Of course, they can see and hear and move and smell better than we can. They have and use languages that do the simple tasks of language, but not languages subtle and strong enough for reasoning in any explicit sense. They have tools, but not tools as powerful as reason. They make tools but not tools as strong as an argument. They have standards of behavior which they enforce by systems of rewards and punishment; but they lack systems of law and codes of ethics because their standards are not so precisely formulated, so general, so sensitive to the special case as good codes can be; their systems are not rewritten in the light of reasons for reform, are not able to be as fast-acting and flexible as a reasoned code can be. Many of our own systems of law are far from fully reasoned, of course; we are here talking of what is possible, proper, and sometimes done.

1-3

Reasoning isn't all done with language, but that's how it's usually conveyed and mostly how it's taught, and certainly how it's written and thus best recorded; and, in fact, it's a help for this text rather than a limitation if we make a virtue of necessity and emphasize the linguistic approach. For you don't want to be able just to reason because reasoning helps you to work out correct answers for yourself. You also want to be able to persuade others of those answers, or of the weaknesses in their own answers because you often need their help or permission, or want to help them. "Let us reason together" is an invitation to communication, not to independent meditation.

1-4

It's essential to a democracy that its citizenry be both independently capable of reasoning about the issues that confront it *and* able to use the social force of reason to persuade one another, so as to reach a social solution that can then be enacted with good support. To help with this second function, we put a great deal of stress on *communicating* arguments, on reasoning with others—much more than most books on logic do. But this isn't an introduction to "rhetoric" in the cynical sense ("mere rhetoric") or debating skills as such; its principal commitment is to improving the reader's ability to give and identify sound arguments (and to criticize unsound ones). Not everyone is persuaded by sweet reason, but not everyone is persuaded by being knocked on the head, either. There are moral advantages—respect for the right of others to make up their own minds as well as political and legal ones—for the use of reason.

1-5

But above all, there's one supreme advantage for the use of reason, privately or publicly. Reasoning is the best guide we have to the truth. That doesn't mean you should never listen to your "inner voice," your instincts, or to authorities; it just means that you ought to use reason to decide when to listen to them. They are sometimes good indicators of truth, sometimes not. Reason is the only way to tell and even it won't tell you for sure, when to listen to instinct or authority. Which is why it's more important than either. There's nothing unreasonable about trusting your own negative judgment about the honesty of a salesperson, even if you can't formulate exactly why

you're dubious. But there would be something unreasonable about continuing to trust that instinctive judgment if it turns out to be wrong most of the
time. Reason is the overall best indicator of the way to the truth, which is
quite different from saying that having explicit reasons, being able to give a
complete sound argument, is always necessary to justify a judgment or an
action. You, or your teachers, or experience, may well have trained your
instincts to be a good guide to the truth.

1-6

How can one be sure that reason is the best guide to truth? Isn't that just a
dogma? We can be sure simply because anything that turns out to be a
reliable guide to truth—for example, the instincts of an experienced auto
mechanic—is what reason tells you to follow unless something better turns
up. Reason operates on the principle of "If you can't lick them, join them."
If you can't find an explicit and virtually bulletproof argument that will
settle an issue, fall back on whatever you have that looks better than nothing; it's still a reason. In short, of course, you have to use a little reason to
decide whether you have something else—like an intuition, a clue, or an
expert—that is better than nothing. So, though you're not always in the
position of having an explicitly statable reason or argument for your decision, action, or conclusion, you should always at least have an indirect argument for it, that is, an argument (a reason) for heeding whatever you're
using instead of a direct argument. Why? Because you want and need the
truth, whether it's about diets, insurance policies, drugs, the use of violence,
or long-distance cruising in sailboats, and that's all that reason is—the best
indicator of truth.

Suppose someone claims to have come up with a rival to reason, a new
magical approach to knowledge. Suppose this person turns out to be able to
predict earthquakes or diagnose illness or prescribe therapy better than all
the experts and scientists we have at the time. What does reason tell you to
do? It demands that you accept the new expert. How did you come to this
decision? By comparing the track records of the old experts with the record
of the new prophet. Which was, of course, the reasonable thing to do. You
didn't abandon reason. You just used it to abandon some old prophets, some
superceded indicators of the truth. Those who offer alternatives to reason
are either mere hucksters, mere claimants to the throne, or there's a case to
be made for them; and of course, that case is an appeal to reason. Reason is
always the ultimate court of appeal—which is not to say that explicit direct
reasoning is always the best basis for judgment.

1-7

You won't find anything in this book that endorses the old prophets, except where their track record is still the best. It's nearly thirty years since I founded the first university-based society for the study of extrasensory perception in the Southern Hemisphere, and I have found the rigidity of established science to be so extreme as to refute every claim for the objectivity of the "scientific method" as advertised by most of those same scientists in their introductory lectures. Closed-mindedness and prejudice are about as rampant among scientists as anywhere else. True scientific method is open-minded, self-critical, flexible. Scientists are, in short, not as reasonable as they would like to think themselves. The great scientists are often true exceptions; they are nearly always attacked by their colleagues for their revolutionary ideas, not by using the standards of reason, but just by appealing to the prejudices then current. Being reasonable takes great skill and great sensitivity to the difference between "well-supported" and "widely accepted." It also takes courage, because it seldom corresponds to being popular.

1-8

So don't confuse reasoning with *calculating* or *measuring* or *ignoring emotions* or *appealing to authority*. Sometimes it involves these things and sometimes it rejects them. Basically, it involves working out, as carefully as you can, the best answer you can find, using whatever has value for that purpose and resisting the temptations of the impostors. Not easy at all, but there's no alternative way to the truth, no short cuts until they are certified by reason. And even then, you have to keep recertifying them, not letting them rest on their laurels.

1-9

What can this book do to help? It can teach you a basic strategy for the analysis of arguments, and hence for their presentation. It can teach you a dozen special tactics for handling traps that are easy to fall into (fallacies), or special situations in reasoning (like debate). It can teach you some general skills that apply to several interesting areas of reasoning, particularly scientific and moral reasoning. It can, incidentally, teach you a great deal about a number of controversial issues. But above all, it attempts to convey to you an attitude, an approach, a skill—the skill of reasoning, the attitude of reasonableness. Neither comes easily; the first requires much practice, and the second is a way of life and requires a lifetime of practice. If you can read these words, you can manage both, and nothing is more important to you and to your neighbors on this planet.

GENERAL INSTRUCTIONS FOR QUIZZES

The A quiz is for self-testing and self-teaching. Use it as follows:

1 Take a plain sheet of paper and cover the whole of the A quiz: this is the "slider" sheet.

2 Then move the sheet down, a line at a time, until you've seen the whole of the first question, and before even looking at the alternative possible answers (most of the early A quizzes are multiple-choice), ask yourself whether you know the answer. If you do, say it to yourself or out loud if you're by yourself; better still, write it on the slider sheet. That is, *make yourself formulate it completely;* don't just settle for "having a feeling," or thinking you know it, or "having a general idea" of what it is. It's essential to write your answer on the slider sheet if you're not dead sure it's correct because making yourself do that will often make you conscious of weaknesses in the answer.

3 If you're not sure what the answer is, move the slider down till you can see the first answer. Is that the correct answer? (Or is it one correct answer?) If you think so, circle the letter *a* that comes before it. You do not need to see the other answers to decide this. If you're not sure, slide the paper down a bit further till you can see the next answer. Think about it. Is it a—or the—right answer? If so, circle the letter *b* that identifies it. Notice that none, all, several, or just one of the alternatives may be correct; it's a weakness in the usual multiple-choice tests that they are unrealistic in that they give you immediately a set of alternative answers without asking you to try to think of them first and that they tell you that one of these is correct and only one. That doesn't correspond to reality at all. In reality, you usually have to think up possible answers yourself, and no one is around to tell you whether you've hit on a good one, or several good ones, or none. Sometimes looking or asking around, or reading ahead a little, will give you some further clues. Our procedure is pretty close to matching that real situation. If the right answer is none of those spelled out, then circle the last alternative ("Other") and write in the correct answer.

Now, pull the slider down a bit further and you'll come to the correct answer(s) and (usually) a short explanation of why it is, or they are, correct and the others aren't. If the explanation isn't enough, turn back in the chapter to where this point is discussed and reread that part. If that isn't enough, complain to the instructor or to me and we'll change the question or add to the text. Keep a copy of your complaints (and any other suggestions you have for improving the text) so that you can submit them as an entry in the Reasoning Prize competition.

The B quiz is an *assignment* quiz. It's usually to be handed in, though it can also be corrected in class, either by yourself or by someone else, while the instructor reads out and discusses the correct answers. Handle this test in the same way as the A quiz if you want to get the most out of it, but this time you'll be handing in the slider sheet, so you have to write the answers on it. Of course, you can correct them as and when the uncovering of more of the quiz leads you to a better answer. But you'll learn a great deal more if you try to answer before looking ahead, and a reasonable person will therefore exercise or develop the strength of mind to do it this way.

The C quiz is an *advanced assignment* quiz (or it may be used as a set of questions for enriching the classroom discussion or your own reflections). It will sometimes open up some of the deeper philosophical issues connected to the topics in the chapter, or it may give more difficult examples on the same issues as the B quiz.

QUIZ 1-A

1   "Reasoning is a particular skill in using thought and language, and it is proficiency in this skill, not the mere possession of language, which distinguishes the human species from the others on this planet."
   a   True (according to this text)
   b   False (according to this text)
   c   Other (explain)

Answer

Other species do possess very highly developed languages (the porpoises, most notably), but so far, they have not appeared to enable the species to perform even moderately complex reasoning tasks such as humans perform by the age of ten. If they do pass on information to one another on which they act (e.g., get out of a trap), as killer whales appear to do, one might call this a very simple kind of reasoning. But it's nothing like what is involved in, say, working out how a complicated toy operates when the instructions on the box aren't very clear—easy for most nine-year olds. So the quote seems correct and the first answer (alternative *a*) is the right one. Note that wolves systematically solve problems, for example, how to spring a cunningly laid trap, and it's useless to insist that they aren't reasoning when doing it. We're merely better at reasoning on most problems. There are many we can solve that no other species can, and a major part of our skill is the capacity to reason with a linguistic representation of the problem. It's a difference of degree, not of kind, but it's a very large difference of degree.

2   Reasoning has the function of helping us achieve the answers to our own individual problems, like which career to try for, which automobile to buy. But it also has another function, which is where the use of publicly accessible (that is, spoken or written) language to set out reasons becomes essential. That function involves:

    a Reflection on the individual's situation in the Universe
    b Using arithmetic
    c Writing poetry
    d Persuading others by argument
    e None of the above, but rather (fill in your preferred answer):

Answer

Meditation about our place in the universe is traditionally associated with Eastern religions and is often highly visual or feeling-oriented rather than verbal. There are speculations by astronomers on the same subject which do require language, but the example of the Eastern philosopher or sage shows that language isn't essential for option *a*, which is what the question asks. So that alternative isn't right.

Arithmetic is being used when we count the number of items in a box and multiply that by the number of boxes to get the total number of items in a shipment. All of that can be done in your head without any "external" use of language, so *b* is wrong.

Writing poetry requires the external use of language, but it's not necessary to set out reasons.

Persuading others can be done with a gun, which is nonlinguistic, but when done with arguments, it does involve the "publicly accessible use of language to set out reasons," so that's the right answer.

3 Dictators with complete power would not have to bother to persuade others, by reasoning, of the truth of any conclusions, since they could force compliance. More open forms of government, such as democracies, must, by contrast, rely heavily on:
    a Legislation
    b Sympathetic understanding of the needs of the people
    c Public proclamations
    d Public presentation of arguments
    e None of the above, but instead:

Answer

The first and third answers could just as well originate from a dictator "laying down the law" as from a democracy. Hence, they are not procedures that a "more open" form of government must use.

The second alternative is certainly a nice ideal for democracies and a useful support for democratic governments. But it's beside the point of the "contrast" requested in this question, which is obviously about the use of rational persuasion. (True statements aren't necessarily right answers.) The appropriate response is the fourth one, and the point is extremely important since it establishes a link between our political commitments and our educational obligations. The lack of curriculum content (in the high school particularly, but also in most colleges) devoted to reasoning about current political issues (as opposed to reasoning about old answers to old problems—history—or reciting creeds and constructs without real understanding of them) shows that we have not yet appreciated this point.

4 The process of systematically and skillfully considering and formulating arguments is a necessary step that must precede coming to any belief that can be called:
   a Reasonable
   b Rational
   c The result of reasoning
   d The result of thinking
   e Not intuitive

Answer

It's often perfectly reasonable to believe that the temperature is above the freezing point just from the feel of the air, without going through any process of argument. So a won't do, and b amounts to much the same, since the term "reasonable" means much the same as "rational," though one might say that the former is a little more warm-blooded than the latter. One talks of a reasonable person, meaning someone who will act reasonably, listen to reason, be moderate when moderation is appropriate, and so on. A rational person is someone with the capacity to reason and who uses that capacity, wherever it may lead. But the difference is usually insignificant.

The process described in the question is the reasoning process and hence the third option is correct, but the fourth describes a much wider class of beliefs including the result of irrational and fantastic thought processes, so it's wrong.

What's the opposite of intuitive thinking? One would normally say "deliberative," and that's pretty much what is described in the question, so the fifth answer might also be checked. But perception or memory or believing an authority fall in between, and if you thought of one of them, you should not have checked e.

Note Don't be lulled into thinking that one or more of the answers given must be correct. Sometimes you will have to fill in one of your own. But by now you have an idea of what we're looking for in your thinking. You shouldn't have much difficulty in Quiz 1-B. You may also find that your instructor has better answers than I do for some of these quizzes. This isn't basic mathematics, where almost everything is cut and dried; it's something more important—more widely useful and more fundamental to our thinking.

QUIZ 1-B

Put a name or a code number (depending on your instructor's request) on your slider sheet, which you should head "1-B." (The code number can be any six-figure number you think of—but make a note of it in your text.)

1 Observations of chimpanzee groups in Tanzania and at Yerkes make it clear they have a highly developed social code. In their relation to this code, they are:
   a No different from humans

  b Different in that the code can't be taught as easily as if they had expressed it in language

  c Different in that they can't change it quickly and advantageously as a result of consultation, discussion of new circumstances, and promulgation

  d Different in that no system of penalties for infractions of the code is known to members of the group

  e None of the above, but

2 "You can't reason without the use of language." Does the text commit itself to this view?

  a Yes

  b No

  c Other (explain)

3 "Verbal persuasion is another name for public reasoning."

  a Yes

  b No (give an example that supports your answer)

  c Other (explain)

4 The crucial general contrasts that are conceded to be legitimate in Chapter 1 are between:

  a Reason and instinct

  b Reason and cause

  c Reason and unreason

  d Reason and feelings

  e Reason and creativity

5 There is no arbitrariness in adherence to the standards of reason because:

  a There is no alternative

  b The alternatives are unreasonable

  c Adherence is required only if you're looking for the truth, and whatever turns out to be a guide to that is what reason requires you to use

  d Alternative approaches are legitimate only insofar as they are approaches to something besides truth

  e Other (explain)

6 "There's a sharp line between reasoning and reading."

  a Yes

  b No

  c Other (explain)

QUIZ 1-C

1 How would you tell whether dolphins or giant insects on an alien planet actually have a language in the same sense as we do?

2 Do sophisticated computers have a language in that sense?

3 Computers calculate (don't they?). Do they reason?

4 a Could one have any good reasons for complaint about government by a totally rational dictator?
  b Could one express them?

5 There are times when one's instincts seem to point in a different direction from one's reason. How might you describe such a situation other than as a clear counterexample to the claim that instinct and reason are compatible?

6 What is the difference between "counterintuitive" and "irrational"?

Chapter 2

Teaching and Learning Reasoning

In a textbook on reasoning, there ought to be some signs that the author has done some reasoning about textbooks on reasoning. You've already done one or more quizzes which illustrate some slightly novel approaches. Let's look at some general aims and special procedures of this text that you may find interesting.

Remember, this chapter has three functions: It introduces you to some unusual features and aims of the book that might otherwise seem puzzling; it will teach you something about the issues and controversies over various approaches to grading and testing, useful knowledge to have as you go on in higher education; and it provides a basis for testing your ability for "reading with understanding," or "basic reasoning," as we've called it.

2-1

The first unusual feature of the text is the very fact that it does treat "reading with understanding" as the basic kind of reasoning. One often encounters students these days who have never been obliged to read meticulously, a process that involves thinking out the significance and implications of what one reads. Such students will have understandable difficulty with a conventional logic or rhetoric course just because they aren't reading carefully. It's important for the instructor to be able to diagnose this weakness as the cause of their difficulties, rather than whatever technical content the usual course incorporates. So the quizzes on Chapters 1 and 2 are essential diagnostic tools for an instructor.

2-2

It's unusual for texts to discuss what texts (and courses) in the relevant subject should do. But students should be encouraged to take a critically constructive attitude toward texts as well as their content, if their learning is to have practical consequences. Of course, they always do this to some extent—they're quite willing to pass a general judgment on whether a text is good, bad, or indifferent. But writing a good text is the result of applied science, or a practical art. As we'll see in this chapter, there are many weaknesses in most approaches to teaching reasoning, at least some of which we're making an effort to avoid here. I'm sure we'll make plenty of other errors, which is why I'm offering $250 in prizes for the best criticisms and suggestions received in the first year of publication. This chapter should help you to think critically (to reason better) about texts and courses in general, and hence should have some value beyond this course; but at least it should make you a more sophisticated critic and user of this book.

2-3

The first chapter may have seemed a little abstract to you. It's really not so. Here are some of its practical implications in terms of the contents and arrangement of this book. First, the emphasis on communication, on the crucial importance of the social activity of reasoning, means that we can scarcely afford any jargon at all. For you can't restrict yourself socially to having serious conversations or arguments only with people who happen to have read this text or, for that matter, any other logic or rhetoric text. We will use, and try to use carefully, the substantial slice of the English vocabulary that already exists for the assessment and expression of argument, of reasoning. We'll use technical terms or symbols very rarely, and when we do, it will be just as a shorthand that you can easily translate straight back into English as you read, and on which you will not be tested.

2-4

Since a main aim of reasoning is to reason with others like yourself, your success shouldn't be judged solely by an instructor who, after years of experience, is probably able to decipher your meaning even when it's very poorly expressed. Hence, at the very least, you should have another student, perhaps a roommate or friend who isn't taking the class, grade some of your assignments (not just the multiple-choice ones, but some of the more advanced ones). Your instructor may want to have you do this as an assignment, as follows: You may be asked to (1) do one of the exercises, (2) get it graded by someone not in the class, with comments explaining the grade, (3) add your own comments in reply, and (4) submit all this to the instructor, who will determine a grade "for the record." Or you may do this in class, perhaps at the beginning of a class when everyone has brought in some assignments; in that situation, the instructor may ask you to pass your assignment to the person behind you or two seats to your left (far enough away so you aren't tempted to "help" with the grading), each of you then grading someone else's answers, with a few comments, and signing the grade. (It doesn't matter whether you did the same assignment or not; in fact, it's sometimes more realistic if you didn't.) Then the assignments might be returned to the author for reflection and (written) reaction, and then handed in. The graders of an assignment will then be graded individually on (1) how well they graded it, as well as on (2) how well they did their own assignments, and on how well they reacted to the grades and comments on their own work.

There are two reasons for doing this kind of exercise. First, it makes each of you remember that you're ultimately writing for your peers, not for a professor. Your fellow students have to be able both to understand your presentations and criticisms (your writing, for openers!), *and* to be persuaded by them. Second, it makes you begin to think about the practical aspects of evaluating the arguments and criticisms of other real people, not just exercises in a book. You'll find you will be considerably more careful to explain your points fully when you remember that someone else in the class is going to read your argument. And many of you will find that your appreciation of the task and of the comments of the instructor will improve considerably. It's easy to feel that "It's obvious what I meant, even if I didn't say it exactly right," when there's just an instructor to argue with; but if one of your classmates also couldn't see what you "meant," you have to think more seriously about expressing your meaning better.

After a fair amount of this kind of practice, the instructor may feel confidence in the class's ability to grade assignments and may do this once in a while without reviewing all the papers; that way, each student can get almost instant feedback on the latest assignment before it is discussed in class. This will often greatly increase your appreciation of the discussion.

If you happen to be using this text on your own, remember that you can still get much of the benefit of the peer-grading system just described by having someone else in your family, a friend, a coworker, or a roommate grade your assignments for you every now and again. It can be interesting for them because most of the topics of the arguments are pretty interesting in themselves, and perhaps also because it's interesting to play the role of the teacher (which is not so easy to do well as one might think).

2-5

A fatal flaw about most texts in this area is that they only give you examples for criticism that deserve criticism. That seems sensible enough, but it's a mistake. What is the skill we are trying to improve? It is not just the capacity to distinguish, without help, between defective arguments and sound arguments. Long ago I discovered that a number of students in a reasoning course, who had become quite good at critiquing all the arguments I set them, ran into tremendous trouble when I asked them to go out and find a defective argument in a current newspaper, magazine, or book. About a quarter of them couldn't find one at all because I had spent no time on teaching the skill of discriminating between good and bad arguments; I'd spent all the time on teaching them how to criticize arguments which they already knew were bad in one way or another, which meant that all they had to do was select the right kind of error out of the list they knew about. In short, I'd converted the task of choosing between good and bad into the task of choosing among sixteen kinds of bad, which isn't the *realistic* task at all. That's very like the basic flaw in the usual type of multiple-choice exam where you only have to pick the best answer of that set, rather than think up the right answer, without a list of candidates, as in real life. Letters to the editor in newspapers don't come marked "Unsound—decide in which way." But exercises in logic books are usually like that—they present sets that you know are unsound in one way or another.

In fact, the situation is usually worse than that, because usually the exercises come at the end of a chapter on one particular kind of error, so the reader has to apply only what has just been learned. When I first caught on to this, I tried interspersing a few examples of good arguments amongst exercises at the end of a lesson. The results were amazing; people discovered the most astonishing and nonexistent errors in them. Desperate to answer the (unwritten) call to condemn, they laid charges that were patently absurd and spent disproportionate time to establish them. Obviously the "hidden agenda" of the course were more influential than what I thought I was teaching. Something had to be done.

In this book we use "scrambled" exercises as one of three ways to handle this and some other problems. Although there are always some exercises at the end of a chapter to give you a chance to apply what you have just learned, there may be some examples which have nothing wrong with them (as far as I can tell), some which illustrate points from earlier chapters, and even some which deal with topics which are as yet undiscussed. I don't say there will be such examples in each set, because that would tell you more than you'd know in real life. I just say there may be some like that. So don't be sucked in by the context; treat each just like examples of argument that you'd see outside of a logic/rhetoric/reasoning text.

2-6

Moreover, the "progress" questions—as opposed to the "practice" ones— usually don't have any cues at the beginning. Students often say, "Well, you have to tell us what you want us to do with these examples." Nobody tells you that when you listen to the radio commentators or read a political circular just before an election. You have to treat them "as is appropriate"; something along the spectrum from tossing them into the literal or mental garbage can to saying "Right on." To make sure which treatment is called for, you'll usually have to do some analyzing, and in a text on reasoning, you'll have to set that analysis out as your justification for your conclusion, just as you'd have to in real life if you were trying to persuade someone in discussion or to write a report on a proposal. So the instructions before the progress questions are minimal; maybe nothing at all, maybe "Comment as seems appropriate." That's part of your task—deciding what's appropriate. In fact, you ought to be able to withstand the pressure of misleading instructions. If you are told to criticize a perfectly good argument, are you confident enough in your judgment to be able to withstand that pressure? You should be, since you'll often encounter hints or instructions that are at least that misleading in real contexts. So watch out for deliberately misleading "hints" later in the book.

2-7

Apart from scrambled and uncued or miscued exercises, our third move toward realism involves requests for "field research"; you will be asked to go out and find examples, perhaps of a certain type, to criticize. There's no question that this proves to be one of the hardest things for most students. But of course it is also the most valuable, because it is nearest to the real use of reasoning.

2-8

When talking about test questions, one kind was probably most puzzling to you. Why would we ever use examples which bear on material not yet covered? How else would we find out that you can already handle that material and hence that we can drop, or drastically cut, that section? And how better can we persuade you that there is something useful in that later chapter than by having you find yourself in difficulties when trying the type of example it covers? Texts and courses need to offer these opportunities to justify or improve themselves. The extreme case of this—hard for instructors (and textbook writers) to accept—is the "challenge" system, where students can take the final exam(s) without taking the course and get credit for the course if they pass them. Taking an exam made of B and C quizzes, before sitting through the course or before reading the text, should either result in your passing and getting the credits, or failing and seeing that the course or text (which gets most students through the exams) has some justification.

2-9

There's something else this text does that isn't often done to the same extent, which is to give some examples of typical, usually real, *bad* attempts at analyzing arguments and other statements. Texts are full of neat examples of the correct way to do the things they're teaching, but one doesn't always catch on to that by being inspired by the instructor's performance. It helps quite a bit to look at how people blow it, not the people who commit fallacies, but the people (you) who are trying to prove that someone else committed a fallacy. You'll thus get some practice in evaluating other students' work even if the peer-grading procedure suggested earlier isn't used.

There's a school of thought in educational technology which believes that good texts should never exhibit examples of bad work because students tend to remember errors just about as well as they remember the right approach. There are times when that may be correct (in writing sophisticated programmed texts, for example), but students often say that no single experience was as illuminating to them, when perplexed about their lack of progress, as that of seeing criticism of an attempt by another person at the same problem.

2-10

In commenting on the examples of good and bad work illustrating this book, an "absolute" standard of grading is used, either Pass/Not Pass (as on the basic multiple-choice quizzes) or, with the harder examples requiring extended analysis, A–F. This marking system simply means that a correct and completely adequate answer for practical purposes gets an A; one with minor blemishes, a B; one that does an adequate basic job but misses some important points, a C; a marginal one—definitely unsatisfactory, with serious omissions or errors but still getting hold of a reasonable proportion of the important points, a D; and anything below that, an F or Not Pass. Those standards are the realistic ones, the informative ones, and they have nothing to do with age or effort or background or IQ or how other people do on the same question. Of course, there will be some subjectivity on the instructor's or author's part in deciding between an A and B, and so on, but the point is that I'm not supporting the use of "curves" or "norms" or any other "relativizing" of the grade given to you during the course, since that just misleads you; it isn't the useful, relevant information for you. You can be the best in the class, but still not be doing the job well and should only get a C; that'll tell you there's some way to go before you've mastered reasoning skills. And you could be the worst in the class and still deserve nothing less than an A. Remember that an A refers to practical standards; very often, a few lines of answer is all it takes to get the A—it's just a matter of hitting the right nail on the head, and showing that you have.

On easy questions, like the basic quizzes, we just talk about passing or not passing; there's no real way to distinguish on an A-F scale there. We don't mislead you into supposing you're doing A work just because you pass a basic quiz; but we also don't downgrade you to a C, when you couldn't do any more than hit the right answer. Sometimes we use the fancier kind of multiple-choice questions where all, none, or some of the alternatives given could be correct, and you may have to fill in the right answer; on some of those the quality of work can be high enough to get you into the A-F scale.

Now none of this has much to do with the final grades that your instructor "gives you" (i.e., gives the registrar in your name) on the course. The instructor might then take into consideration the age or background level of the students, the amount of time (load) they have for the course, the amount of personal help they get, and so on. In particular, it might be appropriate to take into account the standards of the college or department. Why should you be penalized for taking this important course when you can take some Mickey Mouse course somewhere else and get a more-or-less guaranteed A? And, for that matter, why should your instructor, and the department which is offering this crucial course, be penalized by the administration (as they normally would be) if the enrollment in this course drops when it gets around that the standards are tough? (They may be penalized by having the number of positions cut, which may mean your instructor's job.) These considerations have led to "grade inflation" in the past few years that has made grades from some colleges and/or departments meaningless.

But this situation can be changed. The system I use in my courses simply puts the responsibility for controlling grade inflation where it belongs—on any administration which uses enrollment instead of quality of content and teaching as the basis for rewarding and punishing departments and teachers. Throughout the course, while dealing with the students, I allocate grades as devices for passing back useful information to them, using the absolute standards just described. When it comes to sending in grades to the registrar, I merely adjust them upward (if necessary) so that they have the same average as the college average. To be a little more exact, I consider two other matters. First, I make the adjustment only when I am convinced that the class members have worked as hard as it's reasonable to expect them to work, given their overall load. (I find that they usually work harder than that, since they're quickly convinced of the importance of the course.) Second, if I can get a look at their entering grade-point average, I can make sure that if they are already an above-average group, they will have their grades kept above the college average. It goes without saying that where, as sometimes happens, they perform better on the absolute standards than they would on the corrected-average basis, their grades are not down-rated.

Now one can go even further than this. In what I call the "ruthless counterattack" response to grade inflation, one would adjust grades to the average of the highest-grading department (or large course) in the college, unless there is good evidence that that department or course is either enrolling geniuses or out-teaching everyone else on campus.

Of course, it is the administration or the joint efforts of the faculty and administration that ought to be controlling runaway grade inflation. The easiest way is to get faculty support for some very simple limitations, such as a maximum of roughly one-third A's, or two-thirds A's and B's combined, in courses with twenty or more enrolled, unless they can qualify as an exception on the basis of exceptionally talented students or exceptional teaching effectiveness.

In order that students should not be unduly discouraged by their early grades, especially their pretest grades, on the absolute scale, I usually issue a correction sheet showing the general picture I expect, based on prior experience. This sheet might look, in part, as follows:

> If you got a D+ on this test, you can expect that putting in a reasonable amount of work on the course will at least lead you to improve to about the C+ or B− level by the end of the term, and the grade-adjustment process will then mean that you get a B to B+ as your official term grade. You have a good chance of doing better than this, especially if you work hard; you are unlikely to do worse except by goofing off.

And so on with other grades.

Someone who gets an F− on the pretest (or a clear Not Pass on the basic quizzes on Chapters 1 and 2), might, however, deserve some special counseling. Such students may be in over their heads or hyperanxious, and in some cases should be counseled out of the course.

2-11

A feature of some importance is that I've tried pretty hard to use examples for discussion which are interesting in themselves, so that (1) you learn something about a number of worthwhile topics "on the side"; for example, this chapter takes up issues about teaching and grading student work (and teachers); (2) you have a sense of applying your developing reasoning skills to cases which matter.

Naturally this means that the topics will be more controversial and perhaps a little harder than the artificial ones we could easily make up to illustrate the points. That's better than becoming a master of trivial examples and having no idea how to apply your skills to real examples, to problems where your career or health or society is at stake. Reasonableness hardly gets a real test if it isn't tested under pressure, which means emotional pressure, which means controversial issues.

For much the same reason, I occasionally use terms which, while they're not technical jargon, won't be in every reader's vocabulary. You'll be able to pick up their sense from the context and thus increase your reading vocabulary a bit even if, occasionally, you have to look them up in a dictionary. They will be terms worth knowing for other purposes than reading this book.

2-12

There are several modest innovations in the approach to testing. You've already noticed that the quizzes, the A quizzes especially, are designed to do some teaching as well as to help you and the instructor find out how thoroughly you understand the material. This is one illustration of a general theme of the text, namely that testing and evaluation—in particular, critical evaluation—should be done and regarded as a benefit, not an assault. It's something you have to learn to value—not necessarily enjoy—if you value anything else. For it is an essential means to improvement. One of the hardest lessons for some students to learn in a course on reasoning is that they are often wrong and have to be told so. It's easy to see how you can be wrong in an elementary calculus course; in the first place, you've never had the subject before and can't be blamed for not learning it instantly; in the second place, it's hard; in the third place, the teacher has a degree in math and that proves special skill; in the fourth place, one can prove what the answer is by an impeccable and watertight proof.

Contrast a calculus course with a philosophy course, or a course like this which involves the discussion of controversial issues on which you probably have some strong opinions. You don't like to admit your reasoning could be at fault on issues where you already have committed yourself. You know very well that expert opinion is divided on such matters. Your instructors' degrees—probably in philosophy or the humanities—don't show they're almost certain to be right on such matters. And, indeed, you're not even convinced that there are any objective standards in the area. But, before you start getting tough with the instructor, remember two things. First, you may find that there is some subtle skill involved here, and if you stay around a while, you may begin to see that your C−, when you expected an A, was richly deserved, that you've found out why, and that you won't make *that* mistake again.

Second, and this is a plea from the heart, don't forget that complaining about your grade can have (and often does have two) extremely bad results for you. It puts pressure on for grade inflation (it's much easier to give everyone an A than have to hassle about grades). And, if everyone gets an A, most people, probably including you, are not being informed honestly about the quality of their work, which is the most precious information you can get from an instructor. Remember that the "in-course" grades are for your benefit; don't make them meaningless. (It's another question whether you should argue for restandardization of the grade before it goes to the registrar.)

Another very bad result of complaining bitterly about your grade is that it increases the pressure on your instructor to switch to teaching you something that's more like mathematics than practical reasoning. Most introductory logic courses in the best universities today are simply introductions to symbolic logic, which is essentially a branch of math. That puts the instructors in a safe position because it's a subject which they *certainly* know more about than you and it's one in which the answers can be proven right. There's just one catch. It has almost no known practical use.

So be nice to your instructor in this course—don't force her or him to give up on honest evaluation of student work and on practical courses. Reasoning is something we've all done for years, and it is an ego shock to accept the possibility you're not as good at it as you thought. But it has been my experience that most professors really are a good deal better at it than most students, even though they will still be wrong at times. Stay with it; you may learn some things about yourself and about how to stay cool when criticized, as well as about how to reason better.

2-13

Remember, too, that there are no ideal teachers, there are only ideal combinations of teacher (or text) and student; the merits of texts or teachers depend as much on you as on them. The quizzes here, for example, are only potentially valuable; they're only actually valuable if you use them to your best advantage, which doesn't mean with the least effort. The same holds for your instructor. The question is not what he or she succeeds in stuffing into you; it is what you can get from the teacher. You have to work at that. An instructor (or text, or subject) may strike you at first as dull or as turning you off because of some mannerisms or attitudes. The next question is whether you have the ability to overcome that initial reaction. You can usually bet that your instructor (or the text) has some things to teach you that are worth learning. Are you incapable of absorbing them? Sure, you're entitled to try to change the instructor by direct request, or by the student-evaluation system, or by complaint. (You're being directly asked to change *this* text for the better and rewarded for doing it.) But there's also the question of whether that's the only direction where you should make an effort. Part of the effort may better be put into improving your adaptability as a student: your capacity to learn from books without five-color illustrations, to learn about crucial subjects that happen not to be as groovy as some of the "touchy-feely" courses. A reasonable person always has to consider both alternatives seriously, self-change as well as other change.

2-14

The text uses, or suggests that you or your instructor use, a number of devices, memory aids, display techniques, and learning games. They can be thought of as a more practical substitute for the technical terminology and complex calculi of the traditional approach to logic, as devices that are oriented more pedagogically than philosophically. For example, we use checklists to remind you of the various steps you should be sure to cover in argument analysis; we suggest you tape-record political debates on television so that you can replay them slowly for dissection at leisure. We recommend the use of multiple colors in setting out complex arguments for readability; the use of roommates as trial audiences; and the use of role playing or simulation games to handle violently controversial material and other debatable questions. This is the *procedural* side of the practical emphasis of the course; the *content* emphasis on practicality is covered in previous remarks and includes the use of realistic examples, of examples from which you can learn about something besides reasoning, of scrambled exercises, of "field trips," and similar devices.

2-15

Finally, it is essential to understand one point above all others about the approach in this book. The basic belief here is that thorough and decisive analysis of practical prose, and particularly of arguments, is an extremely sophisticated subject, not an elementary one. That doesn't mean it's fearfully difficult for you to do, with appropriate training, but it does mean that the theory behind it is very difficult. The study of the English language is an extremely sophisticated subject. You can use it very well, but no one has yet succeeded in providing an adequate grammar for it, let alone a comprehensive theory of its development or of the psychology of language learning. So the emphasis of this book is on practice rather than theory, though there are plenty of opportunities provided for excursions into theory, should you or your instructor so choose.

The other consequence of this view of the study of reasoning as an extremely sophisticated subject is again a practical one. The history of the subject has consisted of accounts of people hopping quickly over the apparently simple, everyday examples of practical reasoning and moving on into the interesting-looking theoretical woods surrounding it. As a result, they have vastly underestimated the complexity of everyday reasoning. Analyzing the reasoning in some comparatively short examples turns out to be at least as hard as trying to analyze the "deep grammatical structure" of some short sentences, a task which is now notorious for its difficulty. The practical consequence of this is that you will often find that the discussion of an everyday example is many times longer than the example itself, especially when you are beginning to learn the techniques. Most books on reasoning— texts in logic and rhetoric, for example—attempt to provide labels or calculi to handle these examples swiftly. But those devices turn out to handle them inadequately, in my view,

So you won't find your speed in logical analysis going up at first. It will go down. When swimmers or tennis players come under the guidance of a professional coach for the first time, they are often disappointed to find that they have to change the way they were doing things, and they think the new way feels more awkward, doesn't work nearly as well. But the coach has seen a basic flaw in the approach and knows that unless it is corrected, good and quick performance will never be attained by the pupil. In the same way here, although in the end we shall have sharpened up your logical wits and your instinctive reasoning skills so that you can react much more quickly and accurately than now, at first you'll have to go slower than ever before, just to get the steps right. Be patient. When I first started work in a lumber camp the axman who taught me said, "Learn to understand every piece of timber first, before you attack it. If you understand it thoroughly, it will do half the work for you." The master diamond cutters in Amsterdam will spend many hours studying a big stone in preparation for the few seconds it takes to cleave it. You must learn to spend as much time as it takes to study, and perhaps discuss, a key argument before you attack it. Speed builds slowly.

QUIZ 2-A

1 Most textbooks on logic introduce a great deal of special terminology—jargon. The major practical disadvantage of this, when you want to criticize arguments put forward by your peers, is that:

a You may soon forget a new terminology.

    b Different texts use different terminologies.
    c The people with whom you are trying to communicate often haven't been to college.
    d Other (explain).

Answer

The first and second answers are true but they are just extra reasons against jargon, not the major reason. Don't forget them, though! You might get a later question on a quiz which asks you to list several arguments against a "technical" approach to logic. These aren't the major reasons because, even if you didn't forget, and even if all the books used the same terminology, there would still be an overwhelming difficulty.

    The third option may or may not apply to you, but it's not the major problem, because even if these people have been to college, it's very unlikely they have taken the same course and used the same text—and that's the big disadvantage, which you should have put in as **d,** Other, and should have explained.

2 "It seems pretty silly to ask someone who isn't even taking a course to act like the instructor—who presumably knows more (not less) than the people who *are* taking the course—and grade one's assignments. Isn't this carrying the worship of the know-nothings to an extreme?"
    a For most courses this would be a good criticism.
    b For courses whose main aim is to teach procedures for solving problems that require knowing a technical subject, it would be a good criticism.
    c For courses where the final result is an achievement which can be judged—not taught—by the nonexpert, it's an irrelevant criticism because the teacher's skills don't automatically make the teacher a better judge of the product. Cooking courses, handwriting, reading and speaking courses, drama and portraiture courses, and even courses in the repair of motorcycles or fractured limbs, should produce improvements which can be reliably detected by the untrained observer/customer/patient.

Answer

We can surround the answer with a number of words, so that you won't see it as soon as you see the question, but the fact is that all three options are correct.

3 The quizzes at the end of the chapters in this book are often "scrambled" and/or "uncued," which means they may include which of the following?
    a Tests on material from earlier chapters
    b Requests to comment on or criticize perfectly satisfactory arguments
    c Incomprehensible or chaotic material
    d Arguments or passages of prose with no instructions as to what you should do with them
    e Tests of material from chapters you haven't yet read

Answer

Let's begin by extending the question somewhat. The answer as it stands is easy, since all these types of questions except **c** are examples of scrambled or uncued questions: type c might or might not be, hence should not be checked. Can you now state clearly the educational reason for including each of types **a, b, d,** and **e**? If so, you've just done question **3** in Quiz 2-C.

QUIZ 2-B

1 The argument against using any substantial amount of special terminology in a textbook on reasoning arises because of which of these functions of reasoning?
   a Reasoning as a process for arriving at the most probable conclusion
   b Reasoning as a process for persuading others of the probable rightness or wrongness of given conclusions or arguments
   c Reasoning as a process involving language

2 Knowing that someone else in the class or a roommate will grade some of your assignments may have a good effect on you as you do the work, because.
   a You know that the person will have to be able to read it and may not be as good at reading other people's poor handwriting as someone who does it all the time.
   b You'll try to make your points understandable to someone who is nearer to the eventual audience for your reasoning than a college professor.
   c You'll figure the person is pretty easy to con, so you won't put too much effort into the assignment.
   d You want to make a good showing to peers as well as professors.

3 The trouble with setting quizzes that are strictly on the material covered in preceding chapters is that:
   a The student doesn't know what kind of comments would be relevant.
   b The teacher is not assisted in determining whether later material is superfluous.
   c Retention of material from earlier sections is regularly tested.
   d Material you run into in the real world is not usually full of clues that tell you one particular chapter in this text is relevant.

4 Read the following passage and answer the questions that follow.

   Until about thirty years ago, the village of Nayon seems to have been a self-sufficient agricultural community with a mixture of native and sixteenth century Spanish customs. Lands were abandoned when too badly eroded. The balance between population and resources allowed a minimum subsistence. A few traders exchanged goods between Quito and the villages in the tropical barrancas, all within a radius of ten miles. Houses had dirt floors, thatched roofs, and pole walls that were sometimes plastered with mud. Guinea pigs ran freely about each house and were the main meat source. Most of the population spoke no Spanish. Men wore long hair and concerned themselves chiefly with farming.

The completion of the Guayaquil-Quito railway in 1908 brought the first real contacts with industrial civilization to the high Inter-Andean Valley. From this event gradually flowed not only technological changes, but new ideas and social institutions. Feudal social relationships no longer seemed right and immutable: medicine and public health improved; elementary education became more common; urban Quito began to expand; and finally—and perhaps least important so far—modern industries began to appear, although even now on a modest scale.

4.1   Why were there primitiveness and self-containment in Nayon before 1910?
   a   Social mores
   b   Cultural tradition
   c   Biological instincts
   d   Geographical factors
   e   Religious regulations
   f   I don't know

4.2   By 1948 the village of Nayon was:
   a   A self-sufficient village
   b   Out of touch with the outside world
   c   A small, dependent portion of a larger economic unit
   d   A rapidly growing and sound social and cultural unit
   e   I don't know

4.3   Why was Nayon originally separated from its neighbors?
   a   Rich arable land
   b   Long meandering streams
   c   Artificial political barriers
   d   Broad stretches of arid desert
   e   Deep rugged gorges traversed by rock trails
   f   I don't know

5   Comment on the following news story in any way that seems appropriate.

MORE REFUSALS: U.S. SURVEY FINDS BIAS IN HOME LOANS

The federal agency that regulates institutions making the bulk of the nation's home loans reported yesterday that lenders refuse mortgages to blacks more than twice as often as whites.

The Federal Home Loan Bank Board, which drew no conclusions from a survey of lending practices in five cities, said that black home loan applicants experience the highest rejection rate of any racial or ethnic group.

The bank board's survey was the latest in a three-pronged effort launched by major federal regulators of commercial and savings banks. The three agencies conducted the surveys as a prelude to drafting forms that would be used in enforcing federal restrictions on discrimination.

The Federal Reserve Board reported in May that its six-area survey showed minority applicants were rejected about twice as often for home loans.

Senator William Proxmire (Dem-Wis.) released last month comptroller of the currency results which Proxmire said "strongly suggest that mortgage lenders are discriminating against blacks and other minorities."

The comptroller's study, which broke down rejections and acceptance rates by income level, showed that even among applicants with assets in excess of $20,000, blacks were rejected 21.6 per cent of the time and whites 14.1 per cent of the time.

The Home Loan Bank Board, which regulates savings and loans but included all types of home loan institutions in its time survey, said blacks were rejected 18 per cent of the time and whites 8 per cent of the time.

The Home Loan Bank Board study covered 53,705 loan applicants in Buffalo, Chicago, San Antonio, San Diego and Washington, D.C.

Overall, 84 per cent of the applications were approved and nine per cent turned down. The rest of the applications were either withdrawn or no action was taken on them.

Whites had the highest acceptance rates, 85 per cent, and the lowest rejection rate, eight per cent. Blacks received acceptance in 77 per cent of the cases and rejection in 18.

For Asians the proportions were 83 per cent accepted and ten per cent rejected. American Indians were accepted 83 per cent of the time and rejected 13 per cent of the time. The acceptance rate for Spanish-speaking applicants was 81 per cent, the rejection rate 12 per cent.

The report also showed that men of all races were accepted 84 per cent of the time and rejected nine per cent. For women the acceptance-rejection rates were 81 per cent and 11 per cent.

QUIZ 2-C

1 Under what general conditions is technical terminology justified in a college or high school subject? Someone defending a technical approach to logic would probably make the best case by arguing—how?

2 a The Chinese cultural revolution involved replacing a large proportion of the faculty at colleges with lay people. A number of "alternative schools" in the United States have done the same. Set out the pros and cons of this move and relate it to peer-grading as described in this chapter. (Developing a good statement of pros may take a little research.)

   b If you know what the peer-review system is in Big Science in the United States, relate peer-grading to it.

3 See the answer to Quiz 2-A3.

4   "The double standards approach to grading is deceptive packaging, too—to the registrar. It is incompatible with a proper professional approach to teaching and faculty responsibility." Discuss.

5   "Giving misleading instructions to students on quiz questions is a violation of the trust relationship that should exist between student and teacher and is therefore unprofessional conduct."

6   a   Would or wouldn't it be unfair to good students to impose "grades quotas" of the kind suggested in the text (not more than one-third A's, and two-thirds A's and B's combined, with two possible bases for making exceptions)?
     b   What are significant differences between this proposed system and the old "curve" system?

Chapter 3

The Foundations of Argument Analysis

After some preliminaries we will get into the main business of this chapter, which is to set out the basic approach to examples of reasoning that you wish to assess, or to the production of good arguments that you wish to use in persuading other people. Later chapters, one or two of them longer, but some shorter, will expand on some of the more difficult steps in this basic checklist of procedures, and will also develop special techniques for handling particular types of arguments, such as very long arguments, debates, and certain types of moral argument.

3-1

Reasoning is not only concerned with arguments, however. Arguments are just one of the products of reasoning and one of the objects to which reasoning is applied. But it is applied to more than arguments; in general, its relevance is to what we might call "practical" prose, by contrast with (most) "literary" prose. For example, the way in which instructions are written, say for the operation of a complex piece of equipment like a high fidelity preamplifier or Dolbyized receiver, can be criticized from a logical point of view, in terms of whether the sequence of steps is one that corresponds to a sequence of possible actions in operating or assembling the device. An extended instruction manual is much the same as a textbook; and logical criticism of a text (such as this one) is one example of applied reasoning. The reports written by correspondents describing items of major news importance around the globe are often such that they cannot be understood by a reasonable person because they would make sense only if certain circumstances were true, although they are said not to be true in the opening paragraphs of the report. (To be fair to the news services, the incomprehensibility of these reports is often due to editing at the local level.) Spotting that kind of defect is an exercise of the reason.

There are, in fact, substantial parts of the body of literary prose which are subject to assessment in terms of their rationality, reasonableness, and similar qualities. This is most obvious in something like a detective story, where what is supposed to be produced by the end of the story is (typically) a proof that a particular individual was guilty; if it isn't a proof by the standards of reason, then the story is flawed as a literary work just because it fails to meet the standards of good reasoning. In science fiction, the problem of maintaining consistency while describing an imaginary world is one that has defeated more than one budding author.

So the range of impact of the type of critical analysis with which we are concerned in this text is considerably wider than that of arguments as such. Nevertheless, setting up a list of procedures for argument analysis is a good beginning, because almost all the other circumstances in which we apply logic (i.e., the standards or principles of good reasoning) are ones where we can formulate the essential point of the material we are assessing as an argument. In the remaining cases, the point is essentially that what we are doing is applying the standards of reason to the material, or to the individual, or to the group in question, and the punch in these standards, indeed the one basic criterion to which they all refer, is the *avoidance of inconsistency*. Criticism of arguments depends crucially upon appeal to the need to avoid inconsistency, as we shall see, and the criticism of other types of practical prose in rational terms depends on consistency in order to avoid incomprehensibility.

We will begin with straight argument analysis and quickly show how it can be extended to cover a good deal of prose. For example, much advertising prose is intended to persuade you of a certain conclusion, although if you look at it in grammatical terms, it does not have the grammatical form of an argument. Finally, we will say something about the rational assessment of types of prose that are simply not reducible to explicit or implicit arguments.

So the basic threat behind the rational analysis of practical prose is the threat of inconsistency. In this section, let's look at the question of why we should try to avoid inconsistency, why the threat is a serious one; and then, in the next section, we will look at the question of how inconsistency is brought to bear in the analysis and improvement of reasoning.

The avoidance of inconsistency is crucial simply because consistency is a requirement of communication. If you want to talk to people, if you want to convey information to them, if you want to learn something from them, indeed if you want to be able to learn something from the world itself—to perceive something, or know it, or remember it—there is no alternative to respecting the requirement of consistency. Look at a simple example. Suppose a friend said to you that the house where the party is on tonight "is one you can't possibly miss because it's the only one on the street with a red roof and without a colored roof." The sentence is meaningless to you, gives you no information which will help you find the house. It's as if you asked what the weather was like outside of a man who just came into the basement of the library where there aren't any windows, and he replied, "It's pouring rain and as dry as a desert." You don't know what he means. Of course, one makes every effort to find a meaning in apparent contradictions and inconsistencies; if your friend had said that the party was on at a house which is "in Berkeley and not in Berkeley," you would probably have thought to yourself that it was on the borderline between Berkeley and a neighboring community. If the man coming into the library had said that "it is raining and not raining," you perhaps would have thought that he was trying to convey the fact that there were showers, or a very heavy mist with drops of condensation falling through it. But, in hard-core contradictions, you can't "make sense of them," and consequently you can't learn anything from them. Of course, the individual words make sense; it is not as if somebody had uttered a sentence in gobbledygook or just a series of noises without meaning. But the sentence as a whole doesn't have any sense because it is inconsistent, contradictory. The whole point of conveying information is that one is describing a situation which *is* the case, and is thereby excluding certain situations which might conceivably have been the case. If you are told that a certain situation is the case and also that it isn't, the contrast between what is really the case and what isn't has evaporated and you no longer know what you are being told.

The avoidance of inconsistency is thus essential for communication. The sort of inconsistency we have been talking about so far is what is sometimes called "logical inconsistency"; it is an inconsistency which can be detected by anyone who speaks the language, without any other special knowledge. But, of course, exactly the same point would apply with respect to what we might call "factual inconsistency." Supposing somebody tells you that the party is going to be in a house that is in Berkeley *and* in San Francisco; then, if you know the geographical relationship of these two areas, you know that that description is inconsistent. If, on the other hand, the description had been "in Berkeley and in Albany," you could make some sense out of it since these are adjacent cities and the house could well straddle the line between them. It is a little less than precise to describe the house as being in both these cities—it would be more precise to say that part of it is in one of the cities and another part is in the other. But, without nitpicking too much, you can make sense of the description. On the other hand, given the geographical fact that there is no point of Berkeley which is less than several miles away from any point of San Francisco, you can't possibly make sense out of the description of the house as being in both these places. Factual inconsistency is really logical inconsistency between what is said and an unstated extra fact.

A still weaker type of inconsistency, really a borderline case which might more accurately be described as "improbability," or "implausibility," or "quasi-inconsistency" than as strict inconsistency, arises when something is described as having two properties which are almost certainly incompatible. For example, one might describe something as being red all over and also green all over, a statement that would certainly be confusing for most people. But there are certain types of shot silk (or opals) which are red all over when viewed from one angle and green all over when viewed from a slightly different angle, and people who know this fact might immediately think that you were talking about silk or opals. A really good Russian alexandrite, a rare gemstone, will appear dark green in daylight and dark red by artificial light. So here we have a kind of borderline case where the description has the appearance of logical inconsistency but might possibly be excused on the ground that it can be, so to speak, "given a sense" by people who know about some of these odd situations.

The main point of argument presentation is to show that some kind of inconsistency or implausibility is involved in *accepting the premises* of the argument and *rejecting the conclusion.* Arguments are meant to be persuasive; and they succeed in being persuasive if they begin with assertions that the listener or reader is known to accept, and if they continue by showing that acceptance of those assertions (which are called the *premises* of the argument) requires the acceptance of the conclusion. And what "requires" means here is simply that it would be inconsistent in one of the senses just described, to accept the premises and reject the conclusions.

The power of an argument depends upon two things; first, that it should start off with premises that are known to be true or can be shown to be true; and that it should proceed to demonstrate or exhibit the way in which these premises "force" one to accept the conclusion or conclusions. The "force" here is the force of wishing to avoid contradiction, or inconsistency of a weaker kind ("contradiction" is another name for "logical inconsistency"). In *criticizing* an argument, as opposed to *proposing* one, what we try to do is to show that there is no inconsistency between accepting the premises and rejecting the conclusion. (Or, of course, we may criticize an argument by showing that even the premises aren't true.)

So both criticism and presentation of arguments are duels in which the weapon is logic and its cutting edge is inconsistency or contradiction.

Let's look at a very simple example. Someone might be arguing that the true cost of a particular boat that his friend is thinking of buying is nearly twice as much as the friend has stated. The argument would consist of pointing to a number of indirect costs, such as licensing, docking, maintenance, insurance, and the interest cost on the loan involved (or the lost interest from investing the cash that was used to buy the boat outright). Each of these assertions about indirect costs is a *premise,* and it can be challenged directly or conceded. If it is conceded, the function of the argument is to show that the total sum of all these indirect and overlooked costs is approximately the same as the amount said by the friend to be the cost of the boat. In working out that sum, of course we use the rules of arithmetic (which are transformations based on avoiding inconsistency). In identifying the indirect costs, we use various factual sources, possibly including our own experience and the words of experts. We are really putting up a proposition to our friend which consists in telling him either to point out something wrong with our factual premises or something wrong with the laws of arithmetic; or else to concede that there is something inconsistent between his cost estimate and ours. If that inconsistency exists, and if he concedes that the indirect costs to which we are pointing really occur, he "must" concede that he is wrong. His conclusion is really inconsistent with the real facts of the situation, which are exhibited in the premises and conclusion of our argument. In this particular case, the step from the premises to the conclusion we drew relied only on the extremely reliable laws of arithmetic. It could therefore qualify as a case of "logical deduction."

In another situation where the steps from our premises to our conclusion might involve certain rather plausible assumptions, say, about the way in which taxation is likely to go up or the cost of repairs is likely to rise, we would have to say that our conclusion was only "made probable" by our premises. That type of argument is sometimes called an "inductive" argument, by contrast with the "deductive" one given earlier. (It is sometimes also called a "probabilistic" or—somewhat inaccurately—a "statistical" argument.) The difference is not really very important from the point of view of practical reasoning because exactly the same choices are open to the respondent. The opponent must rebut either the premises or the chain of reasoning that takes us from those premises to the suggested conclusion. That chain of reasoning may be merely a matter of rules of language or of arithmetic, which are normally thought of as bulletproof (which would make the argument *deductive*), or they may involve claims that are somewhat less certain, possibly laws of science or generalizations based on experience (in which case the argument is *inductive*). You don't need to memorize the terms "inductive" and "deductive"; we mention them only because you may run across them in some of your background reading. A slight juggling of the premises (by adding some unstated ones) and the conclusions can always convert an inductive argument into a deductive one without any essential loss of the "point of the argument," so the distinction isn't one you would want to build very much on; and, to make matters worse, some of the most respected professional logicians in the country today think there aren't any pure examples of deductive argument anyway. What we need to keep in mind is that a given argument normally involves some premises and some steps to get from these premises to the conclusion, and that if it's going to be attacked, either the premises or the steps (which are known as the inferences) have to be attacked. Premises are attacked in the straightforward way in which one attacks any factual claim, that is, by producing evidence that it isn't true. The inference, on the other hand, can't always be attacked in just that way. A great part of this book is concerned with the assessment of inferences, either with the intent to improve their clarity and reliability or to expose their weaknesses.

So the weapon behind logical analysis, behind the appeal to reason, is nothing more serious than the sharp edge of inconsistency. If people have no interest in communication, no interest in the acquisition of information, no interest in the truth, then there would be no reason for them to concern themselves with avoiding inconsistency, and the practice of reasoning would have no function. But, since we are all pretty much interested in survival, indeed in improving our welfare or that of others, and since, in order to achieve those aims, we have to determine what is the case and what is not the case—for example, what sort of diet is healthy and what sort of medicine is helpful and what sort of clothing will last and what kind of people can be trusted—then we are all in the business of trying to determine the truth about something or other, and hence we are all in the business of reasoning. At least, we "should" be, meaning that if we are not, the price we pay is not mere abstract inconsistency, but a simple practical loss of the things we value.

3-3

It's obvious that you have to speak consistently in order to convey information to others. Be sure that you understand why consistency is also necessary for you yourself to know anything at all. If you believe that there is a God and also that there isn't, you don't know what you believe. And certainly you can't be said to know (and you can't yourself say that you know) either one of these propositions. Knowledge is possible only in the absence of inconsistency in your beliefs just because "knowing" contradictory things only shows you haven't yet worked out which things to believe.

One can make (some kind of) sense out of claims like "I know there's a God and that there isn't," that "human beings have free will and yet don't," and so on. The sense that one makes out of such remarks is that there is *some* sense in which one of these claims is true and *another* sense in which it is not. That's just a way of saying that you've converted each claim into two claims, and that the denial of one of them isn't the denial of the other. In short, you have salvaged consistency in order to be able to make sense of the claim to knowledge.

3-4

You will have noticed in the last couple of sections that we frequently use a rather long-winded way of expressing the fact that reasoning can be used in the service of criticism or in the service of persuasion or communication. It is time for us to look carefully at this double function of reasoning, and once we have understood it, we will be able to avoid this rather verbose way of putting points so as to make clear that we are not talking about just the critical function of reason or just the persuasive function of reason.

People often imagine that rationality and logic are essentially negative or critical enterprises. It is extremely important to understand why this isn't so. There are two quite separate arguments against this "negative" view of logic. The first is clear enough in what's been said earlier; logic or reasoning is the means whereby we reach new conclusions, gain new knowledge, uncover new and important facts. When you sit down to work out exactly what it would cost you to own a boat, you are engaged in a logical process, you are reasoning about the matter, and the result that you come to, if you are good at this kind of reasoning, is a *discovery,* a new and important piece of information, for you. So reasoning is a constructive and creative activity that leads us to new knowledge. Moreover, it is not only with respect to our own knowledge that it's important; as we previously stressed, reason is a means of persuasion, a means that is uniquely important in that it does not deny the right of others to make up their own minds. It is not brainwashing or propaganda or threat, but simply the production of considerations which— in their own interest—should lead them to agree with you (assuming that you have put forward a sound argument), and thereby come to new knowledge themselves. So logic is an important part of the communications web of a just society.

But there is a completely independent reason for rejecting the view that there is some kind of contrast between rationality and creativity, between the use of logic and the use of intuition or imagination. Let's look more closely at the procedure for criticizing an argument. The argument consists in a set of premises which are said to "imply," that is, "lead to," a conclusion or set of conclusions. Suppose that we are concerned only with the criticism side of logical activities. Even here the creative element is inescapable. Let's look at an example. Suppose that somebody is arguing that the intrusion of herbicides into the ecology of the Snake River Valley area in Idaho has been the cause of the drastic decline in the population of birds of prey, especially the golden eagle, in that area. The evidence the person presents is simple. We have the records of naturalists going back fifty years, which show this area to have carried an exceptionally heavy population of birds of prey, ranging from the golden eagle and the bald eagle down to the smaller falcons. We know that, in a relatively short period of time, corresponding almost exactly to the period of introducing chemical herbicides and powerful pesticides into the farming communities nearby, there has been a very serious decline in the number of young hatching and the total population of adults.

Now, what is the exact force of this argument? Why does the speaker suppose that these facts "oblige" you to accept the explanation that she believes follows from them? The force of the argument lies in the fact that it is very difficult to think of any other explanation of the phenomenon of the decline in the population of birds of prey, and since we believe that these situations don't occur without some explanation, it looks as if you are forced to accept the speaker's.

But you are forced to accept her argument only if you cannot think of any other. If you can think of another explanation that is comparably plausible, then, until it is ruled out, she does not have a case. The process of trying to think of alternative explanations of a set of facts—the premises in an argument—is an entirely *creative* process. It is exactly the process which the great original scientist goes through in coming up with a novel theory. There are no precise rules to guide one in such a search, and it requires imagination nurtured by a rich and varied experience to generate the novel hypothesis here. So the very process of criticism necessarily involves the creative activity of generating new theories or hypotheses to explain phenomena that have seemed to other people to admit of only one explanation.

As you begin to think about the example we have been discussing, a number of other possible explanations may occur to you. For example, farmers in that area may well have shifted the type of crop they were harvesting to a crop that provides less adequate sustenance for the small birds and mammals that are at the lower end of the food chain from the birds of prey. There might have been a shift from grain crops to, say, soy beans, which won't support the same number of rodents, finches, and other small creatures. So, although human beings are in some sense responsible, it is only in the sense that their previous activities maintained an unnaturally high level of predator population, and the new crops have resulted in this decline to approximately the level that existed before the first settlers began farming those plains. Naturally, one would have to do some investigation to find out whether this alternative explanation is really a live candidate, but even thinking of such a possibility shows that the issue is not quite so closed as the arguer supposes.

To sum up our point, then, it is a great mistake to suppose that imaginative and creative thought processes are somehow separable from critical and logical ones, since to do good criticism, one must in fact be capable of the imaginative and creative production of new ideas.

And the other side of the coin is that creative or imaginative abilities are useless if they are not combined with the possession of critical skills, since one could not recognize a creatively generated solution to a problem unless one had the critical skills necessary to identify it as a solution to that problem. It's easy to generate new theories of gravitation or new ways to transport people faster than the speed of light if you are not very critical about whether your ideas will work! Critical skills go hand in hand with the creative ones; creativity is not just a matter of being different from other people, it's a matter of having a different idea that works as well as, or better than, previous ideas. If originality just meant novelty, it would be of no value; it means novelty *and* validity.

3-5

Now that we are about to begin serious argument analysis, it may be appropriate to review our use of a number of terms that we have been using until now. We have already made clear that we treat the terms "rational" and "reasonable" as being more or less equivalent. They are also roughly equivalent to "logical." But the term "logic," although it is, in informal speech, more or less equivalent to one sense of "reason" (one can equally well say that "logic dictates that we believe so and so" or "reason dictates that we believe so and so"), also has a more technical sense. The technical *subject* of logic, as the term is employed in philosophy departments for example, refers to what we might more usefully call "formal logic" or "symbolic logic." This may range from a discussion of the rather elaborate and very ancient tradition of syllogistic logic, which began with Aristotle, to more recent developments, particularly to modern symbolic logic which developed into a very substantial subject in its own right in the twentieth century. It can be regarded, however, as essentially a part of mathematics; it is an extremely precise and formal discipline, and not one that can be readily, if at all, applied to the analysis of everyday argument. When we talk in this book about logic, we simply mean the discipline or principles of careful and systematic reasoning. We are concerned not with the abstract type of logic but with the more practical species.

There is another distinction which is connected to these terms and which should be brought in here. We often talk about an argument being "logically sound" in order to contrast it with its being "factually sound." To say that the argument is logically sound is to say that the *reasoning* in it is sound, that the *inference(s)* from the premises to the conclusion(s) is/are sound, without saying anything about whether the premises are themselves sound. To say that it is factually sound is to say that the *premises* are in fact true. As we have mentioned before, if you want to criticize an argument, you can do so by focusing on two points; the truth of the premises, or the goodness of the inference. These correspond to the question of whether the argument is factually sound and the question of whether the argument is logically sound. Determining the truth of the premises is the main task of the subject-matter disciplines in science and the humanities; it isn't our main task here. Our focus is particularly on the reasoning process that moves one from premises to conclusions. And it is quite appropriate that this should be referred to as the "logic of the argument." One will often encounter looser uses of all these terms, but these few remarks should indicate the principal differences that we have in mind when we refer to them in this text.

Another pair of terms that need to be used with some care are "implications" and "inferences." The *implications* of a statement are, of course, what it implies, i.e., what follows from it or is supposed to follow from it. At the most subtle end, the implications may amount merely to what the statement suggests or is intended to suggest; at the strict end, they mean just those things that necessarily or logically follow from it. *Inferences* are the steps from premises to conclusions, but the term is also used to refer to the conclusions themselves; for example, one talks about someone making certain inferences from the clues that are available at the scene of the crime. This is essentially equivalent to saying that the person is drawing certain conclusions from that evidence, or is seeing certain implications in it. But there is one distinction between "infer" and "imply" that is grammatically essential. Premises imply conclusions, they do not infer them. People infer conclusions (from premises, evidence, and other things), which is the same as saying that they "draw" the conclusions. And this activity of inferring is not at all the same as that of implying conclusions, which people can do in other circumstances. For example, when somebody—in a suitable context—says in a belligerent tone that Jones got his doctorate at Harvard, one may take the speaker to be "implying" that Jones knows what he is talking about on the subject under dispute. The *speaker* is not inferring anything, but wants *you* to infer that. We will run through some exercises at the end of this chapter which will clarify this for you. But it is important to introduce you to these distinctions now because, in the next section, we will be using these terms with some care. Now let's get down to the paydirt.

3-6 THE SEVEN STEPS IN ARGUMENT ANALYSIS

What we will do in this section is first to list the Seven Steps, and then explain them in a little more detail so that you will have a general picture of the approach. In subsequent sections, we will go into considerably more detail about the various elements and skills that are involved in each of the Seven Steps, and apply them to various special types of argument. But notice from the very beginning that there isn't anything highly technical or particularly hard to understand about these steps. The difficult thing is to follow them carefully and skillfully. And acquiring that care and skill is a matter of practice and still more practice. Nobody gets to be good at mathematics without a lot of practice; nobody gets to be good at physical skills without a lot of practice; and nobody gets to be good at reasoning without a lot of practice. You have had a lot of practice in casual reasoning, and what this course tries to do is to convert that practice into a considerably more sophisticated, systematic, and effective process. Learning a new jargon or some technical calculus would give you a sense of having learned something, but it wouldn't teach you something useful for the kind of task we are focusing on in this book: the assessment and presentation of everyday arguments. So remember that the trick here is to do a familiar task better, not to learn a new terminology for talking.

The Seven Steps are as follows:

1 Clarification of *Meaning* (of the argument and of its components)
2 Identification of *Conclusions* (stated and unstated)
3 Portrayal of *Structure*
4 Formulation of (Unstated) *Assumptions* (the "missing premises")
5 Criticism of
  a The *Premises* (given and "missing")
  b The *Inferences*
6 Introduction of *Other Relevant Arguments*
7 *Overall Evaluation* of this argument in the light of **1** through **6**.

Let's elaborate on each of these steps, so that we can follow them more fully.

1   Clarify Meaning

This step includes clarifying the meaning of:

Terms
Phrases
Sentences
Suggestions or implications
Arguments

Method

   a   Read most or all of the argument or passage under consideration before trying any clarification.

   b   Replace unknown terms by reference to a dictionary.

   c   Rewrite any unclear parts, using clearer language.

   d   In particular, identify vague or ambiguous terms that you suspect the argument is "exploiting"; e.g., by shifting from one meaning to another. Translate the clause or sentence containing each occurrence of these terms into other language that conveys the correct meaning of the term in each context. That will show up any shifts in meaning.

   e   Write out any important unstated but intended implications or suggestions of the premises, the conclusions, and the argument as a whole. (What's it trying to get across that isn't actually spelled out?)

   f   Ask yourself if you really understand how everything fits together. In other words, have you a "feeling" for the argument or passage as a whole (even if you don't accept it)? Don't let any hostility you may have for the position expressed mislead you into misrepresenting the argument—say, by making it more stupid than it already is (you think).

   g   Look over results of **a** through **e** and criticize the passage for unclarity where appropriate. Most of Step 1 is laying ground for later analysis. But this part, **g**, is a component of your final criticism.

Remember

   a   The "meaning" of an argument (or word, or other expression) is not what the arguer *intended* but what he or she *said,* taken as a native speaker of the language would hear it.

   b   Still, you want to make the best guess at the arguer's intended meaning, and we can take account of context. In one context, "Dogs bite" may mean "All dogs bite"; in another, "Most do"; and in another, "Dogs sometimes bite." That is, the meaning of words or phrases isn't to be found in those words all by themselves. Look at the context; if the speaker is present, ask for clarification. If not, treat the words as having their usual meaning.

2 Identify Conclusions (Stated and Unstated)

Method

  a Some of the unstated conclusions turn up in Step 1(*e*) while you're trying to get the meaning straight. Set them out now: write them in below the passage of text, or fit them in (perhaps in the margin) where they come in. Are there any more, perhaps unintended but unavoidable ones? Get them all stated clearly and fairly. Which are the most important ones? Is there one main conclusion? (There usually is.)

  b To locate the stated conclusions, look for indicator words like "therefore," "because," "so," and "thus," and for placement cues such as location at the end of a paragraph. (These cues are by no means always reliable: you also have to depend on your sense of the meaning of the passage as a whole.)

  c Notice that there may be several conclusions in the argument, each building on the previous ones. And a passage may also contain several entirely separate arguments.

  d Within any one argument, try to decide if that argument has a *main* conclusion (or conclusions) and if the others can be ranked as to their importance. We can call the second group "secondary" conclusions, some of which may still be quite important, others more or less incidental.

3 Portray Structure

That is, set out the relationships between conclusions and premises, in the parts of the passage that are arguments. You've already identified the conclusions. Now you just need to ask yourself what assertions are being put forward to support each of these conclusions. These are the *premises*. Typically, there will be other material in the passage that is neither a premise nor a conclusion. It may be instructions, rhetoric, repetition, flourish, or other statements. The following procedure is unnecessary for very simple arguments, and it should be applied to very long ones a page or paragraph at a time.

Method

  a Number each separate *assertion;* note that one sentence may contain several assertions—for example, this one contains two, as well as an instruction. Put square brackets at the beginning and end of each assertion, and number it in the margin or above the line of type.

  b Do not give a number to repetitions of the same assertion; repetition often occurs for good reasons (as a reminder) as well as bad (not recognized as repetition).

c Do not number irrelevant statements ("asides"). Remember that your judgments of irrelevance or repetitiousness are crucial to your evaluation of the argument, and you must be ready to defend them.

d Do give a number to the implicit conclusions you first located in 1(*e*) and 2(*a*).

e Set out the relationships between the relevant assertions in a tree diagram like the one shown here. It is read downward on the page.

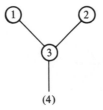

If 1 and 2 are claims put forward to support 3 and are not themselves supported by any other assertion, and if 3 is supposed to support 4, but not vice versa, the diagram looks like the illustration. If 4 might be an unstated conclusion, you might put it in parentheses, as shown.

f For a "balance of considerations" argument, where we say that 1, 2, and 3 suggest the conclusion 5, "despite" 4 (which points the other way), use symbolism as shown in this diagram.

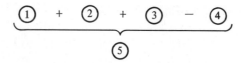

g Sometimes, you can set the structure out on a single line, e.g., (1 + 2 + 3 + 4) → 5 or 1 → 2 → (3 + 4). The arrow then stands for "implies." Sometimes the suggestion is made that, for example, (1 + 2) imply (3 + 4) and are implied by them; then use a double-ended arrow, thus: (1 + 2) ↔ (3 + 4).

h *Terminology*: If statement 1 implies statement 2, we can also say 2 "follows from" 1, or "is a consequence" of 1, or that we can infer 2 from 1. It is incorrect to say 1 infers 2: statements *imply* but can't *infer;* people can do both (but not at the same time).

i While doing this, begin to look for places where there are significant, unstated assumptions ("missing premises"). You can locate them by adding circles to the tree diagram with letters in them at the appropriate places, thus:

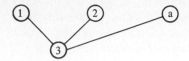

(*a* is an assumption that is needed to support the inference from 1 and 2 to 3)

To formulate them exactly, see the next section.

4 Formulate Unstated Assumptions

The most difficult part of reconstructing an argument is fair and clear formulation of the "missing premises," i.e., unstated assumptions. You must distinguish between:

a The *arguer's assumptions,* what he or she consciously assumed or would accept as an assumption if asked.

b The *minimal assumptions of the argument:* whatever is, logically speaking, necessary to make it possible to get from the premises to the conclusion of the arguer.

c The *optimal assumptions,* usually stronger claims than **b** which are logically adequate *and* independently well-supported. (We'll give examples of all these soon.)

5 Criticize Inferences and Premises

Criticism of expression is already covered in 1(*g*).

Criticizing an inference from statement 1 to statement 2 means criticizing the claim that 1 supports 2. You do not need to know whether 1 is true or not in order to consider whether it supports 2. You just have to ask, if 1 were true, wouldn't 2 then have to be true, or at least very likely be true? (Understanding this point is also the key to testing a hypothesis, for when we say, "If Jones did kill Mrs. Robinson, he would have had to run a mile in five minutes to be in the restaurant by 9:10 P.M.," we're not saying he did or that he didn't, but we are suggesting that it's reasonable to infer from the claim that he did it to a certain conclusion. By checking on whether he could run this fast, we are testing the hypothesis that Jones was the murderer.)

Criticizing a premise requires that, if the argument is going to be any good as a way of marshaling support, the forces it calls up had better be strong, i.e., the premises must be reliable. When the premises are technical claims, you aren't expected to comment on them in the course of logical analysis. When they are definitions or analyses subject to logical criticism, or matters of common knowledge, you are expected to assess them.

Good criticism of an argument requires that you look at both the reliability of the inference and the reliability of the premises. You might think that there's no point in looking at the inference if the premises are false. But your criticism of the premises may be either in error or fairly easily met by minor modification; you must guard yourself against this by covering both types of criticism. Good criticism also involves *selective attack;* first attack the main conclusions (via the premises and inferences that bear on them), and spend less time on the others. And attack with your strongest weapons first; do not start by making picky points, following the order of the statements in the original. Start in on the key weaknesses: start with your strongest criticisms. Strong criticisms are those that could not be met except by extreme modification or complete capitulation.

Criticism strategy involves the key move of "counterexampling." It applies to many types of premise and all types of inference, and it is an exercise in imagination. Here's an outline of the procedure that you can refer back to later. It may be hard to follow in this brief summary, but we'll explain it with examples in the next section.

a To counterexample a generalization—say, "All A's are B's" or "Any A is B"—you think of indubitable cases of A that are definitely not B. (It is irrelevant to think of B's that aren't A's, since the claim wasn't that all B's are A's.)

b To counterexample a definition ("A means the same as B"), treat it as a two-way generalization (i.e., "Any A must by definition be a B" and "Any B must by definition be an A") and look for counterexamples in the realms of possibility as well as actuality, since a definitional truth must hold whenever the language can be clearly applied, not only where it has been applied.

c To counterexample an inference, treat it like a one-way generalization. (It will be a definitional generalization in the case of strict deductions, as in most mathematical inferences; a factual generalization in the case of most scientific inferences.) That is, if the statement A is supposed to imply statement B, try to think of cases where A would be true but B would be either definitely false or unlikely.

d To counterexample an interpretation or analysis, treat it as an inference from that which is interpreted to the interpretation itself, and handle it as in *c.* (It may be intended as an equivalence, that is, a two-way inference.)

Remember

If you have extensively reconstructed an argument by filling in many missing premises and conclusions, you will have done so partly by asking what it would take to make up a good argument. Hence you often won't find much to criticize about the inferences in the reconstructed argument—your criticism will fall instead on the extra bolstering premises you had to add.

6 Consider Other Relevant Arguments

If you stopped after Step 5, you'd have a thorough critique and sometimes that's all that's called for, but you wouldn't know what to think yourself. For to discover that a particular argument has some defects is not to discover that it shouldn't be given some weight, perhaps a good deal. Perhaps enough to act on. At this point, then, you must step backward and try to get a perspective on the argument. First, ask yourself whether there are arguments on the same issue which point in another direction, perhaps to the opposite conclusion or to a somewhat different conclusion. (In the case of argument from analogy, you may even find that the very same analogy can be viewed somewhat differently and taken to support the opposite conclusion.) Next, look for other arguments that support the same conclusion.

7 Overall Evaluation

Go back to your criticisms. How devastating are they? Could they be met by modest modifications of the original material? Even when devastating, do they cover all the original lines of argument? Look at the results of Step 6. They not only should help you decide what you think but they also may help you to see what the original argument was after. Have you overcriticized it?

Now, make your final judgment on the argument. Grade it, in several dimensions if you like, but then make yourself give an overall grade. It's a cop-out not to. You must decide whether it does have force, and how much, for *you*.

QUIZ 3-A

1 You read a newspaper report of an experiment which, the headline said, showed that marijuana has damaging effects. In the experiment, a number of college students (who were paid quite handsomely for participation) smoked twenty joints (marijuana cigarettes, as if you didn't know) a day and exhibited significant loss of motor coordination, problem-solving ability, and so on. What is the relevance of argument analysis to this?
   a It has no relevance, since the report merely tells us new facts.
   b It has some relevance, because the question of whether grass is harmful is a very controversial one.
   c Nobody with any common sense smokes twenty joints a day, so the experiment isn't relevant to normal use of pot.
   d This experiment was supposed to show that something (a conclusion) follows from some evidence, that is, that the report on it really constitutes an argument, and hence it can be appraised by using the techniques of argument analysis.

Answer

The first response applies to the first sentence describing the report, taken alone, which says that marijuana had been claimed to have damaging effects. And it applies to the second sentence, taken alone. But the second sentence is said to describe the evidence which was given to support the first claim. Hence we have evidence and a conclusion which is said to follow—in short, an argument. So argument analysis is relevant to the reported argument. You're not criticizing the newspaper report (it may or may not have been accurate), but you can criticize the argument on which it reports.

The second response is wrong because the mere fact that a controversial issue is involved doesn't mean that an argument has been given. There are plenty of controversial claims (like "Marijuana is a dangerous and highly addictive drug") which argument analysis can't help you with, as they stand, because they are mere statements. It's only when someone begins to try supporting them, or attacking them, that we have an argument to criticize.

The third option makes a very relevant point about this particular argument, which would be worth mentioning if you were being asked to criticize it. But you weren't asked that; you were asked to say whether the newspaper report was something to which argument analysis is relevant. Don't rise to the bait of checking responses just because they're true, or relevant to something; the only issue is whether they're true and relevant to the question asked. This isn't being picky, it's being logical.

The fourth response is exactly right.

2   "If you talk to the *professional* tea-tasters, you'll find that *they* prefer Lipton's."
   a   This is a simple argument of the common form "If . . . , then . . . ," where the first clause contains the premises and the second the conclusion.
   b   This is a conditional statement (a prediction, in this case) which tells you what would (supposedly) happen if you did something or other. Since it's just a statement, it can be challenged only on factual grounds, not for the quality of the reasoning, i.e., on logical grounds.
   c   There's a clear implication here, even though it's not stated. The implication is that Lipton's is the best tea, presumably, in fact, the best tea for *you* (the reader or listener or viewer—to whom this advertising is directed). So it is best treated as an argument with a single stated premise and a single (unstated) conclusion; hence argument analysis can be used.
   d   Other:

Answer

Arguments are often set out in the "If . . . , then . . ." form, although, to be precise, this form represents only the *reasoning* step in an argument, that is, it asserts that the premises of a particular argument do imply the conclusions. The argument itself, stated in full, consists in first asserting that the premises are true, and then asserting the reasoning step or the inference—that is, asserting that the premises imply a particular conclusion—and hence, in light of this, affirming the conclusion. So an argument is actually a little more complicated than an "If . . . , then . . ." statement. But such a statement does express a key element in an argument (and sometimes is used to express a whole argument). The element expressed is indeed the one that is of particular importance to us in studying reasoning. However, this particular statement, beginning with "If . . . ," is not a claim about certain premises implying a certain conclusion. It's not a claim about implication at all. Supposing I say to you,

"If you would get out of the light for a minute, I could see what I'm doing." I am uttering a conditional or a hypothetical statement, just as I might say, "If we had more money, we could afford two cars," but it isn't at all an implication statement, a claim about something following from something else. "Getting out of the light" makes something else possible, but it doesn't make it necessary. Reasoning is all about what "necessarily" (in either a strong or a weak sense) follows from something else, and many "If . . ." statements are about what will or might in fact happen: they're often just predictions, which are statements of fact about the future. "Having more money" makes possible the purchase of the second car; it doesn't imply or make necessary the purchase of the second car. "If you feel up to it, we'll go home through San Francisco so that we can pick up some of the inexpensive wine that we like so much" is introducing a proposal, a possibility for us to consider. It isn't suggesting that "feeling up to it" requires that we go home through San Francisco in order to avoid inconsistency. So the first alternative is not the right interpretation of this little quotation.

We've really covered the second alternative as well in the preceding discussion; this is, intrinsically, just a hypothetical statement—a statement about what would happen if (on the hypothesis that) you did something or other. The only problem is that the context of statements like this, which is obviously part of an advertisement, is a good deal richer than the second alternative gives credit for. This is not just a pure hypothetical statement, taken in context; it's a hypothetical statement which is meant to convey something else to you. Hence, the second alternative, which says that it is "a conditional statement" is oversimplifying the matter, and the third alternative answer is the correct one.

Don't feel bad if you didn't get this one right immediately, or if you find the discussion of it to be not entirely convincing to you yet. You're just beginning to make a distinction for which you have to develop a feeling, and it will take a good deal of practice before you feel confident about it. In the next chapter, we'll get on to some more examples that clarify this and related distinctions.

3   "There's only one person, other than the victim, who was within 50 yards of the place where the murder was committed at the time when it was committed. That person is Royce. So there's no question about who did it. Royce is the murderer."

This is an example of your being "forced" to accept the conclusion in order to avoid which of the following?
a   Logical inconsistency (contradiction)
b   Factual inconsistency (factual impossibility)
c   Improbability
d   Asserting that the victim's violent death might have no explanation at all
e   Having to produce another explanation that is more plausible

Answer

The type of argument is a scientific, a practical, or—as it is sometimes called—an *empirical* argument. It rests upon what we know about the world, not upon the rules of language. If you say that Jones is childless and hence cannot possibly be classified as a parent, you're stating a consequence of the meaning of the terms themselves, that is, a consequence of the rules of language. It would be a *logical* inconsistency to assert that Jones was childless and a parent. But it isn't a logical inconsistency to assert that a murder can be committed by somebody more than 50 yards away from the event. For example, somebody can be shot at a range of 800 yards, or killed with an arrow at over 100 yards. Since we aren't given any facts about the way in which the murder was committed, we can only assume (to make sense out of the argument at all) that it was committed in some way that one normally associates with close contact, such as strangling or stabbing. But of course one can imagine ways in which a body can be given the appearance of having been strangled by somebody close by, although in fact the death was caused by somebody at a remote distance. These are far-fetched possibilities, indeed; one can think of knives thrown by a crossbow, or strangulation produced by a bola, the South American gaucho's weighted cords, or other way-out murder instruments. These are certainly improbable; but they are not factually impossible. The line between what is *inconsistent* with the facts and what is made *unlikely* by the facts is not a sharp one. Hence, either the second or third alternative would be a justifiable answer here, provided that you were clear about your reasons for picking the particular alternative you did pick. It is physically impossible for a house to be in San Francisco and Berkeley at the same time, given the way those cities are separated at the moment, but it's only physically unlikely (improbable) that a person could be in San Francisco at one moment and in Berkeley 60 seconds later. There are a number of rocket and jet-powered devices which could reconcile those claims, though it's extremely improbable that any ordinary citizen would have access to them.

Of course, all the preceding discussion rests upon the assumption that there must have been some explanation of the victim's violent death. Certainly one of the pressures on you to accept a conclusion is your wish to avoid the possibility that there might be no explanation at all of the results. Hence, you should have checked option **d** as one correct answer. Similarly, if you're going to avoid accepting this conclusion, you can do so only by producing a more plausible explanation than the explanation that Royce did it, so you should have checked option **e** as well. How does all the talk about explanations relate to inconsistency? In the following very simple way: It is by discovering or inventing alternative explanations that you avoid the inconsistency involved in saying, "There must be some explanation, but I won't accept the only possible one." If there's only one possible one, and there has to be one that's true, then that one is it.

4 Which of the following (a) represent correct usage of the terms and (b) are true?
  a "Logical" means roughly the same as "rational" or reasonable.
  b "Logic" can refer to a highly technical subject or just to the principles of sound reasoning.
  c Premises infer conclusions.
  d People infer conclusions.
  e Some statements have implications.
  f Contradictions are statements made up of meaningless words.
  g The avoidance of contradictions and inconsistencies is a main goal of being logical.

h It's important to avoid inconsistency if you want to have knowledge or be able to communicate information to others.

i Criticism of arguments does not, whereas creation of arguments does, require imagination.

j Creativity or originality can be distinguished from random novelty or mere variation only by the use of critical standards.

k A logically sound argument might have false premises.

l A factually sound argument must be logically sound.

m If you took a course in technical logic, you would probably learn something; the only problem is whether what you learn would have any relevance to the abstract theory of argument.

Answer

Most of these statements require no comment; they just follow immediately from material in the text, to which you should refer again if your answers were wrong. The alternatives which you should have checked as correct are: **a, b, d, e, g, h, j, k.** The only answer that needs any explanation is **m,** and the best way to explain why it should have been marked incorrect is to say that it would have been correct if the last part of it said: "would have any relevance to your capacity for practical reasoning," instead of what it in fact says.

5 Apply the steps of argument analysis, as best you can, to the argument we reconstructed in the second question in this quiz. (*Hint:* it's a really simple example.)

Answer:

Step 1: *Clarification of meaning.* No problem here with the stated material.

Step 2: *Identification of conclusions* (stated and unstated). The implied conclusion is that Lipton's Tea is the best, and if this is to have any significance for the reader—as advertisements are supposed to—it must mean "best for *you.*"

Step 3: *Portrayal of structure.* This is a simple structure with one premise and one conclusion, and we can abbreviate the somewhat long-winded presentation of the premise by stating it as follows:

Professional tea–tasters prefer Lipton's tea. (Premise)
_____
Lipton's tea is best for you. (Conclusion)

Step 4: *Formulation of (unstated) assumptions.* Now that we have the argument set out in very simple and clear form, it's obvious that it won't work, that is, that the conclusion won't follow from the premises unless you assume something. The assumption is, roughly, that the taste of professional tea-tasters is a good guide to your own taste. Actually, it's a little stronger than this, because the conclusion is about what *is* (supposedly) best for you, not what you'd like best. So there's a second assumption—that your taste is a safe guide to what's good for you. (Or you might combine them if it's assumed that the professional's preferences are a good indication of what's best for you.) The structure, if we keep the assumptions separate, now looks like this:

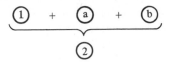

Step 5: *Criticism of the premises and the inferences.* The premises now include the "missing premises," that is, the unstated assumptions that we've discovered are needed in order to make the argument work. Since we've constructed these so that they *do* make the argument work, we won't have anything to criticize under the heading of inferences, so let's concentrate on our criticism of the premises.

The first premise is the one that was stated, and we really aren't in any position to deny it. Maybe it's true, maybe it's not; but, from the logical point of view, there isn't anything to be said about it. The main question is whether, assuming for the moment that it's true, the (implied) conclusion follows from it.

Well, it will follow *if* the assumptions on which it depends are correct. If it's true that the taste (the preference) of professional tea-tasters is a reliable guide to what's good for you, then the argument is just fine.

There are two problems about these assumptions. The first is that there's a distinction between the taste of professional tasters and that of ordinary tea-drinkers. Very often, those who are professionally required to drink huge quantities of a substance develop a quite different taste from those who drink it only occasionally; for example, they will sometimes demand a tea (or a whiskey, a cheese, or a wine) that is stronger, more distinctive, subtler, or smoother than the usual run-of-the-mill version. Whether you know this to be a fact or not, you can easily see that it's a possibility, which is all that you need in order to see that the assumption isn't something one can wholly rely on.

Second, people's tastes are not necessarily a very good guide to what's good for them. For example, for a great many years Camel cigarettes were the most popular brand, not only among the general smokers, but also, it is said, among the professional tobacco buyers and blenders. But Camels were, in fact, not very good for you, and indeed, appear to have been among the worst for whoever smoked them. Once you've seen that the taste of the professionals is not necessarily a good guide to your own taste, and also that taste (of anybody) is not necessarily a good guide to merit or benefit, you have seen that there are serious weaknesses in the two missing premises. And you have expressed some convincing criticisms of the argument. They may not be fatal criticisms, because evidence might be produced to refute them, that is, to establish the truth of the assumptions; but it's not going to be easy, and, as far as I know, it isn't available at the moment. So you have shown that the argument is a very weak one at the moment. (And probably forever, since it's unlikely that tannic acid does your stomach much good.)

One might have gone about this criticism in a slightly different way. Instead of adding missing premises, and thereby making the inference satisfactory, one might have left them out and criticized the inference instead of the assumptions. Either method is exactly the same in its net effect. It turns out to be a little more effective, practically speaking, to try to formulate explicitly the assumptions that would be required in order to make the argument good, than just to accept the stated premises as all the premises there are and then try to criticize the inference. For "criticizing the inference" is shooting at a rather hazy target; stating the assumptions forces you to clarify the criticism considerably, and this clarification often turns up some new loopholes (extra assumptions).

Step 6: *Introduction of other relevant arguments.* It's possible that one might want to introduce questions of *cost,* which is relevant to the conclusion of what's best for you, at least in a pragmatic sense. If we were talking about wines or spirits rather than tea, we would surely have to consider cost, since it's a substantial factor there. However, this isn't the kind of topic on which there are a large number of entries for Step 6—unlike an argument about a topic like the best schools for you or your children. (The comment about the probable general effects of tannic acid is a second relevant, though speculative, consideration.)

Step 7: *Overall evaluation.* Here we have to employ some judgments. How serious are these difficulties that we've raised with the missing premises? Are they really just nit-picking points, or do they represent serious possibilities that make the jump from the given premise to the implied conclusion a pretty speculative one? In this particular case, one really has to conclude that they raise pretty serious possibilities and that the obviously intended implications of the quoted passage are not well supported by it.

QUIZ 3-B

1 Literary prose, as distinct from practical prose:
   a Can always be assessed in terms of style, originality, and other literary standards
   b Can sometimes be assessed in terms of the standards of reason—but not always
   c Can always be assessed in terms of the standards of reason
   d Other

2 The power behind the throne of reasoning is said here to be the requirement of *consistency,* which:
   a Means the avoidance of contradiction
   b Has little force for people that aren't hung up on a highly scientific, rationalistic approach to life
   c Can always be ignored, at some price
   d May be recognizable only if one knows something about the facts
   e Is one step less severe a constraint than the avoidance of improbability
   f Obliges one to accept the conclusion of a sound argument, with all its assumptions stated, if one accepts the premises

3 If you're criticizing an argument, rather than giving one, the appeal to inconsistency often comes in because you are:
   a Showing that it's inconsistent to accept the premises and reject the conclusion

b Showing that the conclusions (or the premises) are intrinsically inconsistent

c Showing that it is not inconsistent to accept the premises if you accept the conclusion

d Other

4 Logic or reasoning:
   a Does not generate new knowledge
   b Is the only route to new ideas
   c Requires imagination in order to criticize certain types of argument
   d Often requires you to think up new explanations of particular facts, that is, to be an inventor, to be original

5 Argument analysis involves:
   a Either criticizing the premises of an argument or (alternatively) criticizing its conclusion
   b An early effort to find the conclusion(s) among the assertions in the argument
   c Accepting whatever meaning the arguer gives to the terms being used
   d Classifying every assertion in the argument as a premise or a conclusion
   e Sometimes dividing sentences up into several assertions in order to reveal the structure

QUIZ 3-C

1 A.E. van Vogt wrote a series of science-fiction novels about what he called the "World of Null-A," centering on heroic figures who had achieved the capacity to think in "Null-A" (non-Aristotelian) terms. He defined these terms to mean thinking which abandons the assumption that every claim has to be either true or false (the Aristotelian Law of the Excluded Middle).
   a Can you give some examples of claims that are neither true nor false? (Don't confuse this with the question of whether they are now known to be true or false.)
   b In general, what do you think can be meant by "alternative logics"? Are there, could there be, totally different "ways of thinking"? Give an extract of a few sentences from an imaginary tape-recorded dialog between your New Logic hero and a supporter of the Old Logic (our present one). Or can't this be done, and if not, what is the significance of that?

2 Isn't there some sense in which creativity does not involve critical skills? Make the question specific; think of a particular type of creative person (writer, painter, musician, scientist, or designer) and start defining what they do that establishes them as creative. Does that same process or sequence involve critical ability? Could there be instinctively original creative artists? If so, would their existence settle the question?

3 How would you settle the question of whether studying technical logic helps one's practical reasoning? Suppose a study showed people who had taken the technical

course to be better, on the average, at practical reasoning than people who had not. Would this finding settle the matter? Would a positive answer justify teaching technical logic?

4 Find a short example of reasoning in today's paper, and run it through the Seven Steps.

Chapter 4

Developing the Concepts of Argument Analysis

By now you have a general picture of the Seven Steps approach to argument analysis. What remains is to become so familiar with it that it becomes an instinctive approach; and to develop some refinements in it; and to learn how to apply it to some special cases. There's obviously nothing very technical about it, it's very much a matter of common sense. But acquiring real skill with it is a matter of a great deal of practice and a much deeper understanding of the steps that we have so far provided. If you do feel, however, that you have a good grasp on what it's all about, remember that you can skip through to the end of this chapter and try yourself out on the A quiz to see if there's any need for you to work through the chapter in detail. (If you do well on it, perhaps you can turn in your answers to the B quiz right away, and skip some lectures while doing some extra reading or working on a C quiz question for a term paper, depending on what arrangements for acceleration your instructor has made.)

You won't ever be required to memorize the Seven Steps. In fact, you'll come to remember them without making any effort, because there aren't very many and you'll get plenty of practice. But there's no reason to feel bad about going back and looking them up, even if you have to keep on doing this indefinitely. Remember that some of the most sophisticated, highly trained, skilled people, for example, airline pilots, use checklists as a basic part of their operating practices, checklists which they never count on being able to memorize and always have available. Whenever an airplane lands or takes off, its pilot is required to go down the appropriate checklist, item by item, just to be absolutely sure that nothing has been forgotten on this occasion. There, the checklist is a matter of life and death. In argument analysis, it's usually not quite that important, though when the arguments are legal ones about capital crimes, or hearings about the adequacy of field tests of a new drug, it is also a matter of life and death. And argument analysis is very frequently crucial for decisions of great importance, involving property and the welfare of others as well as yourself, and hence, it does no harm to make yourself go back and check the list step by step, however many times you've worked with it. It's extremely important to realize at this point that making yourself do argument analysis in a step-by-step, systematic way, is exactly what leads to doing it better than if you did it in just a casual way. The business of formulating the assumptions, for example, will time and again make you realize that the argument depended on an assumption which you hadn't noticed until you made yourself try to state it *exactly*. In the same way, the procedure for "structuring" the argument, which forces you to decide exactly which premise is related to which conclusion, and which sentences are essentially irrelevant, will time and again lead you to realize something of the greatest importance about the argument which escaped your notice at first. It may, for example, lead you to realize that there's a secondary argument buried in the primary one, an argument which throws a red herring across the track of the main argument and must be separated from it in order to be able to cope with either effectively.

In this chapter, we'll expand on a number of the concepts and procedures involved in the steps, with illustrations, and we'll also introduce some further refinements. In particular, we'll have to work very hard on the basic concept of the soundness of an inference and on how it is related to the truth of premises and conclusions. Later chapters will focus on particular steps in the argument analysis procedure and on particular types of argument, in still further detail.

4-1

Let's begin by reviewing the relationship between *argument* and *inference*. The simplest possible argument consists of a single premise, which is asserted as true, and a single conclusion, which is asserted as following from the premise, and hence also to be true. The *function* of the argument is to persuade you that since the premise is true, you must also accept the conclusion. This persuasion will be powerful if it is clear that the inference from the premise to the conclusion is sound, that the premise does in fact imply the conclusion. (Other ways to put this are to say that you can legitimately infer the conclusion from the premise, or that the conclusion is in fact a consequence of the premise.) Since that argument rests for its strength entirely on the strength of the premises and the strength of the inferences, these are naturally the two points to attack, if one is operating in the critical mode; or the points to reinforce, if one is operating in the expository mode (that is, setting out an argument instead of criticizing it). Once you have finally formulated an argument, these two lines of attack are entirely independent. (Until then, you can always "convert" inferences into parts of complex assumptions, plus simpler inferences.) To say these lines of attack are independent is to say that the premises can be true *or* false and the inference still be sound; and, on the other hand, the inference can be sound or unsound whether the premises are true or false. For example, from the premise that the moon is made of green cheese, it does in fact follow that the moon has a high protein content. The premise isn't true, but the inference is just fine. On the other hand, from the fact that the moon's surface consists largely of rocks and dust, which is true enough, it does not follow (that is, an argument which drew this conclusion would be invalid, unsound, no good) that the moon is uninhabitable. Nor does it follow that the moon is inhabitable. The question of whether it's habitable or not (by our species) depends primarily on its atmosphere, not on its physical composition.

So any combination of the premise being "good" or "bad" (that is, true or false) with the inference being good or bad is possible. But, if we bring in the question of the truth or falsity of the conclusion, then, although we can still have various possible combinations, one combination is ruled out. The whole point of arguments, you remember, depends on the fact that if you go from a true premise by means of a good inference, you have to arrive at a true conclusion. (We can modify this a bit to say that if the premise is just probable, then the conclusion will be just probable.) Hence the one combination that is ruled out is the combination of *true* premise(s) with a *good* inference and *false* conclusion(s).

Becoming clear about this point is really the crucial step in becoming clear about what *reasoning* is as opposed to what *truth* is, which is really the distinction on which logic rests. It won't hurt to go through this step once more. If you have a true premise and a good (sound) inference, then—by definition—they will lead to a true conclusion. This follows by definition because what we mean by "good inference" is exactly "one that will lead us from true premises to true conclusions."

Hence it follows that the one combination we can never encounter is that of having true premises, a sound inference, and a false conclusion.

The big trap, when one begins to think about this, is that of believing that you can tell that an inference is no good by noticing that it leads to a false conclusion. Suppose I make a number of claims about the results of some field trials on beer-drinkers. On the basis of these measurements about the amount of beer drunk, the length of time that digestion takes, the relative rates of absorption of alcohol, sugars, and the other substances contained in beer, the rate at which the fluid passes through the system, and so on, I draw the conclusion (as was done in a famous published article) that it is impossible to get intoxicated by drinking beer. Now you may know from your own experience or observations that the conclusion is false. You cannot conclude from this that the *inference* I made was unsound. It might instead have been that some of the *premises* were false—that is, it may be that a number of the observations were incorrectly made or recorded. Remember, then, that you can't tell the source of the trouble in an argument from the discovery that the conclusion of the argument is false; it may have been due to a mistake in inference, or to a correct inference and erroneous premises, or to both.

Nor can you tell from the fact that an inference is no good that the conclusion will be true or false. Bad inferences can lead to true conclusions or to false conclusions, since bad inferences can lead anywhere. That is, if you stick any wholly irrelevant conclusion in at the end of an argument, and say that it is the conclusion of the argument, the inference to it will be unsound; and of course, it might have been a true or false irrelevant statement.

Nor, of course, can you tell from the truth or falsity of the premises alone either whether the inference in the argument is good or whether the conclusion is true or false.

Let's sum it up, then, by reminding ourselves of the whole point of logic and reasoning. Reasoning is the process whereby we get from old truths to new truths, from the known to the unknown, from the accepted to the debatable (in order to make it less debatable), and so on. If the reasoning starts on firm ground, and if it is itself sound, then it will lead to a conclusion which we must accept, though previously, perhaps, we had not thought we should. And those are the conditions that a good argument must meet; true premises and a good inference. If either of those conditions is not met, you can't say whether you've got a true conclusion or not.

The other side of this coin is worth noting. If you know the conclusion is false, then you know that something went wrong: either the premises were false or the inference was unsound. Hence, if you know that the conclusion is false and that the inference was sound, the premises must have been false; or, if you know that the conclusion is false and that the premises are true, it must be the case that the inference was unsound. This fact gives us one of our best procedures for checking on the soundness of inferences.

Let's see if we can sum up these points in a table.

First let's set out all the possible combinations and what we can say about them. Then we'll condense them into a table.

1 If the premises of an argument are T(rue) and the inference (the reasoning) is S(ound), then the conclusion must be T(rue).

(This is the main justification for improving one's reasoning skills.)

2 If the premises are, on the other hand, F(alse), and the inference is still S(ound), the conclusion may be T or it may be F—no way to tell.

3 If the premises are F and the inference, on the other hand, is *un*sound, the conclusion may be T or F.

4 If the premises are, on the other hand, T while the inference is still U(nsound), the conclusion may be either T or F.

Now suppose that we happen to know something about the truth of the conclusion. Can we—or *when* can we—say anything about the truth of the premises?

5 If the conclusion is F, and the reasoning is S(ound), then we know the premises must have been F (because, if they had been true, the conclusion would have had to be true, from point 1 above).

6 On the other hand, if the conclusion is T, and the reasoning S(ound), we can't say whether the premises are T or F. (This one is a bit surprising to most people.) How could one possibly get a T conclusion by sound reasoning from an F premise? Surely, one feels, any falsity in the premise would carry through into the conclusion? Not so; the premise may be false because it claims more than is true: Vienna is 1,000 miles from Milan, from which there certainly follows any more modest claim; for example, "Vienna is more than 100 miles from Milan" certainly follows from (is implied by) the assertion that it's 1,000 miles from Milan; and the more modest claim may be true (as in this case). So false premises may imply true conclusions, and so, of course, may true ones. Hence, the opening statement of this paragraph is correct.

7 If the conclusion is T, and the reasoning U(nsound), the premises may be either T or F. (This is obvious enough, since any statement whatsoever, whether T or F, can be the premise of an unsound argument with a T conclusion).

8 If the conclusion is F, and the reasoning is U(nsound), the premises may be either T or F (for the same reason as in point 7).

Finally, let's suppose that we have information about the truth or falsity of the premises and of the conclusion. What, then, can we say about the soundness of the inference? As before, there is only one case in which we can say something definite.

9 If the premises are T and the conclusion is F, then the reasoning must have been U(nsound) (from the definition of sound inference). Here is a key way to check out the reasoning in an argurment, if we happen to be in possession of the required knowledge about the truth or falsity of the premises and conclusion. Of course, since an argument is usually employed to help us decide whether the conclusion is T, we usually do not know in advance that it is false, and we have to use other standards to tell us whether the reasoning (and the inference) was sound. We'll get to them later.

10 If the premises are F and the conclusion is F, the reasoning might have been S(ound) or U(nsound). (Take any two unrelated false statements you like, call one the premise and the other the conclusion, and you have an example of unsound reasoning that fits this pattern. But the inference from 5 = 6 to 5 + 1 = 6 + 1 is Sound, though both premises and conclusions are F; so either option is open.)

11 If the premises are F and the conclusion is T, you can't say whether the reasoning was S(ound) or U(nsound). (Look at points 3 and 2 above and make up your own example.)

12 If the premises are F and the conclusion is T, you still can't tell if the inference was S(ound). (For example, the premises and the conclusion might be about entirely different topics, in which case the reasoning would be unsound; or they might be components of a perfect argument.)

The table follows; the facts you know at first are underscored.

	Premise	Inference	Conclusion
* 1	T̲	S	T
2	F̲	S̲	?
3	F̲	U̲	?
4	T̲	U̲	?
* 5	F	S̲	F̲
6	?	S̲	T̲
7	?	U̲	T̲
8	?	U̲	F̲
* 9	T̲	U	F̲
10	F̲	?	F̲
11	F̲	?	T̲
12	T̲	?	T̲

The asterisks in the table indicate the only cases where we can make a definite decision. If you look at them carefully, you'll see they are really just different ways of saying the same thing, or expressing its consequences; that *a good inference from a true premise leads to a true conclusion.* (As we've mentioned before, you have to qualify this slightly if you want to talk about probably true statements, but the general pattern remains the same.)

So far, we've mainly talked of "basic arguments," that is, arguments with a single premise and a single conclusion. What we've said applies equally well to complex arguments, those with more than one premise and/ or conclusion, provided that you remember one thing. If there's more than one premise, for example, they are all being asserted to be true jointly; hence, even if only one of them is false, the joint assertion of all of them is no longer true. So, to take an easy illustration, if we have an argument with several premises of unknown truth which, by means of sound reasoning, lead us to a conclusion which is false, we know that there's something wrong with the premises. If there was only one premise, we'd know that it had to be false (see the above table). If there are several premises, all we can conclude is that at least one of them must be false. We can't conclude that all of them are false, nor that only one of them is false. You can read the table in just the same way, as long as you remember that where it says that the premise (or the conclusion) must be false, with a set of several premises or several conclusions, it means that there is something wrong with the set as a whole; that is, at least one of the component statements is false.

Another type of more complex argument has already been illustrated in the last chapter. This is what we can call a "chain argument," that is, an argument where the conclusion from one argument becomes the premise for another. The simplest possible form of this is an argument with a single premise which leads to a single conclusion, which in turn leads to another conclusion. The only thing you have to remember about this kind of argument is that the conclusion of the first subargument is a premise in the second subargument. Hence, you should treat it as consisting of two separable arguments. These will be covered by different lines in the table above, depending on which argument you're looking at in detail. Notice that the simplest possible chain argument is quite different in structure from an argument with two premises and one conclusion, essentially because it involves two inferences instead of one, and hence is open to attack on the soundness of its inferences at two points instead of just one.

4-2

If you have a firm grasp on the contents of the preceding section, you will have no difficulty in mastering the following distinction, which is quite important when you want to speak precisely about arguments. Suppose that we want to talk about the inference in an argument, as opposed to the premises in it, or the argument as a whole. Suppose that we let the letter p stand for the premise(s) and the letter q stand for the conclusion. Then the argument as a whole involves at least the assertion of the premise p and the assertion (explicit or implicit) that the premise implies q. It may also involve the assertion of q, or it may just leave this as an unstated implication of the two preceding claims. The point of the argument is, of course, to establish q. We do it by marshalling, in its support, the premise p and the claim that p implies q. There's an admirably brief way to express an argument of this basic form, which is, "p, so q" (or "q, because p"). In this very concise expression, the part that is implicit is the inference itself.

Now notice the crucial difference between "p, so q" and "If p, then q." The first asserts that p is the case, and it asserts that q is the case. The second does *not* assert that either p or q is the case. The second only makes a hypothetical claim; on the assumption (hypothesis) that p is true, then q would have to be true. The first claim, the most concise possible expression of an argument ("p, so q"), actually involves the second as one of its components—in this case, as an unstated component. But it goes much further; it also asserts the truth of the premise(s) and the truth of the conclusion(s).

It follows from all this that you have to be very careful not to attack the statement "If p, then q" on the grounds that p isn't the case, or that q isn't the case. The hypothetical statement in quotes (sometimes also called a conditional statement), asserts only that there is a connection between the truth of p and the truth of q; this is the sort of connection whose meaning is illustrated in the table above. It says only that if p is true, then q has to be true; but it doesn't say that p is true, or that q is true.

Conditional or hypothetical statements are a way of expressing the inference on which an argument depends. They involve a much weaker claim than the claim involved in an argument, because they assert only that a connection exists between two possibilities and not that either of them is an actuality.

Now a conditional statement ("If p, then q") may express a connection which is true as a result of the meaning of the terms involved in p and q, which would make it a "logical (or definitional) truth"; or the connection may be one which depends for its truth upon laws of nature or particular facts about the world, in which case it is a scientific or empirical truth. And, as we've previously mentioned, the line between these kinds of truth isn't a sharp one; they are just conveniently distinguished.

4-3

We're now in a position to clarify a pair of terms that are common enough in the language, extremely useful in assessing arguments, definitions, scientific relations, and so on. These are the terms "necessary condition" and "sufficient condition." To say that p is a sufficient condition for q is to say that the truth of p suffices to guarantee the truth of q, or that "If p, then q." As a simple example, let's say that p might be the claim that a supertanker has broken up in a storm in the western Pacific, and q might be the claim that the rainfall west of the Rockies in the United States will go down by 50 percent in the ensuing nine-month period. It has recently been suggested that one of the really big supertankers—the ones displacing more than a half million tons—could spill a big enough oil slick to cover some millions of square miles, and that this spill would sufficiently affect the evaporation rate so that the water intake into the cloud system would be very seriously affected. That cloud system, originating in that particular area of the Pacific, is what feeds the West Coast with moisture. Hence, it is being asserted that a supertanker breakup in that area would cause the loss of a great deal of rainfall (and probably also nearly all the crops, including those dependent on irrigation, since the irrigation comes from the snow pack which also depends on precipitation). Here's a case of an (alleged) sufficient condition. A certain state of affairs is, or is said to be, sufficient to produce another state of affairs.

The p here would be the assertion that a state of affairs occurred since we have arranged to use p as an abbreviation for an assertion. But we normally say that the state of affairs to which p refers is a sufficient condition for that to which q refers. These are called, respectively, the *antecedent* and the *consequent* conditions or circumstances. The "assertion" p is of course only a hypothetical assertion here, and is sometimes called the *hypothesis*; the assertion q is said to be a *consequence* of that hypothesis. Of course, this is an empirical sufficient condition and not a purely logical one (that is, one that depends purely on the meaning of words). Even though it's a disputed question whether there are really any "purely logical" sufficient conditions, it's clear that there are some that come so close that it's a useful approximation to treat them as being purely logical; for example, it would ordinarily be said that having a daughter is a sufficient condition for being a parent, in virtue of the very meanings of the words involved.

A *necessary* condition, on the other hand, is a condition which must obtain (is necessary) in order that another condition obtain. Someone might say that it's necessary (or essential) to provide typhoid patients with enormous quantities of fluid, in order that they will survive. One can express this by saying that a necessary condition for survival of a typhoid patient is the intake of very large quantities of liquid. (Thousands of deaths resulted from the failure to recognize that it was the dehydration resulting from the dysentery associated with typhoid fever that was causing the deaths of many victims.)

Necessary and sufficient conditions are not, of course, the same. Providing a great deal of water for typhoid patients doesn't guarantee, that is, isn't a sufficient condition for, their survival, but it is a necessary condition for it. The breakup of a supertanker in the western Pacific isn't a necessary condition for a catastrophic reduction of rainfall in the western United States, since other things, such as a shift in the jetstream, could also cause it, but it is (allegedly) a sufficient condition for it. Banning the sale of spray cans containing Freon may not be a sufficient condition to prevent the destruction of the ozone layer in the atmosphere but (it is often argued) it is a necessary condition. That is, we have to do that, it's *necessary* to do that, in order to prevent that disaster; it may not be enough, but we must do it or else we can't avoid that result.

All these assertions about necessary and sufficient conditions can be expressed using the terminology of "implies," "consequences," "can be inferred from," and the like, but they are useful abbreviations for what is often a complicated circumlocution expressed in those other terms. *Wherever it's true that q follows from p, it's true that q (and the state of affairs referred to in p) is a sufficient condition for q (and the state of affairs referred to in q).*

Which leads us to an interesting discovery. If p implies q, which means that p is a sufficient condition for q, then p guarantees the truth of q, that is, it makes the truth of p necessary. Hence, p can't be true unless q is true, so q is a necessary condition for p. So, whenever p is a sufficient condition for q, q is a necessary condition for p. Reread that sentence, because it shows the way in which these concepts are completely complementary. Notice that it does not say that if p is a sufficient condition for q, then p is a necessary condition for q. It says that if p is a sufficient condition for q, the q is a necessary condition for p. The terms are opposites in the same way that "taller than" and "shorter than" are. If Jones is taller than Smith, then Smith is shorter than Jones. If p is a sufficient condition for q, then q is a necessary condition for p. (The technical term for these is "converse relationships.")

Referring back to our previous examples, we can see that, while the supertanker spill is not a necessary condition for the reduction of rain, the reduction of rain is (allegedly) a necessary condition for the supertanker spill. That is, according to the claim being made here, the reduction of rain is a necessary consequence of the spill, that it must necessarily occur if the spill does occur; that is, it is a necessary condition for the spill. This sounds a little odd, in this particular case, because the reduction in rainfall will occur after the spill, and we usually employ the necessary and sufficient condition vocabulary to refer to conditions which occur before or concurrently with whatever they are said to be necessary and sufficient conditions for. But that's not an essential part of their meaning, it's just usually so. The exact way to formulate the condition is to say that the reduction in rainfall over a certain period is a necessary condition for the spill to have occurred earlier. In the same way, when we've said that the ingestion of a very large quantity of water is a necessary condition for recovery from typhoid, it follows automatically that recovery from typhoid is a sufficient condition from which we can infer that there was at an earlier stage a substantial intake of water.

When we turn to examples of *logically* necessary and sufficient conditions, we don't have to worry about these somewhat awkward sounding changes of tense. If we assume for the moment that arithmetic, and mathematics in general, is a rigorous, logical development from the definitions of the basic concepts of mathematics (the usual view), we can give plenty of examples of necessary and sufficient conditions from arithmetic. For example, it's a sufficient condition for being divisible by 3 that a number should be divisible by 9; but of course it isn't a necessary condition. Since it's a sufficient condition, however, the converse must be a necessary condition; let's see if this is true. Is it a necessary condition for being divisible by 9 that a number be divisible by 3? Of course it is.

There are many cases where a condition is both necessary and sufficient. For example, it is both a necessary and a sufficient condition for being divisible by 9 that a number should be divisible by 3, leaving a dividend that is itself divisible by 3. If either of these conditions is met, then the other is met. Each is a necessary and sufficient condition for the other. They are sometimes said to be "equivalent conditions." Conditions that are both necessary and sufficient for each other occur in the empirical realm as well, though they are somewhat less common there. In the field of medicine, a pathognomonic symptom is one which is a unique identifier of the particular disease or condition. If the condition is present, then that symptom is present; if that symptom is present, then the disease is present. Each is a necessary and sufficient condition for the other. (Most symptoms are neither sufficient nor necessary conditions for the disease of which they are symptoms, but the collection of symptoms, known as a syndrome, which definitely identifies the standard form of the disease, is a sufficient condition and sometimes is a necessary condition.)

The most useful employment of terms like "necessary" (and "sufficient") conditions in the empirical realm occurs when we wish to make a distinction between the relationships of certain conditions to an effect. It is often very important to make it quite clear that, whereas the provision of a certain type of medication is essential (necessary) in order that the patient should recover from a certain disease, it by no means guarantees (is sufficient for) recovery. Similarly, in talking about the analysis of circuits or economic conditions, we often need to be very careful to distinguish sufficient conditions for a certain state of affairs from necessary conditions for it.

We started off this discussion of sufficient and necessary conditions by using the letters p and q to stand for statements or assertions. Along the way, we occasionally used them to stand for states of affairs, and even for properties. There are certain circumstances in which it's really important to distinguish statements, for example, from properties, but this doesn't happen to be one of them. When talking about sufficient and necessary conditions, one can always convert the possession of a property into an equivalent statement to the effect that that property is possessed by the object in question, and vice versa. So we can say either that certain states of affairs whose occurrence is expressed by statements, or that certain properties, possession of which is a state of affairs, are necessary or sufficient conditions for other states of affairs or properties. The language is equally useful in either case.

4-4

You are now in possession of a fairly precise vocabulary for the major part of argument analysis. It should be stressed again that some of the distinctions that we will be using, and have already introduced, are not absolutely sharp ones. We have pointed out that the distinction between factual inconsistency and logical inconsistency isn't a sharp one. We've talked about the way in which some "If p, then q" statements (conditional statements) are statements of implications, whereas others are statements of causal connection and others are not even clearly that. Those distinctions aren't sharp, either. Nevertheless, you can see that a conditional statement is sometimes telling you about an inference that you can make, and on other occasions it seems to be telling you something about the connection between possibilities. In the context of a complete argument or a conversation in a particular setting, you will rarely find any difficulty in making the distinction, so don't worry that it isn't possible to give an abstract definition of the distinction.

But you need to be on your guard against another (related) word or two that can mislead you seriously in the analysis of practical prose. Just as the form of words "If p, then q" is often, but not always, an indication that somebody is telling you something about what can be inferred from what, so the form of words "q, because p" is often an indication that q is the conclusion for which p is the reason—but not always. Sometimes it's just telling you what the cause of a particular event was. For example, "I got wet because the top on the car is leaking" isn't telling you about a premise from which you can infer a conclusion; it's telling you about a physical cause for a physical effect. "He picked up venereal disease because he would insist on joining every swinging group in range" cannot be reconstructed in the form of an argument with a statement about the man's activities as the premise and his contracting venereal disease as the conclusion; the first didn't "lend support to" the second, or even make it very likely it produced it or caused it. (It only increased the possibility of it, not necessarily to a very high level.) The very word "because" obviously has an origin that is connected with the origin of the term "causation"; but it has become one of the principal words that we use in order to indicate the connection between reasons and conclusions. And there are plenty of intermediate cases where it's very hard to say whether "because" is being used to indicate a cause or a reason, but again that doesn't prove to be very bothersome in the full context of an argument. And you can always cover yourself in argument analysis by considering both alternatives explicitly. The main point to remember is that you have to keep your eyes open to see whether we're looking at a case which is clearly one where a mere causal connection is being asserted, or a case where we clearly have a reason that is being put forth for a certain conclusion.

The final irony is that even the word "reason" is sometimes used to indicate a cause. "The reason why the cooking stove in the boat won't work is that somebody put kerosene into it instead of alcohol." This is really a factual claim, a causal claim; it's just like "He died of a heart attack." It doesn't give you reasons for you to accept the conclusion, it gives you an explanation of an event. Most heart attacks are not fatal, but this one was.

Compare that with "I think this stove was made in Switzerland, because it has the word "Berne" stamped on the base, though the rest of the stamp marking is pretty well impossible to read." Here, somebody is giving you a reason for drawing a certain conclusion, the reason being that the name of a Swiss city is stamped on the stove, and one of the missing premises is, of course, that it's quite common for manufacturers to stamp the place of manufacture on their products. (What's another missing premise in this argument? Quiz 4-B, 5.)

In general, you won't have too much difficulty with identifying real arguments for argument analysis, as opposed to complicated descriptions and case histories, as long as you constantly bear in mind the importance of getting a general sense of the purpose or function of the whole passage before you start the analysis. Don't lose the woods for the trees, don't be misled by the words like "because" or "reason" or "since" or "if . . . , then. . . ." None of these will guarantee that you're looking at an argument. They should make you prick up your ears because they are often used in arguments, but they don't guarantee the presence of an argument; they're not a sufficient condition or a necessary condition for the presence of an argument.

4-5

Let's look at this question of identifying arguments in a slightly broader framework. One of the quiz questions at the end of Chapter 3 required you to go out and find an argument for criticism. Some of you, if you did that, will undoubtedly have brought back material that looked like an argument to you, but you couldn't sell the instructor on it. Let's look at a few of the usual mistakes that people make in identifying arguments.

First, they tend to pick on something that is argumentative, that is, controversial or emotional. But often people who are talking about a disputatious subject do so by means of a long harangue, which is merely emotional discourse "expanding on the theme" of their point of view, but which doesn't provide arguments (not even bad ones) for the conclusion which they are espousing. Patriotic speeches, lengthy condemnations of the evils of our times, often look like very good material to the eye of the inexperienced argument analyzer. But they frequently don't pass the test of providing reasons for a conclusion, reasons that can be separated from the conclusions. Sometimes, though, you can work out an implicit conclusion and reconstruct them as arguments. Keep asking yourself whether what you are about to identify as the premises of the argument could be established independently of the conclusion. If they can't be established independently, then they're really just another way of expressing the same facts, and all you have is a kind of verbal translation of one sentence into another. Here's a letter in a national magazine, commenting on an article it had published on aviation safety. The writer says that the article is:

> The most distorted, ill-conceived and damaging piece of sensationalist journalism I have ever read. As an air-traffic-control specialist as well as a commercial pilot, I feel qualified to comment. Through the efforts of many knowledgeable and dedicated professionals within the aviation industry, a rapidly increasing number of people and organizations are recognizing air transportation as the safest, most efficient and most economical means of moving people and cargo.

The writer is obviously in an argumentative mood. But what is he presenting in the way of an argument? He is saying that he personally thinks the article was very bad, and he does know something about the subject. Now you can't write controversial articles without somebody disagreeing; that's what it means to call them controversial. And they would hardly qualify as controversial if the only people who disagreed were people with absolutely no knowledge or experience in the areas. So the fact that this person, with considerable experience in the area, disagrees doesn't give us a reason for rejecting the arguments in the article. The next sentence of the letter is really just another plug for aviation, and all it does, again, is to say that a large number of people think air transportation is great. Did the original article say that it wasn't great, or just that it had a lot of serious things wrong with it which ought to be corrected? We don't know and, in the absence of any specific quote from the letter writer, what he says here doesn't appear to count against anything that you can tell was in the article; hence, it isn't an argument against the article.

As a matter of interest, the letter, analyzed as straight prose, makes a number of extremely dubious statements; for example, the claim that air transportation is the safest means of moving people. Even the Air Transport Association's own statistics place trains ahead of planes as safe carriers.

The letter illustrates an important point to watch when you're trying to develop criticism. Don't confuse it with letting off steam, with merely announcing that you and perhaps many others disagree. Nobody's going to be very surprised by that. What the writer should have done, of course, is to show that some claim or passage or general implication of the article is in fact wrong by appealing to independently gathered or faultlessly objective evidence. Indeed, if you think carefully about the piece, you'll realize that his very appeal to experience contaminates him as an independent judge. It turns out that he is an air traffic control specialist, that is, somebody who earns a living from the success of the airlines. However conscientious people may be, it's hard to be sure that they will be unbiased in assessing claims about the industry which supports them. Similarly, the fact that the letter-writer is a commercial pilot also shows that he has considerable investment in the continuing success of aviation. The fact that he disagrees with an attack on its safety may well show only that he feels severely threatened by the attack, not that his experience objectively shows the attack to have been wrong. As we'll see when we get to a more detailed discussion of bias, one can't act as if everybody involved in or dependent on a field is automatically biased about it, but one also can't act as if the connection doesn't introduce a serious possibility of bias, and hence, a serious weakness in this kind of "argument," which merely consists in giving one's own opinion.

Reflecting further on the piece, we see that, apart from the letter-writer's certainly false claim about the safety of air transportation, there is an implied claim that an increasing number of people are using it. But the statistics show that the airlines are in trouble, apparently because of a decrease in use rates per 1,000 head of population (which is the appropriate index, incidentally, rather than absolute numbers).

Thus, even though he doesn't present anything that really qualifies as an argument, it's possible for us to do some criticism of the ways in which he fails to present an argument, so the example is not without some potentiality as an exercise. But it certainly isn't an example of a good, or even good-looking but fundamentally fallacious, argument.

The Acting Administrator of the Federal Aviation Administration, the key agency in this area, also wrote in to complain about this particular article. And, for a change, he quotes a passage from the article; he then produces facts to refute it, the right approach. It turns out that he doesn't do very much better, although his approach is a very much better one. Here's what he says:

> I take particular exception to Gonzales' gratuitous remark that generally "the F.A.A. won't issue an air-worthiness directive (which has the force of the law)

until something terrible happens." As a matter of fact, the F.A.A. issues or revises around 200 air-worthiness directives (A.D.'s) every year as a result of its regular surveillance program, . . .

That looks like a good, straightforward, honest refutation of a careless generalization, doesn't it? But as you look at it really carefully, you notice a couple of words which weaken its impact a good deal. Before you read any further, look at the passage and see if you can identify the two key qualifying terms that greatly weaken this attempt at refutation. Both key words appear outside the passage that is being quoted from the original article. The first of them is "generally," from which we can infer that Gonzales did not categorically state that the F.A.A. won't issue an A.D. "until something terrible happens," but that he only said that this was generally or usually the case, presumably meaning that this was more often than not the case. Now what has the Acting Administrator got to do to refute this? He has to show that most of the A.D.'s that are issued by the F.A.A. are based on something other than a terrible occurrence. What does he in fact show? Assuming for the moment that the facts are exactly as he describes them, "the F.A.A. issues or *revises* around 200 A.D.'s every year." So the second term that weakens the apparent refutation is the term which I've italicized in this quotation, the word "revises." If Gonzales was talking about *issuing* A.D.'s and if the Acting Administrator is talking about *issuing* or *revising,* the one claim hardly refutes the other. They are about categories of A.D.'s that overlap to an unknown extent, but might overlap only to a very small extent. That is, most of the 200 A.D.'s that change in some way every year may be revisions. The case against Gonzales is looking weaker.

Nor is that the end of the trouble. Remember that Gonzales's basic claim, as far as we can infer from these letters which are intended to be read by people who don't have the original article in front of them, is that it takes "something terrible" to get the F.A.A. to produce an air-worthiness directive. The reply from the Acting Administrator would be a relevant counterargument if there were many fewer than 200 terrible events in the aviation industry every year. It looks as though the Acting Administrator is operating on that assumption because if there are, for example, 400 air disasters each year, the fact that 200 A.D.'s are issued hardly shows that it doesn't take something terrible to produce one. But there are more than a few hundred crashes, near-crashes, near-misses, or structural failures in the course of a year in the aviation industry, so that figure of 200 doesn't cut much ice as a counterargument. The best interpretation one could make in favor of the Acting Adminstrator is to say that the key point here, although it's not well brought out, is that these 200 A.D.'s come from the F.A.A. "as a result of its regular surveillance program," and that a "regular surveillance program" has nothing to do with the kind of event that we would refer to as "something terrible." That may be so, but it's not too obvious, since one would think that the regular surveillance program would involve, amongst other things, investigation of wrecks and structural failures which could be regarded as something terrible.

So here are a couple of examples of careful reasoning at work, the first devoted to showing that what looked like an argument really was hardly worthy of the name, whereas the second one showed that what looked at first sight like a good tight criticism was in fact very weak (which is not to say that further investigation might not show that it could be improved). Our verdict must be, on the evidence available, that the first letter really makes no significant contribution to the discussion at all, and that the second one raises a point which it certainly fails to show is a conclusive argument against the original article.

You'll have further opportunities to try out your skill in distinguishing arguments that are worth examining from those that aren't, and in particular from those that are mere rhetoric, in the quizzes at the end of this chapter. One impression that you should not pick up from this discussion concerns the relevance of emotional and "loaded" language to logic. It's often thought that logic is somehow a cool and precise discipline, in which emotion has no place. On the contrary, there are many occasions where reason forces one to the conclusion that an outrageous crime has been committed and should be condemned as such, or to one that fully justifies enthusiastic and affectionate support of some person or resolution. In the same way, it's a complete mistake to automatically criticize arguments on the ground that they use emotional or highly loaded language. That language serves a function, it has a meaning, and whatever that function or meaning, it may be appropriate or inappropriate in certain circumstances. The task of the reasoner is to determine whether, and when, that language is appropriate to the evidence or the situation, and to criticize it only if it's not appropriate. Most of the really interesting uses of reasoning center on highly controversial and emotional issues; they're interesting not just because it's often harder to handle this kind of argument but also because it's often more important, since issues where people get upset and deeply involved are likely to be more crucial.

Another point to remember is that the fact that a passage may consist intrinsically (that is, taken just by itself) of a rhetorical tirade does not justify supposing that it shouldn't be reconstructed as an argument; after all, it's quite likely that it is, in that context, meant to support a particular conclusion. If you can see what that conclusion is, then state it, and begin to ask yourself whether the rhetoric supports it or merely reaffirms it.

Perhaps you are now beginning to see just how much importance there is to the first two steps of argument analysis ("Clarify the meaning" and "Identify the conclusion"). It's often not easy to do these, and the whole apparatus of your analysis depends entirely on getting these steps right, although not necessarily at the first try. The crucial point to remember is that both meaning and conclusion must be worked out by consideration of the *context* of the passage, not just by looking narrowly at the words in it. You are an extremely sophisticated language user, and you have no trouble at all, in practical terms, in sensing that somebody who tells you about the experts' opinion of Lipton's Tea is trying to sell you the stuff. What is a little harder is the business of formulating exactly what the implicit message is. We're in the business of judgment here, and there will be times when what I have to say in this text will strike you as not the most plausible interpretation of the passages that I am quoting. You may well be right about this; ask somebody else to give you an opinion. Write it up from the point of view that seems best to you. Remember that in many actual situations, you'd be able to confirm which interpretation was correct by talking to the person who had spoken or written the passage, or by reading or listening further. Additional disagreements between us about the relatively short passages that we deal with in a text would likely diminish with this further exposure. But, even if we disagree now and again, perhaps on important points, it doesn't mean that we won't agree about most of the important points in analyzing arguments. Don't carry away the picture that a single error in argument analysis is always fatal. It is much more likely to be fatal if it occurs at the point where you're trying to get a general sense of the meaning of the passage. But even then, you may pick up a number of valuable criticisms further down the Seven Steps.

4-6

Now it's time to introduce you to what we might call the ethics of argument analysis. The dominant principle here is what we can call the Principle of Charity. The Principle of Charity requires that we try to make the best, rather than the worst, possible interpretation of the material we're studying.

That is, even if, as a matter of strict grammar, we could shoot the writer down for having said something that doesn't follow or isn't strictly true, it may be more charitable to reinterpret the passage slightly in order to make more "sense" out of it, that is, to make it mean something that a sensible person would be more likely to have really meant. We'll do this all the time. It doesn't mean letting people off the hook entirely by assuming they couldn't possibly have meant something just because it turns out to be unsound or untrue; most of us make such mistakes quite often. What the Principle of Charity does mean is that "taking cheap shots" is something we shouldn't waste much time doing. Other words that come in from ordinary language about this point are "nit-picking" and "attacking (or setting up) a straw man." These terms all refer to poor argument analysis, either to making irrelevant criticisms or to making criticisms that are not relevant to the main thrust of the argument or that are unfair in some other way.

The Principle of Charity is more than a mere ethical principle, but it is at least that. It requires you to be fair or just in your criticisms. They can be expressed in heated terms, if that is appropriate; they may involve conclusions about the competence, intellectual level, or conscientiousness of the person putting forward the argument, all of which may well be justified in certain cases. But your criticisms shouldn't be unfair; they shouldn't take advantage of a mere slip of the tongue or make a big point out of some irrelevant point that wasn't put quite right. So the Principle of Charity does coincide with good practical advice about powerful and efficient argument analysis. It tells you that you want to interpret the argument's meaning in whatever way makes the most sense and force out of it, because otherwise, *it can easily be reformulated slightly in order to meet your objections.* That's why it is sound practical advice. "Setting up a straw man," means setting up—for the purpose of attack—an argument which is not the real one to be discussed but a poor imitation of it, which is easier to criticize, and which is sloppy argument analysis because it can so easily be rebutted. There will no doubt be political occasions where you can get away with this kind of thing, but it's a very cheap victory when you do, because it's not only unethical but so highly vulnerable to counterattack that it's a dubious strategy even on selfish grounds.

We'll make a good deal in this text of the difference between "strong" and "weak" criticisms of arguments. Roughly speaking, the difference is that a weak criticism is one that can be refuted by rather modest changes in the argument, or that depends upon a rather dubious interpretation or on what is, at best, a possibility. By contrast, a strong criticism is one that gets at the heart of the argument, hits it in a way that can't be evaded without giving up the main thrust of the argument, rests on indubitable interpretations and highly likely claims, and so on. You're on your way to making strong criticisms rather than weak ones when you take account of the Principle of Charity in these early steps where you're trying to get both a sense of the general meaning of the argument and everything in it and a sense of what its main point is, that is, what conclusion it's trying to establish.

Suppose somebody says, "It's a good thing that President Ford wasn't assassinated in Sacramento in July 1975, because then Rockefeller would have become President, which would have been a disaster." An example of a cheap shot would be to say something like: "You mean that you don't care at all about the life of a man who's given many years of devoted service to his country, that all you care about is the political situation after he is infamously killed? And you don't care about the fact that this would have been a vicious and pointless act of violence—you're more interested in the balance of power in the Republican Party?" That kind of response is very common, and it can't be justified on the basis of the passage quoted. The speaker who is worried about President Ford's successor may very well have deep concern for these other matters, but simply be focusing on one of the several dimensions of the effect of such an assassination, when making this comment. It's easier to criticize the speaker by bringing in all these other points because they all are very relevant to the conclusion and important. If you can successfully accuse an arguer of having overlooked relevant and important points—for example, if this speaker had claimed to be giving an overview of all the reasons why the assassination would have been unfortunate—of course you have a strike against him. But you have no real basis for that line of criticism, so we regard it as a cheap shot, and certainly as violating the Principle of Charity.

The example quoted serves as a pretty good illustration of some of the difficulties that people have with Step 2, Identifying the Conclusions. In one of the trial classes using these materials, several students identified the claim that Rockefeller would have been a disastrous President as the conclusion. One of the reasons they gave for making this identification was the importance and the controversial nature of that claim. But the force of a claim doesn't show it's the conclusion of an argument. It's true that we often try to establish (that is, make into a conclusion) the most controversial claim in an argument because it's the one that most needs support, but sometimes, too, we use controversial claims as premises. In this case, it is *because* the arguers believed that Rockefeller would have made a bad President that they concluded that it was fortunate that Ford wasn't assassinated in Sacramento.

4-7

What we're doing in this chapter is exploring the general procedure for argument analysis in enough depth to give you a good understanding of the basic logic behind it, and some examples of its application. We're still talking about fairly general logical issues that come into argument analysis; in later chapters, we're going to get into some of the detailed procedures that fall under each of these headings, but first we need to get the basic conceptual framework set up solidly.

One of the "basic framework" questions that seriously bothers beginners concerns drawing the line between factual criticism and logical criticism. You will have noticed in some of the examples we've just been discussing, about aviation safety, for example, that I occasionally make some reference to facts that bear on the argument under discussion which you may not have known. While it's a good general principle that the main function of argument analysis is to concentrate on errors of logic rather than on errors of fact, and while it's certainly true that you, the student, are not going to be held responsible for knowing all sorts of details about the operations of the Federal Aviation Administration and a million other subject matters of examples that you'll come across, there are two points to bear in mind. First, even if you are not certain about the exact facts in a particular case, it may be a matter of common knowledge or belief that there are some exceptions to a generalization which is being quoted as a premise to an argument you are scrutinizing; it's perfectly appropriate for you to raise these possibilities of error. You're not saying that the premise is definitely wrong, but that it would need to be checked out carefully in certain respects, which you are pointing to. So don't underestimate the extent to which you know a little bit about a lot of things and the extent to which this knowledge can be useful in pinpointing possible weaknesses in an argument. Argument analysis doesn't always score big by mentioning such possibilities, but it has done a useful task because it has indicated where the argument needs further support or clarification. If you're the person who is putting the argument forward, this indication is helpful, just as it's helpful if you're investigating the argument to see whether it ultimately stands up. And there is one important type of argument where discovering a possibility is completely fatal to the argument. What is that kind of argument? (Quiz 4-B, 6.)

The second reason why I sometimes bring in a few extra comments of a factual kind that I wouldn't expect every reader to know about is simply that they are interesting and worth knowing for purposes of assessing other arguments, or even the particular ones under discussion, for their impact on your own behavior and beliefs. Of course, it's reasonable to suppose that I'll be wrong about some of these so-called facts that I produce, and you should be on your guard against accepting them from me any more than from the authors of other textbooks, or from arguments that you encounter. Regard them as interesting and relevant claims, and if the matter has considerable importance to you, check them out further before relying on them.

What you are expected to know about is the meaning of terms, because you not only speak the language but you certainly have access to a dictionary which you can use if the term either has a technical flavor or is a relatively uncommon one. With arguments that you are going to consider seriously, for a written assignment perhaps, it's strongly recommended that you turn to an encyclopedia and not just a dictionary, because you'll often find that facts and possibilities will emerge from the articles in there that will sharply affect your appraisal of the arguments, including even your appraisal of the inferences and not just their (factual) premises. Certainly you are in a better position to criticize arguments about a technical subject if you know a good deal about the subject matter; but you may still be able to criticize them on purely logical grounds although you know nothing about the topic. One often reads discussions or sees television shows in which the justifiability of a certain type of surgical operation is being debated, and without knowing anything at all about the specific details of the medical risk, you may easily see ways of handling the problem of whether and how much to inform the patient. Or, accepting the figures produced by the admittedly biased advocates of the surgical procedure, you may still see analogies with other risks in our society, such as the risk of death in traffic, which can lead to a very different viewpoint on the advisability of the operation in question. Or you may see loopholes in the experiment that is being quoted as supporting a position. Errors of reasoning occur even in the heart of science; and indeed, they are surprisingly common there, particularly errors of reasoning about the practice and the funding of that particular branch of science, rather than errors of reasoning within the science itself. Scientists are very prone to think that their care, skill, training, and frequently high intelligence will automatically carry over, for example, to the administration of science, the funding of science, or the application of science to human affairs. It's an open question whether these experts are as good at arguing about such matters as an intelligent lay person, and on the track record, we have to conclude that they are very often highly unreliable there, just as is the lay person.

The question of how to draw the line between factual criticism and logical criticism, which we've been discussing in this section, naturally leads to the question of exactly how to distinguish between the premises and inferences in an argument. Much of what we were discussing in the opening sections of this chapter bears on this point, and as we are now about ready to consider the steps of portraying structure (Step 3) and identifying the missing premises (unstated assumptions) (Step 4), it's appropriate for us to turn to this point.

4-8

Here we are, then, facing a great big slab of argument—perhaps a paragraph or a page from a book, or even an entire article. Let's review the preliminary assessment procedures. We've read the piece through very carefully, trying to get a sense of what it's about. We've decided that there are several arguments involved in it. That is, there are several conclusions put forward as following from certain other statements which are obviously the premises (since they're not themselves in turn supported). Some of these conclusions turn out to be used as premises in a later argument, so we're looking at a passage of argument which involves some chains of argument. Studying the material still more carefully, we see that some of the sentences merely involve reviews of things that have been said or have been proved earlier and do not need to be taken into account as fresh material for purposes of analyzing the whole passage. We also notice that some parts of the argument involve historical allusions to earlier thinkers or politicians, and that they are not intended to add new evidence, but only to be of general or passing interest. So we drop them from our serious analysis, along with the repetitions. A sentence or two is obviously intended to be a rhetorical flourish, perhaps a rephrasing of one of the conclusions that has just been established, in more flowery or stirring language. Careful consideration shows that nothing is being added here. There are a couple of terms in the argument which we're not too familiar with, and we've taken the opportunity to jot down at the top of our page the relevant dictionary definitions of them. Looking carefully at the passage in the light of these dictionary definitions, we're pretty confident that there hasn't been any shift in the meaning of these terms all the way through the argument, from one dictionary definition to another, or from the dictionary definition to some illicit but attractive alternative. If in any doubt about this, we've translated the clauses in which these terms occur into other words, to see whether a switch has occurred. It's also clear that all the conclusions that are being "aimed at" by this passage of argument are explicitly stated within the argument. If they aren't there, we'll state them as carefully as we can and write them in the margin at the appropriate place on our rough working copy, attaching to them a number corresponding to the place where they occur in the argument, all of whose functioning assertions we have now numbered in sequence. If you're having any real difficulty in sorting out what the arguments are trying to establish or how they go about doing it, now is the time to write down some criticisms of unclarity of expression or structure. Later on, you'll come back to look at whether these are serious criticisms that should be given high priority in the final report, or whether they're relatively minor and deserve just passing mention toward the end of your report. Never expect to be able to write the final report straight off. Write a first draft after you've filled out the working-sheet entries, and then try for a final draft.

Now that your general picture of the passage is beginning to take shape, go back and read it again and see whether you're missing something. Perhaps some of those sentences that you dropped out do add a bit to the argument—perhaps they add a little extra information that should be taken account of as a premise, even if you have to rewrite them into a very condensed form in order to express this little bit of information clearly. Since it saves a lot of rewriting, one can usually immediately number the assertions as they occur in the printed passage that you're considering. If you have to rewrite one of the sentences, cross it out in the passage but leave the number there; then, on your rough working sheet, write out the condensed form with the appropriate number next to it. That way, it will still be easy for you to read down the passage, come to a certain number that's attached to a crossed-out clause or sentence, and know just where to find the condensed version of it. Be sure that wherever there's a vague sentence, whose meaning can be understood only after you have read the whole passage (and have taken into account the Principle of Charity), you cross it out (leaving a number in its place) and rewrite it in a more precise and perhaps more charitable form.

Remember that the crucial difference between premises and conclusions, when you're trying to distinguish them, is that the premises are supposed to supply reasons for believing or accepting the conclusions. The basic premises of the whole argument will not be supported within that whole argument. Later on, you may find assertions that have been previously supported, that is, that were conclusions of an earlier phase of the argument, but which are now being put forward as reasons for yet a further conclusion. These will of course be "intermediate conclusions" in a "chain argument," and in the tree diagram of the argument they will have lines leading down *to* them as well as lines that lead down *from* them.

While you're going through this process, you will of course be beginning to notice places where the argument is vulnerable to criticism. And we'll get on to that in more detail in the next section. First, let's see if we can apply what we've been saying to an argument of a length that's slightly greater than the one about Lipton's Tea, but not yet as complicated as the kind that we will eventually handle.

> We can be proud that America has turned the corner on the depression of the last few years. At last the many indexes of recovery are showing optimistic readings. The rate of inflation has slowed, unemployment has more or less stabilized, inventories are beginning to drop, advance orders are starting to pick up, and—the best news of all—the average income figures are showing a gain. The doomsayers have been discomfited, and the free enterprise system once more vindicated.

Here's a pretty straightforward passage. First of all, we have to see if there's anything there we don't understand. Perhaps you're not certain about what "inventories" are; they're the supplies of raw materials or components that are stored by manufacturing companies from which they draw the materials for production, or at the retail end, they are the supplies of products that are warehoused in anticipation of sales. It's a sign of a depression in your situation if you can't move your inventory, and if it's true in general, the economy is probably in a depression. When you're having trouble selling goods, your inventories remain stable. They should be dropping so that you can start placing further orders for manufactured goods or raw materials and hence, during a depression, a drop in inventories is usually taken to be a sign that recovery has started up. As your inventories drop, you begin to place orders for delivery at some future time; these are called advance orders.

So the general meaning of the passage is clear, but now let's get down to a little more detail. Exactly what is the main conclusion, or what are the several conclusions? This question is not quite so easy to answer and there are three candidates. First of all, to avoid having to repeat long sections of the passage, let's label the assertions in it. It's helpful to use a different color of ink for this, so that the contrast stands out; and you may want to use colored parentheses (to distinguish them from parentheses that are part of the passage) to indicate the beginning and end of each of the numbered assertions. The assertions are really the pieces of the jigsaw puzzle, and your picture of the structure of the argument is going to relate them, showing which are conclusions and which are premises. You separate the ones which you are likely to comment on separately, even if they all serve as premises for the same conclusion and therefore could technically be given the same number. Even with these instructions, a few judgments have to be made in allocating the numbers, so let's look at one way to do it.

1
We can be proud that (America has turned the corner on the depression of the
2
last few years.) At last (the many indexes of recovery are showing optimistic
3   4
readings.) (The rate of inflation has slowed), (unemployment has more or less
5   6
stabilized,) (inventories are beginning to drop,) (advance orders are starting to
7
pick up,) and—the best news of all—(the average income figures are showing a
8   9
gain.) (The doomsayers have been discomfited,) and (the free enterprise system

once more vindicated.)

Let's walk through this, step by step. The opening words, "We can be proud that" are just a rhetorical flourish or an underlining of the significance of the argument. They aren't "what it's all about" and we can skip them right here. The first main assertion is the one that we've labeled number 1. Now we come to the second sentence. I could have just skipped this one on the ground that it merely summarizes what is going to be said with care in the following sentence. However, it does go just a little further than the summary. It says "the many indexes" and then it gives a few of them; hence it isn't adequately supported by the next sentence, which, for example, says nothing about a very popular index, the gross national product (GNP). It also doesn't say anything about retail and wholesale prices, about farm prices and foreign orders, about new housing starts and other indicators from special industries, such as automobile manufacture, that are bellwethers for the economy as a whole. So we scent a slight overgeneralization here, and we need to give this sentence a number in order to make clear that it represents a conclusion that is open to question when we analyze the argument.

In the next sentence, I break out the various claims separately, because the facts about each of them are rather different and we need to consider them separately.

I skip over one little comment in the middle of the sentence, where the writer says that "the best news of all" is that assertion 7 is true. To say that income gain is the best news of all is not just to wave a flag about it but actually to make a claim about it which could be challenged. It would be entirely appropriate to have labeled the phrase and picked up any complaints, about its justification in the analysis of the argument, but one doesn't want to get into too many of the details, and I'm inclined to think of this as being very much like the "we can be proud" kind of flourish. But nobody's going to fault you for having separated it and said something about it. You need to be clear right from the beginning of this game that, except for the very simplest arguments, there's nearly always some room for alternative ways of analyzing them. The way you structure them is only a means to an end, after all. The big question is whether you're going to come out with the really serious criticisms at the end, and not some trivial ones, or some completely unfair ones.

A similar general problem arises about the assertions that are marked 8 and 9. One could argue that these are more rhetorical flourishes, embellishments on the fact expressed in 1. But it's a little more precise to treat them as further conclusions, because they do go a little further than 1. To be specific, 8 draws a conclusion about the prophets of doom, and, after all, no evidence was given earlier in the argument as to exactly what they said other than the rather general claim that we were heading for trouble; and 9 does generalize to vindicating the free enterprise system, which might take a little more than showing that we pulled out of one slump.

Now what *is* the main conclusion, if there is one? The key conclusion is assertion 1. Several pieces of evidence are being marshaled to support it, and they are, of course, assertions 3, 4, 5, 6, and 7. They are summed up in assertion 2. Then, from this key conclusion (assertion 1), we're drawing two further assertions, namely, assertions 8 and 9. So the total structure of the passage looks like this:

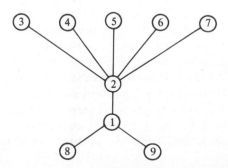

Notice that 9 doesn't follow from 8 or vice versa; they are both conclusions from 1 (along with some other assumptions about what the doomsayers said and what free enterprise amounts to).

Notice, too, that we draw separate lines from each of the various premises 3 through 7 to conclusion 2 and hence 1, not because any one of them is said to be a sufficient condition for 2 or for 1 (a situation which would also diagram the same way), but because each of them is said to support 1 at least to some degree, and we need to look at each such claim separately. We might have used the kind of diagram, illustrated earlier, where a whole set of premises is tied together with plus signs and a horizontal bracket, but it is used primarily in situations where each of the considerations has weight only in conjunction with the others; whereas here, each is supposed to have some weight by itself. Again, the difference is a matter of judgment as to the way the arguer feels about the force of these premises. To call them "indexes of recovery" suggests that each of them has some significance in its own right, so to speak.

Notice that although 8 and 9 are the "bottom line" conclusions, they are not the *key* conclusions. They are, if they can be established, politically and economically more significant than the single fact that the American recovery has begun on this particular occasion, and hence, in some sense, they are more important than what I've called the key conclusion. But that's in global terms; assertion 1 is far more important for the analysis of this argument. If it can't be established, then 8 and 9 are nowhere.

The decision to represent the inferences from 3 through 7 to 1 (with an intermediate stop at 2) by separate lines involves a certain risk which we should now state, to avoid your falling into a particular kind of trap later. It might turn out that the argument from each of these indicators is fairly weak, and we might point that out in the course of our analysis. It does not follow that the argument from all five of them can be dismissed. (That's one reason for using the form of diagram, shown earlier, which reminds you to hold them all together and to look for their *overall* strength.) True, we'll pick this point up as we get further down the Seven Steps anyway, but it's well to be forewarned.

This is a relatively simple argument, compared with many that you'll run into, and one of the ways in which it's simple is that only one person's argument is involved. Often, in reading a newspaper report, you'll see that the report itself is interpreting some facts in a particular way (this usually shows up in the heading), but the people who are being reported on are not arguing in the same way as the newspaper. If you turn back to the last exercise in the B quiz in Chapter 2, a story from the *San Francisco Chronicle,* you'll see that the headline says, "U.S. Survey Finds Bias in Home Loans," but the second paragraph says, "The Federal Home Loan Bank Board, which drew no conclusions from the survey of lending practices in five cities, . . ." So you'd have to separate two lines of argument in doing your analysis of that passage, one corresponding to the line of argument of the newspaper and the other corresponding to the line of argument of the federal agency. There are various ways you might do this, and we'll look at examples like that later, but just remember that you can't assume that all the arguments involved in a passage of argument should be treated as part of a single continuous stream.

4-9

Now we come to what is probably the hardest aspect of argument analysis, conceptually speaking. It isn't usually hard at the practical level, but there will be times at the practical level when you need to understand the conceptual issue in order to be able to proceed, and this need is what we are going to take up. We are now moving to Steps 4 and 5 in the Seven Steps; the steps that require you to identify unstated assumptions (Step 4) and criticize inferences and premises (Step 5). Here's where you begin to be able to use your schematic diagram, your "tree structure" which lays out the form of the argument. It identifies the targets for your attack. Every line on the diagram represents an inference; every number represents a premise. Some of those premises are supported and some aren't. The ones that are supported are the conclusions of an earlier argument and hence vulnerable as a result of criticism of that argument. Your basic targets are set up; now, how do you go about deciding whether they are immune to criticism, or what kind of criticism that is appropriate for them? We've already done a little bit of reconstruction; that is, we've filled in any conclusions that are implicit in the argument or in its context. We now face the question of whether to go further with the reconstruction and fill in what are called "missing premises," namely, the further assumptions that are required, in many cases, to make an inference satisfactory. We call them *unstated* assumptions because some assumptions are stated within an argument and identified as assumptions. It is not these we are talking about in Step 4, but the missing ones.

Let's begin with a simple example. Suppose some woman says, "She's a redhead, so she's probably quick-tempered." Ask yourself right away, what is the missing premise? Before you read any further, try to write it down on a piece of scrap paper. What is the speaker assuming?

A popular answer to this is that the woman is assuming, "All redheads are quick-tempered." That's incorrect; it's much too strong an assumption to saddle the speaker with. By making this the assumption, you're setting up a "straw man," and it seems easy to refute the argument by saying that it depends on an assumption to which you know a number of exceptions.

At this point, you may notice that the conclusion is "she's probably quick-tempered." It occurs to you that to get to this conclusion from the premise, you need only a much weaker generalization, namely, "Most red-heads are quick-tempered." The fact that you know some redheads who are even-tempered doesn't count at all against this more modest ("merely statistical") generalization. So the argument stands up against what at first seemed to be strong contrary evidence.

But you still don't have the assumption correct. There's a feature of the argument, simple though it is, which tells you that you're still saddling the arguer with too strong a generalization. It might be the case that most redheads aren't quick-tempered, but the argument might still be perfectly sound. Why?

The reason is that the argument is about a woman, and to support it, all you need is the assumption that most redheaded women are quick-tempered. Do you really have evidence that the statement is false? Whether it's true or false, you're at least in a much more difficult position to find a weakness in the argument than if you had presented it as depending on the original alleged assumption.

Now let's look at the argument as we've reconstructed it. We've constructed an extra premise ("Most redheaded women are quick-tempered"), which we can add to the stated premise ("She's a redhead") in order to draw the conclusion that she's probably quick-tempered. In terms of diagraming the argument, you should use letters instead of numbers to refer to the missing premises that you have constructed and add them to the diagram at the appropriate points. So, whereas this was originally the simplest possible form of tree diagram, with a single premise and a single conclusion, the diagram shown here is now one stage more complicated, with two premises and one conclusion, the second premise being labeled *a*.

Stand back and look at what we've done. When we first looked at the argument, it had a single premise and a single conclusion. The inference from the premise to the conclusion is not exactly an obvious one. It hinges upon the truth or falsity of what we've called the missing premise. But if we add the missing premise to the given premises, as we have in the reconstructed form, what can we now say about the soundness of the reconstructed argument?

Clearly, the reconstructed argument involves sound *reasoning*. Previously, it was an argument in which the inference was questionable; now it's an argument in which the *inference* is perfectly sound. Surely, it's absurd to reconstruct arguments in a way that completely changes the status of the reasoning in them from unsatisfactory to perfectly sound? That doesn't seem like an appropriate reconstruction of the original argument.

It's appropriate enough, though, because it has simply shifted the target from one place to another. The weakness will now be in that extra premise, whereas, previously, it was in the *inference*. And this illustrates a very general principle about argument analysis. You can either leave the argument the way you find it, in which case a good deal of your criticism will be criticism of the inferences in it; or you can patch it up by adding some assumptions on which it is obviously depending, in which case the inferences will be pretty satisfactory, but the assumption will now come under fire. There is no essential difference between the inferences in an incomplete argument and the missing premises in a complete argument. They both serve as the link between the original given premises and the conclusions of the argument. For this reason they are often said to be "inference-licenses." Laws of nature are a very common type of inference-license. If somebody says that Jones can't be in Honolulu at noon if he was in Capetown one microsecond before noon, the soundness of this inference depends upon the law of nature which states that nothing can travel faster than the velocity of light. We are using that law of nature as a missing premise in our argument, as a license for inferring from Jones's presence in Capetown at a microsecond before noon to the conclusion that he can't be several thousand miles away at noon. If we were to infer from the fact that he was in Capetown a minute before noon to the conclusion that he couldn't be in Hawaii at noon, we wouldn't be relying on a law of nature, but upon a technological truth of the moment, which is that we have no means of transportation that can travel at the velocity required to make this jump. In that case, the missing premise is an assumption about contemporary technology, and its truth serves as a license for the soundness of the inference.

So we have the option of criticizing the inference step as it stands or of converting the principle that underlies it into an extra premise and thereby ensuring that the inference in the reconstructed argument will be sound, although the argument will still be open to criticism because its underlying assumption, now expressed as an extra premise, is debatable. Which is the best way to approach argument analysis?

In cases where the inference steps are already very simple and clear, it's best to treat them as they stand. They may involve mistakes; for example, somebody may make an inference in doing a mathematical problem which involves a mistake because of a failure to put the decimal point in the right place or to transform from one set of units to another correctly. In such cases, one can merely point out that the inference is at fault, with the argument in its original form. Arithmetical errors and other computing errors are typical of these cases. If Jim Black has multiplied both sides of an equation by 7 and erred in multiplying the right-hand side of the equation, it's pretty pointless to say that this step in his argument "rests on the assumption that six 7s are 43." He didn't make that assumption, he just made an error in the mathematical transformation, i.e., the inference.

Another kind of case where it isn't worth reconstructing an argument by adding missing premises is when the missing premise which you are thinking of adding simply restates the whole argument. Suppose Mr. Lyons argues that it was entirely appropriate to discharge a certain patient from a psychiatric ward because her depression had shown marked signs of lifting; it's obvious that he is arguing from a single premise about the lifting of depression to a single conclusion about the appropriateness of discharging the patient. Now you can add a missing premise which says, "Whenever this particular patient's depression is lifting, it's appropriate to discharge her," and of course the argument will now, in its reconstructed form, be *logically* bulletproof. On the other hand, it is somewhat superfluous to have added the missing premise, since it tells you only that the original argument was satisfactory. We haven't obtained any illumination by adding this premise. *All* arguments depend upon the "assumption" that you can get from their specific premises to their specific conclusions, and adding this claim as a missing premise gets us nowhere. (In the example about the redhead, as a contrast, the process of formulating the missing premise led us to see exactly what was being assumed, and it wasn't just "from the premise that she's a redhead, you can draw the conclusion that she's probably quick-tempered.") So here's another sort of case where you don't want to waste your time adding missing premises: where the missing premise simply states that the argument as it originally stood was satisfactory.

In short, where there was obviously an error in calculation, a slip in the logic, or some other kind of error of mechanical reasoning, it isn't worth formulating it as a missing premise, largely because nobody would ever have assumed that. And where the required assumption is formulated in terms of the exact same premises and conclusion as the original argument, it is obvious from the fact that the original argument was put forward that this assumption was being made, and no illumination is achieved by pointing it out explicitly. Identifying missing premises has utility when they are neither trivial claims nor obvious errors in routine reasoning. It is in the large remaining body of cases where the procedure of trying to formulate the assumptions exactly pays off. The discipline of doing so leads one to realize, in a way that no other procedure does, precisely what the assumptions are on which the argument rests. And it sets them up in a form where they can be carefully assessed for essential loopholes.

Of course, once one has added the missing premises, one should not then find any remaining errors of inference in the reconstructed argument. For you have formulated the assumptions just so that they will make the reconstructed argument sound, as far as inferences are concerned. The focus of attention now shifts to the premises alone (as they relate to the reconstructed part of the argument).

Exactly how does one correctly formulate the missing premises of an argument? Here again, we find that imagination and originality are often required in this basic part of the critical process. You can see from the redhead example that a process of careful trial and error will often work. But there are times when the situation is more complicated and it is considerably more difficult to get the missing premises right. Moreover, there are often alternative ways of formulating them when more than one is involved. That's perfectly all right as long as you can produce a set of premises which together convey the essential content of the assumptions underlying the argument. To do this, you have to juggle three quite different considerations.

First, the assumptions have to be strong enough to make the argument sound. Second, they should be no stronger than they have to be, since they might then be too strong to be true, and you would then have constructed a "straw-man" version of the argument, which you would be able to criticize even though the original argument was immune to your criticism. Third, a considerably more subtle point: You also want to try to relate the assumptions as you formulate them to what the arguer would be likely to know or would believe to be true. The principal function of argument analysis is not that of reconstructing the state of mind or body of beliefs of the arguer, but this may nevertheless be a relevant consideration in some cases. You need to decide whether you are arguing against the arguer or the argument. In a dialog exchange, of course, you'll be arguing against a person, and then your best guess at what that person really believes (provided it meets the other conditions for a satisfactory missing premise) will be very relevant. In other cases, you may just have to settle for what you think makes the most sense.

Suppose that the argument about the redhead had gone like this: "She's a left-handed, cross-eyed, 6-foot redhead—you can bet she's a quick-tempered witch." Now, strictly speaking, all that the arguer is stuck with as a missing premise is a very restricted kind of a generalization. You could say that the argument assumes only that most left-handed, cross-eyed, 6-foot female redheads are quick-tempered (assuming that "witch" is a figure of speech). If you look back to the outline of the Seven Steps, you'll see that what we are talking about here is the "minimal assumption of the argument" (Step 4). We don't have any other evidence about the arguer in person, so we can't come to much of a conclusion about the arguer's assumptions on the basis of any specific evidence. However, in general terms, it's likely that the best (the optimal) assumption for the sake of analysis is that redheaded females tend to be quick-tempered, or perhaps that redheaded, cross-eyed females tend to be quick-tempered. We don't need to narrow it down any more by bringing in the 6-foot height and other features because it is extremely unlikely that the person giving this argument has any evidence on the effects of any extra conditions on the probability of a quick temper. Probably, in fact, the evidence that is available bears on the question of whether redheads in general, whether male or female, tend to be more irascible than people with other skin and hair colorations. (That's if there is any evidence at all.) It's possible that there is some evidence on this based on sex differences, so, to be charitable, we restrict the missing premise to females. But it's most unlikely that it is available in any more refined form than that, and it's only a kind of hunch that suggests that people who are cross-eyed might tend to be more irascible than those who aren't. So, with a dash of charity, we might put that in. But the real point is that assumptions ought to bear some relationship to what the available evidence can support, if they are to be the kind of thing that can help the argument along. (And, of course, they have to be logically adequate, so that they will make the inference part of the argument sound.) Hence, we look for the kind of factual claim that is likely to have evidential support, as well as being logically adequate for the argument. This usually means that we go a little stronger than the minimal assumption that would do the job, and thus finish up with what was earlier called the "optimal assumption."

Let's take another example and put it through the hoops. This one will illustrate the way in which assumptions which are put in negative form are sometimes the most illuminating ones. Suppose that we are listening to somebody arguing in favor of decontrolling the price of domestic oil and hence gasoline prices. He says, "The main reason for this is, of course, that we have just got to provide enough incentive to the oil companies to explore new fields, given the fact that the cost of explorations in the marginal areas has now gone up considerably." The structure is pretty simple. The conclusion is that we ought to decontrol oil, and the premises are that doing so will provide enough incentive to explore new fields, and that the profit margin included in the present controlled price isn't enough to cover the cost of that kind of exploration.

Now, what is the speaker assuming? Note first that it's trivial to say that he is "assuming" that from these two premises you can draw this conclusion. Of course he is, and it's a waste of time, space, and words to put it down. The question is, exactly what assumption is he making that he thinks is strong enough to bridge the gap between those premises and that conclusion? This question isn't settled by asking him directly because he may not be very good at detecting his own unconscious assumptions—he might saddle himself with a stronger assumption than he needs. One of the most important functions of argument analysis is to force one to make one's own assumptions explicit, as a result of which one frequently finds that one is assuming more than, or other than, the things one had supposed.

Putting the key question of argument analysis in terms of a vocabulary which we discussed earlier in this chapter, what we're asking is whether the premises as they stand in this argument provide a sufficient condition for the conclusion, or, if not, what we have to add to them to get that.

In the first place, of course, the arguer in the present example is assuming that if domestic oil prices are decontrolled, the price will go up. That's a very sensible assumption in view of the market situation at the moment, but it certainly is an assumption of the argument, and given the fact that overseas producers are having real problems selling their present production, it may not be true for long. Secondly, he is assuming that the prices will go up enough to provide the required new incentives. It's not entirely clear whether that is going to be true. It's a question of whether the demand will hold up at these higher prices. So you might say he is assuming the demand will hold up well enough to get the prices up to the point where they create a profit margin from which exploration in the marginal areas could be financed. But, of course, we haven't come to the end of the assumptions. There is a particularly important one still buried in that argument. Can you see what it is? Take a moment to think about it before reading further. Go back up and reread the argument carefully, and think about what you've heard in recent discussions of this issue.

The further assumption is that the oil companies will in fact put the money into further exploration, if they do succeed in increasing the prices to the level where exploration would be financially possible. Putting it negatively, the assumption is that the oil companies won't simply pocket the profits or divert them into other investments besides exploration. Of course, this really is a big assumption. As a matter of interest, on the track record of the past year or so, it's an unlikely bet. The oil companies have been showing enormously greater profits, and they have also been diversifying (that is, buying into different industries, such as hotel chains) with the profits instead of putting them into exploration. Moreover, they have been doing that with the profits they were making under controlled prices on native crude oil. This suggests they were making enough to do at least a certain amount of further exploration, but not doing it. Well, there may be all sorts of deeper pros and cons about the issue, but a little exploration in argument analysis has laid bare a series of key assumptions here which will direct our further research, and which raise questions in our minds which will substantially impede our willingness to accept this argument immediately.

Notice that we avoided talking about assumptions like "Belief in private enterprise requires decontrol." We restricted the assumptions to the oil companies because the arguer isn't sticking his neck any further out than that, and because there are certain special features of the oil industry that don't generalize across the entire private sector. We haven't destroyed the argument; it's quite possible that the reason oil companies have been diversifying or distributing their profits in recent years is that going into further oil production was not as profitable as these other enterprises, whereas it would be under decontrolled prices. On the other hand, it is by no means obvious that, given an enormously greater quantity of profit, they may not be in a position to make a business choice in favor of other completely new enterprises not related to oil production. Argument analysis doesn't always lead you to the conclusion that an argument is not good; what it may give you is a much better perception of what its strengths and weaknesses are, and that is just what it does in this case.

If you are asked to go beyond criticism to take a position on the conclusion itself, of course you'll move to Step 6 ("Consider Other Relevant Arguments"). In the present example, you would look at the question of what the effects on the domestic consumer will be of substantially increased costs of gasoline. Such costs will not only have a direct impact on the running costs of their cars, but indirect effects on the costs of all their purchases involving plastics manufactured from petroleum residues, on their home heating costs, and the cost of other goods and services whose production or provision involves fuel costs or oil costs. Senator Kennedy estimated in late 1975 that the annual effect of decontrol would be between $800 and $900 per American family; the administration's estimates have been nearer to 10 percent of that estimate. If Kennedy is right, decontrol might produce a new or worse recession. Picking up another dimension of the issue, there is the crucial problem of the nation's dependence on foreign oil and the possibility of a boycott by foreign oil suppliers as a device to impose a particular political position upon the United States. President Ford certainly believed that the nation should be willing to pay quite heavily for independence from foreign sources, which means that we have to develop more domestic sources. In his view, this line of argument might concede the truth of the earlier ones but move in a new direction to avoid decontrol by requiring a great emphasis on using more efficient methods of transportation, heating, and manufacturing. The administration is using a strategy of this kind as a backup strategy, not as a main strategy. It would certainly involve considerable changes in the life-style of most Americans, changes which would be likely to prove politically unpopular even if they were in the long run beneficial.

Having looked at all these considerations (and there are several others that are relevant), one should then be in a position to take Step Seven (Overall Evaluation) and come to a decision as to whether the oil prices should be decontrolled.

Remember that you have to do this kind of thing piecemeal. First you pick up particular arguments and subject them to careful argument analysis. Then you gradually try to assemble a comprehensive set of the main arguments that are relevant to a particular issue—something which you can do from a study of the public discussions and the technical literature connected with the topic. Finally, you are in a position to do the integration or perform a synthesis of all these considerations.

4-10

Let's go back to the example which we spent some time structuring earlier, the one about turning the corner on the depression of the last few years. Let's apply to this some of the discussion of assumption formulation and criticism that we've been getting into in the intervening sections. This is a really important type of argument, because it has persuaded many members of Congress and the media that recovery is just around the corner, or that we have just turned the corner to it, or that we have just begun it, and, as a result Congress is prepared to pass legislation that it otherwise wouldn't pass. If Congress and the media are wrong, we may be in for a much worse period ahead. Even if they are right, they may have been right because they were lucky and not because this argument is any good (which should affect our assessment of their judgment). So it deserves careful scrutiny. And it's also an important type of argument because it's just on the borderline between the technical and the commonsensical; technical enough to frighten off a good many citizens who, in fact, could perfectly well understand it with a slight effort and thus be in a better position to judge the rationality of their elected representatives.

Remember that the argument essentially has the form of quoting five indicators that have changed recently, concluding from them that "the many indexes of recovery are showing optimistic readings," concluding from that statement that we have turned the corner on the depression, and then going on to flights of higher political and economic fancy with conclusions 8 and 9, to which we will turn later.

Let's use the Seven Steps, although, as always, we may be able to pass very rapidly over some of them as soon as we have satisfied ourselves that they don't contribute usefully on this particular occasion.

Step 1: *Clarify Meaning.* We have already said something about the semitechnical terms "inventories" and "advance orders," but it's clear that there's a rather vague phrase at the core of this whole argument. The phrase is "turned the corner" as it occurs in "America has turned the corner on the depression of the last few years." What does "turning the corner" amount to? I suggest that the commonsense meaning of this phrase is the idea that things are getting better. As you will see, a good deal of the argument would look more plausible if all it had to show was that things were getting worse at a somewhat slower rate. But it's no good calling that "turning the corner"; it merely means that we have slowed down our rate of decline, and that we have not even reached the corner. That distinction, simple though it is, is obviously not clear to most headline writers in the newspapers and magazines of the seventies. One constantly sees headlines that suggest that the depression has—to use another phrase—"bottomed out," whereas the fine print shows only that the rate at which it's getting worse has slowed down a bit. The *rate* at which things get worse is of very little interest if it continues to get worse. Suppose that it simply stopped getting any worse. We still wouldn't have turned the corner; we would have stabilized in a state of depression. People all too easily switch from talking about states to rates. And that's exactly the fallacy in the argument from the first of the specific indicators that are quoted. "The rate of inflation has slowed" means merely that prices aren't increasing as fast as they used to; it doesn't mean that inflation isn't continuing. Hence, it in no way shows that we have turned the corner. We may just as well expect inflation to accelerate again as to reverse its direction—there's no way of knowing. Meanwhile, it continues, to our cost.

The second indicator, that of assertion 4, states, "Unemployment has more or less stablilized." The level at which it has stabilized is high enough to produce incredible hardship, including an income below the official subsistence level, for millions of families. If it remains constant at this level, we will not have left the depression at all. Even if it has stabilized at this level, that's no sign that it's going to get better. This may be the permanent level for it, given the present management of the economy. Changes such as decontrolling the price of oil would, in Senator Kennedy's view, start unemployment on the rise again, and there are many other significant national policy decisions which might have the same effect. On the other hand, President Ford may be right, and we may go upward. This argument certainly doesn't show that we have turned to corner yet. Remember, too, that official unemployment figures are highly suspect: they tend not to include people who give up on finding a job after many months of trying.

The third premise is, "Inventories are beginning to drop," which shows only that people are doing some buying, and thus overcoming the excessive ordering that led to overlarge inventories based upon the rate of purchase of a prior and healthier year. The drop in inventories means only that one unhealthy sign has become less unhealthy; that doesn't make it healthy. If the inventory level has dropped to what is now an appropriate point to balance sales, we can't tell whether we are in the middle of a depression or not. Excessive inventories are a bad sign for the business person because so much capital is invested in them, frequently capital that is on a loan at high rates of interest. Again, it is very important not to have larger inventories than you need in order to supply orders as soon as they come in. In a depression, a small inventory will be appropriate, and hence the reduction of inventories is what you expect as you head *into* a depression. It's no sign of one's getting *out* of it. It is a sign that somebody is buying something and, nationwide, it's a sign that a significant amount of purchasing is going on. But that occurs even in the heart of a depression. So the reduction of inventories, although welcome news to those who were holding excessively large ones, is of negligible significance for depression-end predictions. Carried too far, reduction of inventories is a sign that a company is going out of business, and indeed part of the present reduction of inventories is due to that, as the increased number bankruptcies makes clear. When you go bankrupt you completely liquidate your inventory, often at very disastrous prices. So reduction in inventory isn't a very good indicator that we are turning the corner; in fact, it doesn't indicate that at all.

"Advance orders are starting to pick up." This appears to be a slightly better indicator than the preceding one, because it does tell us that some people have got their inventories down to the point where they feel they have to replenish them. So not everybody is going out of business, and indeed some people are betting that they are going to continue to stay in business. But even at the worst depth of the worst depression, there will be advance orders. Moreover, such orders will have picked up quite a bit since the period before we hit the bottom of the depression, because up to that time we were living on the fat of inventories that were too big. Once again, the only inference that can be made legitimately from the fact that advance orders are beginning to pick up is that some sectors of the economy look as if they are not going to get any worse. That's a long way from saying that they are going to get better. It should be a sign that they are going to get better if the advance orders rose to a point above that of the previous healthy year. So far, we are nowhere near that point. So we certainly haven't any evidence from this indicator that we have turned the corner, that is, have begun to climb back up.

Finally, the indicator which is referred to in the argument as the "best news of all": "the average income figures are showing a gain." It's likely that the writer thinks of this fact as the best news because it refers to the eventual effect on the consumer. That opinion shows that he (or she) has a heart but it doesn't say much for the head. What can you tell from the fact that average income is increasing? The easiest way to see the loopholes in this inference is by describing a couple of situations where the average income will show an increase but where one would not be at all inclined to say that the trough of the depression is behind us (the "counterexampling" technique). In the first place, average income will increase at a time of rapid inflation as a result of modest wage increases that only partially compensate for the rate of inflation. This certainly describes the present situation. The number of unemployed may remain the same, or perhaps increase slightly, and those who are employed may be getting less real income than ever before, although it looks more in terms of dollars. If we could be sure that the "average income figures" here were corrected for inflation, we could rule out this criticism; but we have no evidence to suggest that corrected dollars are being used here. The lack of sophistication of the general line of argument suggests that they are not, or the fact would have been mentioned. Secondly, the average income figures may be going up simply because the top 10 percent of the population has been receiving very substantial increases in its income. The fact that the sales figures on extremely expensive luxury cars, bookings at the most expensive resorts, and so on, have not been significantly affected over the past year or so, and indeed have in many cases shown a gain, is a weak indication that we may actually be in a situation in which the wealthiest people in the society are, on the average, doing even better than before. That, of course, pulls the average up, even if the remaining 90 percent are worse off. To mention a third possibility, recent increases in the period during which unemployment benefits may be collected, and in the size of the checks for unemployment and for retirement, will tend to improve the average income figures, in uncorrected dollars, without really producing a durable gain in welfare. So nearly everybody may be eating less, having less to spend, living in worse substandard housing, and still this index might show a gain. It's a sign of extreme insensitivity to the full range of implications of the word "depression" that somebody should think this to be a significant indicator of improvement.

Notice that we haven't made much effort to formulate the assumptions that would make each of these subinferences sound, because they fall into the category of being plain errors of inference, best pointed out as such. Now we come to another inference, where it's more useful to formulate the missing premise. The inference to "America has turned the corner on a depression" is clearly unsound, even if none of the preceding criticisms had any merit. For it is supposed to follow from the claim that "the many indexes of recovery are showing optimistic readings." And that conclusion assumes that the indexes quoted are either all the indexes of recovery, or at least a representative sample of them. Once we have formulated that assumption, it's pretty clear that there are troubles with it. Certainly this isn't the whole set of indexes, or even the whole set that is usually used; for example, the gross national product is not mentioned, nor are new housing starts, the cost-of-living index, the rate of investment in capital improvements and machine tools, families below poverty level, and similar indicators. Hence, we can say only that evidence has not been supplied here that supports this conclusion; it may be true, but as far as this argument goes, it hasn't been shown to be true.

Now we turn to the last two conclusions which are said to follow from America's recovery. The first says that "the doomsayers have been discomfited." Since the preceding argument doesn't show that doom has either been averted or is showing signs of being averted, the doomsayers have scarcely been discomfited. At least, not if they have any capacity for argument analysis. But there isn't anything new that's wrong with the inference to that conclusion.

The last conclusion of all reaches out a good deal further: "The free enterprise system has been (once more) vindicated." There are a number of assumptions required in order to get this conclusion out of the preceding argument, beginning with the assumption that the preceding argument is sound. Since it isn't, a link in the chain of inference is snapped right away. But strong criticism always requires that you go on and look at other possible criticisms as well, and there are other assumptions involved here. It's not too clear what "the free enterprise system" is, exactly speaking, or what it's supposed to do. Is it supposed to guarantee that there won't be any depressions? An extreme laissez faire view wouldn't guarantee the absence of depressions. Is recovery from depressions enough to "vindicate" free enterprise systems? Shouldn't there be some reference to the welfare of human beings in the system? Is a system "vindicated" when it has 10 percent of the population suffering from malnutrition? All these questions need to be answered, and they all bear on the assumption that the free enterprise system has been vindicated if "we have turned the corner on the depression." Perhaps vindication requires that they not last very long—remember that the last Great Depression is usually thought not to have ended until World War II began, so that the free enterprise system, which was somewhat freer then, according to most definitions, didn't pull us out of it even after twelve years. And finally, this last inference certainly involves the assumption that what we have in America is the free enterprise system. Whereas many of the questions that have just been raised are of the kind that would be raised by people of the left-wing persuasion in politics, people of the right-wing persuasion would be likely to argue that we do *not* have a free enterprise system here. And indeed, they might well argue, it is because of the extent of government control that the depression of the 1970s occurred and continued as long as it did. So conclusion 9 is certainly the shakiest of all, depending as it does on all the preceding assumptions as well as these extra ones.

We've built into our discussion of the argument so far many of the other relevant arguments, so there's no need to do so as a separate step. We can sum up by saying that this argument is an extraordinarily weak one, essentially worthless. And that goes for its utility in establishing all the conclusions that it is supposed to establish.

Does that mean that the country isn't coming out of the depression? Not at all. As things stand, further decline is something about which nobody can be confident. By the time you read this, we may have come out of the depression or fallen further into it. Good arguments to show which prediction was correct are not available to us at this stage.

4-11

This completes the general review of the procedures for argument analysis at a fairly serious level. It represents an adequate foundation for handling the great majority of everyday arguments about important matters. The rest of the book will concern itself with refinements, elaborations, and special cases, but by the time you have come this far and have done the quizzes on this chapter, you should be in possession of substantially improved skills in argument analysis, and, in general, reasoning skills that are much more efficient than those with which you began.

QUIZ 4-A

1 Without looking back in the text, which of the following are correct?
   a If the premise(s) of an argument is/are false, the conclusion(s) will be false.
   b If the reasoning in an argument is unsound, the conclusion(s) will be false.
   c If the premise is true and the reasoning unsound, the conclusion(s) will be false.
   d If a conclusion is false, either the reasoning is unsound or (one of) the premise(s) is false.
   e If the premises are false and the reasoning is unsound, the conclusion(s) will be false.

Answer

Just don't read this until you've tested yourself thoroughly by evaluating each of these statements. If you marked any of them true except the next-to-last one, you were wrong. For examples and explanations, refer back to Section 4-1.

2 The reason(s) for getting clear about all the permutations and combinations in the previous question (and Section 4-1 in the text) is so that you:
   a Will be able to distinguish the question of whether the reasoning in an argument is sound from the question of whether the premises or the conclusions are true
   b Won't jump to the conclusion that there's something wrong with the reasoning in an argument just because you happen to know the conclusion is false
   c Will understand that your task in argument analysis is not over just because you think you've discovered a false premise
   d Will be able to see ways to test the truth of a hypothesis when you're not sure whether it's true or not

Answer

It's easy enough to say that the two possible targets in an argument are the premises and the inferences (the reasoning). But students find it exceedingly difficult to keep them distinct when it comes down to cases; they will frequently fall into traps such as thinking that the reasoning in an argument must be sound since they know the premises were true and that the conclusion is true. But in such a case, you have no grounds for this judgment. And when you are assessing the reasoning skill of someone, perhaps an authority you wish to refer to again or a potential employee you'll need to rely on, it would be a serious error to infer that their reasoning is good just because they generated a true conclusion from a true premise; they may have made two errors in the reasoning which happen to be in opposite directions and to cancel each other out, no thanks to the reasoner. Not only people, but also scientific theories, generate consequences; and the standard procedure for testing a theory is to see whether its consequences (i.e., what can legitimately be inferred from it) are true. If they are not true, and if you can be sure that your reasoning was sound, you can conclude that the theory is wrong. For all these reasons, you have to be absolutely confident that you understand the difference between sound reasoning and true premises or conclusions. That's why we make such an issue of this difference at this stage: To understand this is to understand what the study of reasoning is all about and why it's important. All four of the responses given here are true.

3 Circle the letter S for sufficient condition, N for necessary condition, and B for both, in the following cases:

S   N   B   **a** Being born is a _____ condition for someone's being alive now.

S   N   B   **b** Being born is a _____ condition for your dying someday.

S   N   B   **c** Being born is a _____ condition for your being a great poet.

S   N   B   **d** A reduction in the rate of population growth is a _____ condition for the avoidance of eventual overcrowding and wholesale starvation.

S   N   B   **e** Discovering an extremely lightweight and cheap storage battery (say 1 percent of the weight of lead-acid batteries) is probably a _____ condition for stabilizing our national gasoline consumption.

Answer

a Necessary but not sufficient, since a great many people were born who aren't alive now: we all also needed food and care, and we don't live indefinitely.

b Necessary and sufficient, since, empirically speaking (which is clearly what we are doing here), once you're born, it's guaranteed that you'll die, and for you to die it's necessary that you were once born. If we were talking about what's logically necessary and sufficient, that is, guaranteed by the very meaning of the words, the answer would be "neither necessary nor sufficient," since it's logically possible that people might be created full-grown by the whim of a wizard, and that they might be immortal. So birth would neither guarantee eventual death nor have to precede adulthood.

c Necessary but not sufficient; it takes a little something extra.

d Unless an infinitely expandable food supply or an infinite improvement in the efficiency of its use emerges, the mathematics guarantee this result. Since there are no real infinities, this is pretty close to being a logically necessary condition.

e S (probably) but not N—there are other ways to achieve this result, hence this isn't an N condition for it. It's only probably sufficient because weight and cost aren't the only relevant factors; by-products or risks from explosion or leakage rate are all possible sources of trouble. Probably we should just say that this is possibly a sufficient condition; it's a start toward one.

4 Which of the following is an argument or part of an argument; that is, which is the assertion of something as a reason which is supposed to justify a conclusion, a judgment, or an action? Which of them is informative in some other way? And which is or could be both? Circle A for argument, O for other, and B for both.

A   O   B   **a**   The sailplane with a small auxiliary motor is increasingly popular partly because it is economical with fuel.

A   O   B   **b**   Hang gliders quite often crash for reasons that are never determined.

A   O   B   **c**   Private planes most frequently crash because they weren't tanked up or their pilot was.

A   O   B   **d**   If we don't loosen up the penalties for cocaine use and sale, we're going to repeat the savagery and alienation caused by the pot laws.

A   O   B   **e**   If we don't crack down on drug-running, we're going to see a tremendous increase in the power and profits of the underworld.

Answer

In the type of behavior which we describe as rational people do whatever they do because there are good reasons for doing it, and those reasons are what produces or causes their behavior. Thus, reasons are, in such cases, also causes. Take statement **a** above; in part, this property—economy—of the motorized sailplane has caused the increase in sales and it also provides a good reason for purchasing such a machine. So one might set this out as an argument, with one premise about the economy and a missing premise about the increasing shortage and cost of fuel, and we can reasonably infer from those conclusions that these powered sailplanes are sensible purchases. We can't infer that they will become, or are becoming, increasingly popular. That inference would require another premise about people's being rational, one about costs being reasonable, and so on. Whenever, as here, a reason serves as a cause, there will also be an argument which exhibits the fact that it is a reason for the conclusion which the people it has influenced have accepted. But the best choice here is O; for, as it stands, the quotation does not try to *argue* for the conclusion that sales are increasing, it tries to *explain* that situation. If you asked a purchaser—say, Bill Bottom—to explain his action, he'd probably mention the same factor, and it would still be an explanation, not an argument. But if you asked him to justify his purchase, he'd produce the argument, appealing to the same factor but leading to the conclusion that he (or "one") should make this purchase. The appearance of the term "because" thus does not always justify both a causal and a reasoning interpretation.

Look at statement **b.** The claim here is just a causal claim. This statement is informative, and quite significant since there were about fifty deaths of hang-glider pilots in the past twelve months, and there is a move afoot to have the Federal Aviation Agency send in its crash-investigation teams to find out more about the causes of fatalities. It's generally believed that a number of manufacturers are putting out extremely dangerous designs. Be that as it may, there's no latent argument in the statement we have quoted here, and the answer is O. Statement **c** is also correctly identified as an O. Of course, you can construct an argument by adding various extra premises, which will enable you to infer from lack of gas or excess of alcohol to the *probability* of a crash. But that argument is just using **c** as a premise which expresses a *causal* connection. The question here is whether **c** can also be interpreted as an argument of the form "q because p"; and it can't, because you don't *justify* crashes by stating that the pilot was intoxicated, you only *explain* them that way. In **a**, by contrast, you can both explain and justify the purchase of powered sailplanes by appeal to economy, so its classification depends on the exact form of the conclusion.

Let's look at statement **d**. Is this just an empirical conditional statement like, "If you turn that switch to the left, the fanspeed will go down" which just expresses a causal connection. Or does it also (or instead) give you a reason for a conclusion like, "If these fingerprints match, then we'll have to conclude that Sandovan was the thief"? The answer is B (both)—we're providing explanations that are also potential justifications or premises for this conclusion. The same is true of **e**, though here the conclusion is a prediction, not a moral judgment. (*Note:* these are difficult distinctions to make, as hard as anything in this text. Most actual examples are pretty easy to classify.)

QUIZ 4-B

Answer T(rue) or F(alse) throughout questions 1 and 2.

1 a If the conclusion of an argument is false, the premises must be false.
   b If the conclusion is false, the reasoning (inference) must have been unsound.
   c If the premises are false and the reasoning is unsound, the conclusion will be false.
   d If the premises are true but the reasoning is unsound, the conclusion will be false.
   e If the conclusion is false and the premises were true, the reasoning must have been unsound.

2 a "p, therefore q" is an argument.
   b "If p were true, then q would have to be true" is an argument.
   c "q follows from p" is a conditional (or hypothetical) claim.
   d "p, so q" is a conditional claim.
   e "p implies q" tells us that p is a sufficient condition for q.
   f "p implies q" tells us that q is a necessary condition for p.
   g "p is a necessary condition for q" tells us that we never can have p without q.
   h "q is a necessary condition for p" tells us that we never can have p without q.
   i "r is a sufficient condition for s" tells us that we never can have r without having s.
   j "t is a sufficient condition for r" tells us that r is a necessary condition for t.

3 If you were deciding how to structure (analyze) a passage of prose, in which of the following cases would you break the sentence up and show it as involving two components, one of them a reason for the other? (In the remaining cases, you would leave the sentence as a single causal claim.)

a Freud disregarded the danger to his health from his heavy cigar smoking because he was incapable of giving it up.

b Freud should have given up smoking because it clearly was killing him.

c We know that Freud was a compulsive smoker because he tried to quit on many occasions, knew it would cost his life to keep on, and was not suicidal.

d Since 80 percent of California motorists ignore the 55 mph limit despite the California Highway Patrol's tripling its speeding citations and now spending 50 percent of its time on enforcing this one law, it's futile to continue to enforce it.

e Since you went away, it's been blues every day.

4 In this passage, the assertions have been numbered for you. Answer the statements **a** through **k** with T(rue) or F(alse).

> The Ford policy on releasing price control on domestic oil and gas is simply a way to give big business bigger profits at the expense of the average citizen (1). Of course, the *alleged* reasons are to encourage further development of our own resources (2), and to decrease total consumption (3) and hence the need for imported oil with its attendant dependence on overseas politics (4). But there's no need for exploration and development to be funded out of profits; loans are available for that (5). And the profits are in fact not going into development (6)—Mobil just bought a hotel chain, for example (7)—because there are more profitable places for them (8). No, it's just another rip-off of the general public (9)—a tax of over \$1,000/year per family (Kennedy's estimate) (10) to support Big Oil (11) and Ford's desire for power that can't be fettered by the sheikhs (12).

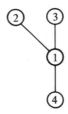

a Mostly emotional polemic, not a rational argument.

b Involves some emotional language, but a good deal of argument.

c It could perfectly well be entirely couched in emotional language and still be an entirely rational argument.

d The main conclusion is assertion 1.

e The main conclusion is assertion 2.

f The main conclusion is assertion 3.

g The main conclusion is assertion 4.

h There's a subargument here, which looks like this: Unstated conclusion: Price control on domestic oil should be abolished.

i This subargument is said to be sound.

j One of the premises of this subargument is said to be false.

k The overall structure consists in refuting the subargument and offering another explanation for decontrol of prices.

5   What's another missing premise in the arguments (a) in the next-to-last para-
    graph of Section 4-4 (p. 66), and (b) on pp. 86–87?

6   For what kind of argument is it a fatal defect if it can be shown that there is even
    a *possibility* of a certain type of situation occurring? (See the end of the second
    paragraph of Section 4-7, p. 74.)

7   "It's worth using some cumbersome or even ungrammatical language to avoid
    sexism, just as it would be to avoid racist or religious slurs. The language is
    committed to sexism far more than it is to other forms of prejudice, so corrections
    are more intrusive in this case. But surely no less important! Grammatical stan-
    dards are not as important as the avoidance of sex-role stereotyping."
    Is this argument or diatribe? Analyze it to answer, and if it's an argument, go on
    through the Seven Steps.

QUIZ 4-C

This quiz is simply a one-step-more-difficult version of Quiz 4-B; it covers the same
ground, instead of getting into more philosophical issues as we sometimes do with
the C quizzes.

1   Without referring to the text, fill in the gaps in the table below when it is possible
    to give one definite answer, using the letters F for false, T for true, and S or U for
    sound or unsound reasoning. Put a question mark where it isn't possible to be
    definite.

	Premises	Reasoning	Conclusion
a	F		
b		S	F
c		U	F
d	T	S	
e		S	T

2   The differences between an argument (let us say, from a premise p to a conclu-
    sion q) and the inference (from p to q) on which it depends are that (mark T or
    F):
    a   The argument but not the inference attempts to establish the truth of q.
    b   The argument but not the inference involves the claim that p is true.
    c   The inference but not the argument is unsound if p is true but q is false.
    d   The inference but not the argument expresses a hypothetical or conditional
        connection between p and q, that is, it asserts only that *if* p were true, q would
        be true.

3   To the best of our knowledge, which of the following is a sufficient condition and
    which is a necessary, condition for whatever follows the blank space? Circle S, N,
    or B (for both) in the margin if and as appropriate.

S   N   B   **a** Overeating and underexercising—premature death.

S   N   B   **b** Heavy cigarette smoking, defined as three packs or more a day—lung cancer.

S   N   B   **c** The number x is divisible by 2—The number x is divisible by 4.

S   N   B   **d** Being a strong supporter of one side in a political issue—being biased.

S   N   B   **e** X occurred before Y—X caused Y.

4 Do a complete analysis and assessment of the argument in question 4 of Quiz 4-B.

5 Suppose two educational experts had the following argument:

"A text which is supposed to teach skill in the interpretation and use of language," one expert said, "should at least be well written, and laid out and printed in exemplary fashion."

"Not if it means a 25 percent increase in cost," the other retorted, "and/or a year's delay in publication, and/or the impossibility of updating the contents at intervals of less than several years, and/or censoring many examples, perhaps not coming out at all—as long as the skills are taught."

"Some skills might still be taught, but the bad example of such writing might *unteach* other, delicate, skills—the skills of writing with style and sensitivity, for example."

"If they can be unlearned so easily, they won't survive long in this world anyway. Of course, it's much better if an author does combine the two—literary and analytic skills—but in an imperfect world, some things may be worthwhile that do just one job well. Or even fairly well, if the job is done better than elsewhere."

"Justifying sloppiness sounds like sophistry."

"Valuing refinements over reasoning competence sounds effete."

Who won, if anyone? Apply your conclusions to this text.

Chapter 5

Clarifying Meaning

You now have some basic fishing tackle in the box; the time has come to add extra reels and lines and rods for a more specialized and powerful treatment of particular cases. We'll do this first by expanding on the main steps in the argument analysis procedure, and then we'll pick up a series of special cases that bring in several parts of argument analysis—for example, special techniques for handling long arguments.

5-1 An Illustration

This chapter on the clarification of meaning has, of course, a great range of application in reasoning outside argument analysis. In all functional and much literary prose, the techniques described here will often turn out to be useful. It must be stressed, however, that we are trying to develop much more than a list of procedures that you can look up in the way you might look up the instructions in a home repairs guide when the plumbing gets stopped up. We are trying to develop a *habit of thought,* an *attitude,* a set of *instinctive reactions* that will become part of your normal thinking patterns. When you hear a commercial that says a particular brand of ballpoint will write "up to 40 percent longer *or more!*" your response should not be to suppose that the manufacturer is claiming savings for you of more or less 40 percent. You should immediately recognize this as an essentially empty claim. Most of you probably do realize this intuitively, but let's look at exactly how your reasoning would appear if we had to "unpack" the claim. Doing so will help us with less obvious examples.

The first key move is to ask "longer than what?" Longer than you sometimes probably get from your present brand? Individual pens of the *same* brand often (as you know from experience) vary by 100 or 200 percent in the length of writing life, so even if you keep using the same brand it will be able to make a better claim than the ad does; its advertising can say "up to 100 percent more." Longer than the most widely used ballpoint? Than the worst of those commonly sold? But *any* brand, even the worst, could make this claim, since some samples of it will certainly write "up to 40 percent longer than others. So the first loophole in the claim is the lack of specificity about the comparison. Let's shut this loophole up and see what others there are, if any. In closing this loophole, we'll learn something about how to express claims like this better when we ourselves want to make them.

Let's add to the claim, after the word "longer," "than the *average* for the *most commonly sold* brand." And, since we should be comparing averages with averages, we'll assume that the claim is to be taken to mean that the *average* performance of the new brand is (so much) longer than the average of the most commonly used brand (Bic, at the moment).

This tidying up of the claim has been done for *our* benefit, to make it easier for us to see if there are any other sources of trouble (that is, unclarity) in the claim. The fact that we've tidied it up doesn't in the least mean that there wasn't something wrong with it as it stood. We have identified the "something wrong," namely, the failure to specify what the comparison is with, and that loophole has now been identified, charged against the claim and put on one side for the time being. (It's charged against the claim, to repeat, simply because the claim is true of any brand as it stands; hence it in no way supports the superiority of the advertised brand, which we know from the context is what it is supposed to do.) Now let's look at the modified claim. The claim, as rather generously refined by us, reads that Brand X (the one being advertised) will write "up to 40 percent longer, *or more,* than a Bic," where Brand X's performance is to be defined as the average performance of a large number of samples of that brand. The remaining problem concerns the meaning of "up to 40 percent or more." Five percent is obviously within the "up to 40 percent" range. So is 1 percent; so indeed is 0 percent. It looks as if the real meaning of "up to 40 percent" is "not more than 40 percent." Since that includes 0 percent, it's a really empty claim. Any brand of anything in the world is up to 40 percent better than any other brand, because it's at least no percent better.

But that's being a little too persnickety. When people say, "up to 40 percent," they certainly are committing themselves to the claim that at least sometimes there's a gain of 40 percent. When we add to this the phrase "or more," we certainly mean that the gain is at least very occasionally more than 40 percent. Now, *what* gain? The trouble is that when we compare averages, as we've agreed to do to make some sense out of the rest of the claim, there isn't going to be any "sometimes" feature about the results. The average performance of Brand X will be exactly 2 or 25 or 43 percent more (or less) than the average performance of the Bic. What has really happened here is that we have so vague a claim that any attempt to clarify one part of it makes the other part senseless, and vice versa. Or are we being unfair? Was our particular way of tightening up too restrictive?

Suppose we hadn't tightened up the implicit comparison by specifying what it was a comparison with and how the comparison was to be made. Then the phrase "up to 40 percent longer or more" would make sense, because particular samples of Brand X will certainly produce results that are anything up to 100 percent better than particular samples of any other brand (indeed, of Brand X itself!). But the claim is now empty just because all it tells us is that particular samples of any brand vary a great deal, which hardly shows any superiority of Brand X over any other brand.

Now that's a fair amount of unpacking of an apparently simple phrase, but it's a phrase that is very commonly used in advertising, and the exact reasons why it is a misleading phrase do take a little sorting out. It's misleading because it suggests that it's a tangible, indeed a quantitative, claim about the superiority of Brand X, but when we get down to unpacking it, we discover that it really doesn't contain any promise of actual superiority at all.

Let's reflect for a moment on what sort of procedure we used in the course of this analysis. We considered various specific and clearly meaningful interpretations of the claim, and then matched them against it to see if we were either missing or oversimplifying some part of its meaning. Then, having identified one particular source of trouble, we tidied the claim up so that it wouldn't confuse us while we were searching for other sources of trouble (in this case, "trouble" meant lack of clarity). We'll find that these procedures are frequently useful as we go further into this chapter. Making something more tangible, making it more precise, more specific, is a most important way of trying to find out if you understand what it means. Conversely, when you want to make something clear yourself, then you try to make it as tangible and specific as possible.

5-2   Real Precision and Fake Precision

The preceding example is one where an exact percentage is quoted, but in a context which takes away from it any real meaning. That's a case of fake precision. Recently we've seen examples of TV commercials showing a small imported car traveling from Los Angeles all the way up through and past San Francisco, with an accompanying patter which shows that this is a specific instance of what it means to have a car that will do "540 miles on a tankful of gas a day (Environmental Protection Agency figures)." That's a slightly different example of fake precision. Since the EPA figures are obtained on a dynamometer and make limited allowance for wind resistance, and the ones being used refer only to highway driving at a speed well below the normal highway driving speed, and since traveling over that stretch of road involves a great deal of city as well as highway driving, there is no way in which any ordinary driver could expect to obtain anything like 540 miles to a tankful. The 540 is indeed a very precise figure; the trouble is that it doesn't apply to the picture. The picture is one of a fantasy performance, not a real one; the 540 miles to a tankful is so specific that it looks like a figure obtained from an actual performance. You are therefore being persuaded that you are seeing photographs of a car actually getting this precise mileage, whereas what you're really seeing is a photograph of a car doing an actual trip, combined with an exact figure that is obtained from calculations that have very little to do with that trip. This is theoretical precision masquerading (or being misrepresented) as practical precision.

Another type of fake precision is involved when somebody quotes a person's height at 5 feet 8.62314 inches. Measurements of a person's height are not meaningful beyond about a tenth of an inch (and perhaps not even that far) because slight posture variations or the length of time that the person has been standing up before the height measurement is taken, or the length of time since the person has had a night's sleep, or the extent of fatigue from other causes, can well produce variations of that amount several times during the course of a day.

There are many other ways in which numbers are used in order to exploit the impression of precision that they give, but in a context which makes clear that the precision is inappropriate. Some of these are quite subtle. In the example of the fake range on a tankful of gas that we've just discussed, the way in which you're persuaded to think of this as realistic is by the combination of photographs of a real car traveling on a real highway with the superimposed mileage figure. Nobody actually said in the commercial that you would really get this mileage from your specimen of this car; indeed, the advertisement even says (in small print) that the figure is based on an EPA estimate for highway mileage. But few of the viewers realize the extent to which that undermines the figure completely. It says 540 miles; the real figure isn't 539 or 538 or 530 or 500; the real figure for that trip, run at normal speeds, would probably be around 375. (We happen to have that car in the family, and it has yet to produce as much as 400 miles on a tankful of gas even on steady freeway driving at or below the speed limit, and dealers as well as other owners agree that this is normal.)

Another style of TV commercial that is currently popular involves the photographed interview with somebody who has been asked to identify which pile of laundry has been washed with the detergent that's being adver- tised—let's call it Bright. A sense of veracity, of accuracy, of completeness of reporting is provided by the fact that you're obviously watching a film or video tape of an actual interview. (Let's put aside for the moment the ques- tion of whether actresses are used to fake that aspect of the matter and assume that, as appears to be the case, it really is an interview with a house- wife.) It turns out that the housewife identifies, in this "blind" test, the whitest clothes as being the ones that were washed with Bright. (In a similar commercial, a housewife identifies the cracker that was spread with Imperial margarine as "the one that was really spread with butter." Should you, or should you not, give some weight to those commercials as supporting the view that there is an obvious benefit from using the advertised product?

Our answer depends entirely on how typical this filmed event is of what happens in reality. That it happened in reality we can conceive. But is this all that ever happens in reality? To be blunt about it, did the ad agency have to film fifty of these scenes before it came across one where the housewife thought that the Imperial was the butter, or the Bright pile was the cleanest pile? If there were fifty filmings and one case in which things went the way the advertiser hoped they would, then we have an extremely misleading commercial, even though what it portrays as happening is exactly what happened. So "the camera cannot lie" is far from the truth, at least is far from the truth that we're interested in. The camera isn't lying about what happened; but it is being used to lie about the significance of what hap- pened. You can't blame the camera, but you can blame yourself if you make the step from photography to interpretation too hastily. So accuracy or pre- cision is a function of context as well as of the use of quantitative measures or photographic reproductions. In short, there's often an element of interpre- tation involved that undoes much of the apparent accuracy or precision that the use of figures or photographs may convey.

5-3 Precision versus Imprecision or Vagueness

Of course, the natural contrast with precision is imprecision, the difference between giving somebody's height in terms of feet and inches, and perhaps the nearest quarter inch, and saying that "the person is quite tall." Just as precision is phony when it represents more accuracy than can in fact be obtained, so it is unnecessary when it represents more accuracy than can reasonably be *used*. It is possible to weigh diamonds to the millionth part of a gram, but there's no real point in doing so, and the process would be immensely complicated and expensive. For example, one couldn't use even the most refined top-loading balance because the kind of air currents that result from changes of temperature in a room in the course of a day, or because of the movement of people in the room, or because of leakage of air around the windows, would deflect the balance by many times a millionth of a gram. How much more absurd it would be to talk about weighing packages of sugar to the millionth of a gram, although it is technically feasible. Precision is, like many other devices in reasoning and in science, a tool to be used appropriately, not a quality to be worshiped blindly. Hence, it is a mistake to criticize an argument or an assertion on the ground that it contains some vague language—perhaps it describes some people as being "pretty tall" or some sacks of sugar as being "heavy" instead of giving a quantitative measure of their height or weight—*unless the lack of precision hurts the argument.*

When people begin to work on reasoning skills in a careful way, when they begin for the first time to become analytical and careful about the analysis of meaning, the three most common mistakes they make all fall under the heading of this chapter. They tend to complain inappropriately about the use of vague terms, about the use of emotional language, and about the failure to define tricky terms. As those of you who have taken courses in science and mathematics will be well aware, they make a good deal of the idea of "the number of significant digits" in spelling out a quantity. You were taught carefully not to give more digits than represent physical reality, or the limits of measurement, or are mathematically appropriate. For example, if you are determining the average weight of thirteen samples of a chemical, and you can measure each of them accurately to a tenth of a gram, you should not quote their average weight to a ten-millionth of a gram just because, when you come to divide by 13, you can nearly always generate as long a string of decimals as you like by just continuing the calculation. We're making the same kind of point here, but in the general context of reasoning. Don't complain about axes because they're not scalpels, don't complain about useful approximations because they're not exact.

On the other hand, there are situations where it's really crucial to have a certain amount of precision in order to justify the conclusions that you need. If you want to determine whether drinking Coca-Cola causes cancer, you'll have to be extremely accurate in your measures of the age of the patients that you put into the experimental and control groups, and as accurate as possible about the length of time that they have been drinking Coca-Cola, and the amount of it they drink. Otherwise, you may well pass over what is actually a very significant result. Or you may be led to conclusions which can't be justified by the degree of accuracy provided in the data. So here we have a case of the exercise of judgment; you have to learn how to judge what an appropriate degree of accuracy or precision is for certain types of conclusions. We'll come back to this point from time to time, with various examples. It's only a matter of refining your common sense somewhat.

First, let's look at the way in which increasing precision can be useful (assuming it can be justified by the appropriate measurements). Suppose that we described somebody as "tall." Let us suppose that the complete sentence says "Jones is tall." What does this tell you? Certainly it's vague, imprecise, but still it tells you something. We might say that it certainly tells you that Jones is more than 5 feet 6 inches in height. But wait a minute. A *man* that is said to be 5 feet 6 inches high wouldn't be called tall, but a woman of that height might be said to be tall. Certainly a Japanese woman of that height would be considered to be tall. Even more certainly, a man from one of the pygmy tribes in Africa would be said to be tall if he was 5 feet 6 inches high. So if you try to translate "Jones is tall" into "Jones is more than 5 feet 6 inches high," you're immediately making some assumptions. You're assuming that "Jones" is the name of a Western European or an American man. Now, Jones is indeed a very common name for people from English-speaking countries, but, though less commonly, it is also the name of people of all races. Certainly one is not entitled to the conclusion that Jones has to be the name of a man, since women are increasingly referred to by their family names in a way that was once upon a time reserved for men. What we see here is a typical example of a *contextual inference,* and a rather shaky one at that. Of course, the fact that this happens to be a shaky example in no way justifies the conclusion that contextual inferences in general are unreliable. Since a very large part of our inference involves the use of contextual cues, and since a great many of these are extremely reliable, it would be foolhardy to draw a generally skeptical conclusion about the inference.

Let's pursue this example a little further. Can we at least conclude that "Jones is tall" means "Jones is at least 5 feet high," if the sentence is encountered in some context which shows that it refers to an individual in, let us say, the North American continent. This takes care of other races whose average stature is considerably less than that of the usual American or Canadian; but it still won't do. It's quite common in certain schools to refer to the children by their family names. And a nine or ten-year-old, or even a twelve-year-old, might well be said to be tall (meaning "tall for his or her age") even though the child was only 5 feet high. So "Jones is tall," even with the help of some contextual assumptions, won't do you much good unless you can definitely count on Jones being an adult. If the context is such that we can tell the "Jones" being referred to is an adult, it is reasonable to conclude that the sentence implies that Jones is more than 5 feet tall (or have I overlooked another possible exception?). And that's quite a significant piece of information. Probably it's correct to say that the sentence contains rather more information than this. For example, one might say that it implies that if Jones is an adult man (and a resident of North America), then Jones is more than 5 feet 6 inches tall; and if Jones is a woman, then Jones is probably more than 5 feet 3 inches tall. It's less and less likely that one would describe a woman as tall as her height gets nearer to 5 feet; hence, the meaning of the assertion makes it virtually certain that the individual is more than 5 feet 0 inches high, pretty certain his or her height is more than 5 feet 2 inches, very likely that it's more than 5 feet 3 inches, quite likely that it's more than 5 feet 4 inches, and likely that it's more than 5 feet 6 inches. Notice that in order to understand the real import of this sentence, you need to know quite a lot about the distribution of heights in the relevant population, so the "meaning" of a sentence will often depend upon the possession of a good deal of factual information. In a very strict sense, the meaning is just what follows from the dictionary definition, which supposedly doesn't depend upon mere facts. But, to be realistic, the meaning of "tall" would shift pretty quickly if the population of North America lost several inches of height overnight. For "tall" is a comparative term, as we've come to see in considering cases of pygmies and children, men and women, Japanese and American. Couldn't we say that the true meaning of "tall" is "greater in height than the average"? We could, but what this comes down to, in terms of feet and inches, will of course vary with the average. A strict logician might wish to continue to argue that "tall" doesn't have as part of its meaning any "feet and inches" content at all. But, in the practical language of everyday life, it does have that content because the description of a person as tall always occurs in a context where it's possible to work out the race, age, and sex of the person, and a contextual inference thus makes possible a conclusion (an interpretation) in approximate measurement terms. If you had to give an "absolute" definition of "tall," one that would work in all contexts, you'd have to say that it refers to the average, whatever that happens to be: that is, it would have to be a relativistic or comparative definition, with no specific content at all. But if you were giving an explanation of what it means in practice in our context, when applied to people and not coastal redwoods, you could do better than the comparative definition.

Thus we see that a vague term (1) has some meaning, (2) often has a good deal more meaning when we have a context from which we can make further inferences, (3) can be given an abstract definition by referring it to another abstract term ("average height"), and (4) can be given a somewhat more precise meaning if we restrict that meaning to uses of the term in particular contexts. All these are important messages about the clarification of meaning, its limitations, and its possibilities, and we'll rely on them on many future occasions.

5-4   Information Content

Why is precision ever valuable? How can we ever legitimately complain about vagueness? It may be helpful to think about these concepts in terms of a notion which we can call "information content." What we shall try to show is that the information content of a sentence, or of a description, or of a descriptive term, goes up with increasing precision, provided that the precision is real, not phony, precision. This will lead us to a general perspective on the meaning of terms and of sentences that we'll call the "contrast theory of meaning." This perspective isn't anything very elaborate or abstract, but it's a useful point of view. You can see what's meant by the contrast theory of meaning if you look back at what we were doing when we were trying to work out the meaning of the assertion "Jones is tall." What we asked ourselves was, What does the assertion exclude? That is, what can it legitimately be contrasted with? The contrast theory of meaning maintains that the best way to understand the meaning of a claim (or a term, etc.) is to work out what it is to be contrasted with. This can be done at various levels; for example "tall" is of course to be contrasted with "short," and also with "average" (in height). That is, it marks one end of a spectrum of relative or comparative heights. Its meaning is to be gathered from what it is contrasted with on this spectrum. When we move to a more specific level where we try to find some kind of feet-and-inches equivalent of "tall," we see that, given a good deal of help from the context, we can (sometimes) contrast it with "5 feet high." So, on this level, the meaning of "tall" is "more than 5 feet high" (and probably more than 5 feet 3 inches, fairly probably more than 5 feet 5 inches, and so on).

Let's try to unpack this notion of the "information content" of a claim a little further. Suppose we're talking about somebody's height. Suppose the context makes it clear that it's an adult Anglo that we're talking about (and *not* one who's a basketball player or otherwise athletic). From your background knowledge of adult male Anglos, you know that the scale of feasible height, that is, physically possible height, runs from somewhere around 2 feet 6, for dwarfs, up through somewhere around 7 feet 6 for giants, with perhaps a very tiny number of individuals going beyond these extremes. So your *background information,* without anybody's telling you anything specific about Jones, tells you that his height is somewhere in this range, and in fact tells you that it's more likely to be in the region around 5 feet 9 or 10 than out toward the extremes. We can actually represent this in terms of a very rough kind of curve, showing the probability that Jones has any height from 2 feet 6 to 7 feet 6, and this curve would obviously start with a very low probability down near the 2-foot-6 end and finish up with a very low probability at around the 7-foot-6 end, and bulge upward pretty strongly above the 5-foot-6 area. (See the accompanying diagram.) This curve is technically described as the distribution of the probabilities that a randomly chosen individual from the population that we're talking about (adult male white Anglos) will have the height that is represented on the line along the bottom: it is shown in a solid line below.

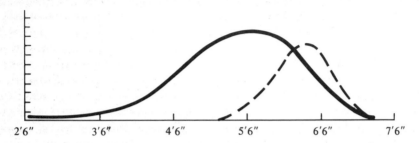

Here's a graphical representation, then, of your *background knowledge* about Jones's height, with your knowing nothing specific about Jones, but only these various contextual facts about the sort of person he is, in very general terms.

Now consider what happens when somebody says, "Jones is *tall*." We can immediately replace the curve that we have from our background knowledge with a new curve that looks something like the dotted one on the diagram. It shows the distribution of height amongst men that might reasonably be called "tall" by someone familiar with both the English language and the facts about the height of North American Anglo males. The information content of the statement "Jones is tall' might, for certain purposes, be said to be represented by this second picture. But it might also be said to be represented by the difference between the first and second pictures. What has happened is that you've been able to exclude, with varying degrees of probability, a whole range of possibilities that previously existed for you. These two senses of information, the first sense referring to what we might call the "intrinsic information content" of a claim, and the second to the "*new* information content" of a claim, are both frequently used in our language. When somebody hears a political commentator tracking down the sources of the large contributions to a particular political candidate's reelection campaign, and comparing these sources with the candidate's voting record on certain key issues, one might respond to these disclosures by saying "very informative," meaning the information that one has learned a good deal that one didn't know before, and that one regards the information as valuable. Somebody else, more of a political specialist in this particular area, might comment that he hadn't found it so. He's telling you that it didn't give him any new information. To say that something is very informative is typically to say that it's telling you something new. The individual who didn't learn very much from the political commentator's remarks isn't for a moment claiming that these remarks have no information content at all. They do assert certain facts, which as far as he knows are true; and there are a great many of these facts, so that, in one sense, a good deal of information was being produced. But it wasn't very informative for this person; that is, it wasn't new for him. So "information" sometimes means "facts" and sometimes it means "new facts." Notice that the content will also not be said to be information if it is false. "Very informative, *if* true," the cynic may say. Information consists of facts or knowledge, both of which terms imply truth; and sometimes it is restricted to novel facts or knowledge, perhaps even to new and relevant or interesting facts and knowledge.

So the information content of "Jones is tall' can be thought of as represented either by the second curve above, or by the crossing out of the part of the first diagram that is excluded by the second curve. That's where we get the "contrast theory of meaning" perspective: the meaning of a claim is what it rules out. Just as there are two senses of information, corresponding to the absolute or intrinsic information content and the new information content, so there are two senses of "meaning," corresponding to the "abstract or purely logical meaning" and to the "practical or significant" meaning. "Jones is tall" has a certain absolute meaning in that it excludes "Jones is of average height or short"; in a particular context, however, it may have an imprecise but substantial feet-and-inches meaning; and in a very specific context, it may have even more "meaning" than that. The great detective is informed that Jones is tall; he says, "Aha!," and Dr. Watson asks him what is so exciting about this rather vague and scarcely exciting description. "Why, don't you see what this means? It cannot have been Jones who was seen by the stage door attendant at the theater; and that means that Jones could not have been the murderer." Logicians have often tended to suppose that using the term "meaning" in this extended sense where it covers the implications of a claim in a particular context is a rather sloppy use of the term; that its proper sense is its acontextual or context-free sense. But recent work in logic, and more attention to the subtleties of common language, suggest that the detective's use is an entirely proper use of the term, and a much closer relative of the logician's sense than was previously supposed. The meaning of a claim, the information it contains, what we learn from it, its significance, what it tells us—all these phrases have the double function in our language of referring either to the changes in our knowledge state that result from adding the new information, or to the strict out-of-context content of the claim. Thus, switching from one of these interpretations of "meaning" to the other, the same claim may be informative and not informative, it may tell us something or not tell us something; "Jones is tall" of course tells us that Jones is tall, but if we already knew this, then we might equally well say that it tells us nothing. Sometimes we use the phrase "tells us nothing that we don't know already" in order to make this distinction;

but sometimes we just say "He told me nothing at all," although of course he told you a number of things which you believed to be true. It was just that you knew them already.

We've seen how even a vague statement like "Jones is tall" can have considerable information content in either of the two senses that we've distinguished. Consider now the statement "Jones is extremely tall." We'd represent that in the same way, with a curve which pushes the probabilities considerably further up to the right-hand end of the spectrum of heights. You might say that it narrows down the range of possibilities for Jones's height considerably. Notice that it's becoming increasingly precise as a description, and that as it becomes more precise, it rules out more and more of the range of previous possibilities. That's the general feature which lies behind the value of precision. Now consider "Jones is the tallest man alive." What you see is a continued shrinking of the range of possibilities until finally it contracts to a dot. The description becomes increasingly precise, has more and more information content for you just because it narrows down the range of possibilities. Thus it excludes more and more of the initial possibilities. The informativeness or information content of a claim is directly proportional to the range of possibilities that it *excludes*. The more it excludes, the more informative it is.

Now look at the situation if we start talking about quantitative measures. Suppose we say, "Jones is more than 5 feet 6 inches tall." We can represent this on the diagram by blocking out all the heights below 5 feet 6. Suppose that the description is now changed to "Jones is between 5 feet 6 and 5 feet 8." Now we can block out all the heights above 5 feet 8, and we've narrowed down the range of possibilities to a 2-inch range. Clearly the information content, the informativeness, of our description has increased dramatically. Now if we say that Jones is in fact 5 feet 7 inches high, we've narrowed it down even further. And, where the precision isn't phony, as we increase the accuracy of the measurement, we exclude more and more possibilities and hence increase the information content of our claim. (Notice that this is true in either of the two senses of information that we distinguished previously.)

This method of conceptualizing precision, information content, and meaning helps one considerably in the reasoning process where one is trying to clarify the meaning of the assertions in an argument that are possible premises or conclusions for the argument; and it also helps one in understanding and appraising merely descriptive prose.

Now let's apply this approach to a general view of the world. Consider the "Conservation of Luck" claim "Good luck in this world is always balanced off by bad luck." It sounds like a philosophical equivalent of one of the conservation or symmetry laws in physics: for every force there is always an equal and opposite force and so on. But what does it really mean? Ask yourself what it *excludes,* what *contrast* it draws. For openers, does it mean that good luck is always balanced off by bad luck for each individual person? Or does it mean that the balance is struck across the whole population of the world? (One might get some pretty lucky people, but there would also be some other people somewhere else who were unlucky.) Until we get some clarification on this point, the Conservation of Luck principle is so vague that it really doesn't tell you what to expect at all. Does it rule out people's being steadily lucky throughout their lives? Does it rule out, for instance, a man's being stupendously lucky—winning the Irish Sweepstakes, for example, and thereby making over a million dollars which he invests in a company which is wildly successful, the only occasion in which he has ever invested in anything, enabling him to retire in his midtwenties in good health which he retain during the rest of a long and happy life? Of course, if it rules out this kind of thing, then it's simply wrong, because there are plenty of examples of both these types of persons. Or so it seems. Perhaps the Conservation of Luck proponent thinks that there's always some hidden sorrow under the surface in these good-luck stories. Does he or she have any evidence for that? Or is this just an article of faith? Of course, such questions concern the issue of whether the claim is true, rather than what it means. But, since people who put forward views like this want them to be true, they often will interpret them in such a way as to make them more likely to be true. And one way to do that is to make it more difficult to falsify them. And one way to do that is to make them so vague that it's almost impossible to see what would falsify them.

So a Conservation of Luck supporter might well interpret the claim to mean that there's always some bad luck in everyone's life, even though it may not be quite as much as there is good luck in some cases (and vice versa in other cases). So the Conservation of Luck claim might be meant to apply to each individual, but it may not be the claim that the amount of good luck is exactly the same as the amount of bad luck. Here we'd have the balancing of good luck by bad luck, but only in terms of the number of good luck events and the number of bad luck events, not the quantity of good luck and the quantity of bad luck.

So there are two completely different questions that have to be settled before we can tidy up the vagueness in this claim. First, is the Conservation of Luck principle meant to apply to the life of each individual? Second, is it meant to apply to the quantity of luck and not just to the occurrence of luck of both kinds?

Notice that if we take it in the "weakest" of the interpretations that we've been considering, the claim becomes almost empty. That is, it becomes the claim that someone somewhere gets some bad luck sometimes to compensate for the good luck that other people, elsewhere, get at some other time. In other words, there is both good and bad luck in the world. That doesn't turn out to be a very interesting claim, since we all know it's true, and it isn't at all what we had in mind when we first heard the Conservation of Luck claim. The phrase "balancing off" in the claim suggested a kind of precision that turned out, under pressure, not to be definitely there.

Notice that, in order to understand what people might mean by this claim, we're asking *them*. If the claim were a simple one, expressed in English, we'd know more or less exactly how to take it, and we wouldn't have to ask the speaker. But a phrase like "balanced off" is a metaphorical phrase in this context; we know exactly what it means when we're talking about weighing one thing against another on a balance, but we don't know exactly what it means when we're talking about weighing luck, especially good and bad luck.

That example is fairly typical of a large number of claims about the world that are expressed in terms sufficiently vague so that one really can't tell whether they are interesting or not. If we took the claim in its most precise form, interpreting it to mean that within the life of any single individual, the amount of good and bad luck exactly balance, then, although it isn't too easy to say how a piece of good luck balances against a piece of bad luck, we could certainly say that this is an interesting claim and perhaps investigate it. All we'd have to do is to find a few truly fortunate individuals whose good luck obviously was far greater than their bad luck, in order to show that it was false. The claim that there are no such individuals does seem pretty implausible; but it's certainly a definite claim, and one that we can investigate systematically, and one that, if true, would be pretty informative. Notice the way in which the reduction of vagueness again increases the amount of information content.

Let's take another example. One constantly runs into remarks in low-grade "Buyer's Guides" columns in magazines to the effect that "you get what you pay for." This axiom is usually offered as a piece of homespun wisdom subsequent to the discovery that certain feature or performance characteristics of some product are fairly expensive. By and large, however, it's a sensationally stupid remark and, into the bargain, fairly vicious. Of course it could be made so vague that it's impossible to falsify it; suppose, for example, that it is interpreted as meaning that what you get when you pay more is something more expensive. Then it reduces to "you get whatever it is that you pay for." Interpreted in this way, it would be true but trivial. Interpreted in the way in which it is usually meant, which can be translated as "when you pay more you get more quality; when you pay less you get less quality," it's not trivial and it's also not true. Any issue of *Consumer Reports* contains a listing of products—usually half a dozen listings—which show that inexpensive products often outperform, and give you better quality (e.g., durability) than, more expensive products. In fact, anyone familiar with the marketplace knows that there are always some products around which are marked up simply in order to be expensive, in the hope that people who are stupid enough to believe that "you get what you pay for" will buy them in the belief that they're better, or on the ground that one achieves status through being able to purchase extremely expensive products, regardless of whether they're worth it. What one should achieve is a reputation for being unintelligent, of course; but we're a fairly badly educated bunch of consumers although we're overcoming that gradually, and we still have people running around acting as if cost is a good indicator of quality.

Look at the sources of error in that assumption. First, it completely ignores any reductions of cost that are possible through large-scale productions. In the automobile field, for example, a new Rolls-Royce Camargue will run you over $70,000, whereas the Mercedes 690 SEL costs half that. But, because the Rolls-Royce is made in extremely limited numbers, its manufacturers are unable to capitalize on the economies of scale that are available to the Mercedes factory, which can afford considerably larger runs of components and accessories from its subcontractors, and hence pays considerably smaller unit costs. In terms of quality of workmanship, it simply isn't possible to argue for any systematic difference between the two. There are a few little goodies on the Rolls-Royce, like the use of solid wood inlays, that will not be found on the Mercedes; but there are a dozen engineering goodies on the Mercedes that cannot be found on the Rolls-Royce, which add up to the fact that the Mercedes 690 SEL handles far better, is a considerably safer car, a far more economical car, and a better-riding car, as well as a better-performing car than the Rolls-Royce. Of course, it isn't a Rolls-Royce. So, in the trivial sense of "you get what you pay for" it's true that you get something for the $70,000 that you don't get for the $35,000 or so. But it's also true that you get not just something but a hell of a lot of things for $35,000 that you don't get for the $70,000. (For those who are interested, these include air suspension, automatic compensation of height as the load of passengers and luggage is increased, the capacity to swerve to avoid an accident and brake to stop before hitting a stalled car, with a huge margin of safety in situations where the Rolls would add to the wreck, substantially better safety-car engineering if it does come to a crash, and many other advantages.)

To give an example from the more humdrum end of the consumer purchasing spectrum, *Consumer Reports* did a nice study of rug cleaners some time ago, in which it compared all the major rug cleaners on the market by doing very careful comparisons of their ability in cleaning rugs made with various kinds of fiber and soiled with various types of dirt. Just as a matter of interest, they also included in the study the use of a dilute solution of Tide detergent. Since rug cleaners are sold in a rather small market, and are sold in a way that resembles cosmetics rather than soaps, they have very high advertising budgets, and also relatively high manufacturing costs, per unit sold. Hence the cost difference between the rug cleaners and the dilute solution of Tide was astronomical—10 or 20 to 1 in favor of Tide. Well, it turned out that Tide beat the hell out of the rug cleaners in terms of performance. What is one going to say about this if one really believes that "you get what you pay for"? Presumably what you're paying for here where the prestige factors that might enter your purchase of a Rolls-Royce are hardly relevant, is rug-cleaning power. And you're not getting more by paying more. There are dozens of examples of this. In the perfume field, it's well known that Jean Patou's perfume "Joy" is inflated in price just so that the manufacturer can use the advertising slogan "the costliest perfume in the world." It's also widely believed that the profit margin on Cadillacs, although this is not publicly released by General Motors, is from 4 to 20 times that on a Chevrolet; that is, a great deal of what you're paying for when you buy a Cadillac is General Motors' profit, rather than quality in the product. This is possible because of the extraordinary prestige position that the Cadillac occupies in the automobile market. It may well be the case that there are certain gains in quality, but they are certainly not present to the extent that you pay for them, i.e., to the same extent as the difference in price.

Once again, we see that if the general claim is made more precise, it becomes less likely to be true; and if it's made more vague, its truth can be preserved but its information content evaporates. This again illustrates the general principle that the informativeness of a statement goes up as its precision increases, but at the same time, the chances that it will be true are reduced just because it has, so to speak, made itself more vulnerable. Thus, the clearer and stronger the contrast between a term or a statement and what it rules out, the more informative it can be (and will be, if it's true). The vaguer the term or statement is, the less it rules out, and hence the less it tells you about the world when a claim is made involving it.

An example you might want to reflect on—you can treat it as a kind of advance exercise from Quiz 5-C—is one that is of great importance to us in our political thinking: "Democracy is the best form of government."

5-5 Exploiting Vagueness

Vagueness is sometimes undesirable, but then it's sometimes necessary. When you don't have enough information to be able to make a precise statement, or the time to express it, you may be able to express the information you do have in a vague statement and be able to convey something very valuable by doing so. Maybe you can't be very precise in locating the reasons why you found somebody an unsatisfactory employee, but even if you say something rather vague like "Somehow she just didn't seem able to accept any responsibility for the work she was supposed to be doing," you may be comveying something very important to a prospective employer just because he needs somebody who is strong in this dimension.

In the preceding section, we discussed a number of cases where rather fancy-sounding general claims are made, whose truth is preserved only by interpreting them in an extremely vague way. These are examples of *exploiting vagueness,* that is, of *using vagueness to preserve truth at the expense of becoming trivial.* The crucial problem in the search for truth in this world is to combine novelty with accuracy. It's never hard to make true statements; you can always say that "either it will rain tomorrow or it won't." The problem is to find a statement which is both true and informative, that is, not already known to be true. The old criticism of a piece of bad research or writing is an ever-threatening one—"what's new isn't true and what's true isn't new."

There are other ways of exploiting vagueness which deserve to be considered, and which are often employed, sometimes unconsciously, in bad arguments. There's a whole family of them that are closely related and that have acquired special names because they are so common. The underlying fallacy—the name for a seductive error of argument—is pretty close to being the same in each case; you can probably tell what it is from looking at a list of the names for it. It's called the "bald man argument," "the slippery slope," "the black-and-white fallacy," the "thin edge of the wedge"; and sometimes less printable terms are used.

Let's take the "bald man argument" as fairly typical of the species of fallacy that we're talking about. The argument goes as follows: Take a man with not a single hair on his head. He would certainly be called bald. Suppose that he had one hair on his head. We certainly wouldn't say that he had ceased to be bald. Suppose that he had two hairs. That wouldn't persuade us either. In fact, the addition of a single hair is never going to make the difference between being bald and not being bald. But the difference between being bald and not being bald is simply the difference that we achieve by adding one hair at a time. Since adding one hair never makes the difference between people's being bald and not being bald, there really isn't any difference between being bald and not being bald. Thus, the argument apparently reaches an obviously unsupportable conclusion from apparently plausible premises, by apparently legitimate inference. In the form we've just expressed it, it's pretty clear that you're not going to buy it. But, in more subtle forms, it becomes a very insidious type of argument. Often it occurs when rejecting an appeal by someone, say a prisoner on an indeterminate sentence who's up for parole. The parole board may argue that, while there are a number of points to be made in favor of the prisoner, these points are rather small, whereas the difference between a truly reformed and faultless record in prison and the kind of record that would be instantly turned down by the parole board is a very large difference. This may be, in particular cases, a version of the "bald man" argument. After all, the difference between cases where, although perfection has not been achieved, enough merit is evident to justify granting parole, and cases where there isn't enough evidence, is only a difference of degree. Hence, it's inappropriate to turn somebody down on the ground that all that has been offered are considerations that amount only to a difference in degree. It would be perfectly all right to say that there just aren't quite enough of these considerations. But it won't do to say that there are "only" differences of degree.

In the same way, there is the obvious fact that one can move extremely gradually from white to black through shades of gray so close to one another that one can't distinguish any two of them; this fact can be used to support the conclusion that "really" there isn't any difference between black and white. Of course, you don't accept that version of the argument, which is why we use the term "black-and-white fallacy" for it. But you may easily be persuaded that the difference between a war of aggression and a war of self-defense isn't really a true difference, because you are led through a series of cases where a country has had to react against the buildup of forces by an enemy preparing to invade it, prior to the invasion, or face certain defeat as soon as the invasion begins. You can, of course, see that these are cases where the idea of self-defense is predominant, so that it can hardly be called a war of aggression. You can also see that one can push this kind of consideration further and further, so that eventually we have a war which is mounted because of hostile "enemy" propaganda which is interpreted as a forerunner of an eventual buildup of arms, and is used as a justification of invasion even though no actual arms buildup has occurred.

Or you may be persuaded that torture is justified in the interrogation of suspected criminals or prisoners of war by somebody who points out that the line between physical and mental torture is not a sharp one, and that we obviously believe that imprisonment and interrogation are in some circumstances justified, so that we really are drawing an arbitrary line when we say that physical torture is not to be allowed; in addition to being arbitrary, this line handicaps the forces of right in their quest to stamp out evil. So we finish up by agreeing that using totally brutal methods of physical torture while interrogating (or standing by while our allies do it) is legitimate. Part of the fallacy here is a "bald man" argument.

Another example concerns the difference between brainwashing, propaganda, and education. It is very hard to draw the line between them, and that fact has often been used to legitimate types of classroom activity which are mindless repetition of dogmatic truths about our country or our value system, treated as if they were of the greatest importance although not supported by any kind of rational argument. They are simply brainwashing or propaganda, not education; and they have no place in the classroom, since they fail to recognize the rights of the individual to autonomous decision making, the right which underlies democracy. This example provides one with a specimen procedure for counterattacking against a "bald man" (or black-and-white) argument. The most obvious counterargument is simply to use the phrases which identify this fallacy and say that the line of argument that's being used would show that black is white or that a bald man really is not distinguishable from someone with a full head of hair. But another type of counterargument is a little more powerful, if you can bring it off. Treating the pledge of allegiance or saluting the flag or reciting a religious code as something that is (1) obligatory, (2) forced upon children who have not been able to make up their own minds yet about whether they wish to take such pledges, (3) important, (4) something the legitimacy of which is not discussed seriously, critically, analytically, and at length is, it might be said, exactly the kind of behavior which a democratic system of government opposes. So, in rebutting the slippery slope argument that tries to show that such activity is really not very different and hence not "essentially" different from educational activity, one turns the tables in order to show that, if this isn't an important difference, the very difference which is extolled in all these propaganda activities is itself not an important difference; that is, it is not the difference between us and our "enemies."

In the same way, in dealing with the slippery slope arguments which are used to legitimate torture by the police or by army interrogators, one should consider the possibility that it is precisely the avoidance of such torture, and similar recognitions of the right of the individual to the integrity of his or her person and freedoms, that constitute the difference between us and our enemies. So, if the slippery slope argument is to be accepted, we must also accept the conclusion that we have no reason to be fighting the enemy (or, in the case of the police, to be fighting organized crime).

Let me run through that once more. This is really a case of turning the slippery slope argument on itself, and in common with a number of other cases of reasoning where one can do this, it's an uncommonly powerful procedure. (Another example is illustrated by the obvious criticism of "nothing is really certain," namely, that criticism applies to itself and hence can't be treated as reliable.) The argument justifying brutal interrogation of a military prisoner has two strands, one of which is the slippery slope argument and the other of which is the moral argument. The slippery slope argument involves saying that we already accept very long and exhausting interrogation, prison camp conditions, shouting at prisoners in the course of interrogation and probably shining strong lights in their eyes, and so on. It's only one step from these to a little cuffing around, or sticking the point of a knife into somebody, and only a step from that to chopping off a finger or shooting off an ear or tying a wire around the throat or applying an electric prod to the genitals. And, on the other hand (the moral argument), our cause is just and the information we extract may be vital in saving lives of our own soldiers who are in the moral right, and we're using these techniques on somebody who represents the enemy, who is morally wrong. The tough line of counterargument that we're considering now runs as follows: First, we say to the person who has put forward the preceding argument, you're arguing that there's only a difference of degree between what we would anyway accept and what is being questioned here (the use of physical torture); and then you say that although this is a difference, it is only a difference of degree and that it is overwhelmed by the moral differences that are involved. But the problem is that there's only a difference of degree between the moral position of the enemy and that of ourselves, and hence your very same argument would show that that moral difference isn't a real difference or a really important difference, and hence that it can't be used to justify the difference between yelling, shouting and shining lights, and shooting off an ear or electroshocking the prisoner, which is an absolutely unmistakable, clear, visible, and painful difference.

So you have attempted to argue out of existence the one difference that is really obvious by appealing to another difference which is only a matter of degree, and the way you've chosen to do this is by arguing that matters of degree are not very important. But the moral difference is most certainly a matter of degree, and if such differences are not really important, then they most certainly cannot be used to justify differences of treatment which are quite clearly not just a matter of degree at the sensory level of the sufferer, that is, at the most obvious level of direct sense perception. (In case you think that the difference between, say, the communist and the anticommunist sides is not just a difference of degree, then it would be worthwhile trying to spell out just what features of life under the anticommunist regime in South Vietnam could be said to be more democratic or more beneficial to the people than corresponding conditions in the communist North at the height of the war in Vietnam. The fact is that the difference here may have been not only a difference of degree, but it may have been a difference in the opposite direction from the way the arguer is assuming it goes, which of course opens up another line of counterargument.)

In the case of using torture on a suspected criminal, the problem is that "suspected" is not a category of criminality, but just an indication of the way that the evidence points prior to careful examination by a judge, jury, and the adversary system. To apply torture to somebody in such a situation is to treat the person as somebody who has been proven guilty of criminality beyond any reasonable doubt; that is, it is to treat "being a suspect" as one of the most serious crimes in the book (since very few jurisdictions allow torture for anything except the most serious crimes, even if then). So the attempt to justify torturing suspects, in order to get either a confession or information, by use of the slippery slope argument is open to the "fast switch" counterargument that if there isn't any real difference between brutality and interrogation of the more verbal kind, then there isn't any real difference between the behavior of the interrogator and the behavior of the criminal, if indeed the suspect is a criminal. Hence one slippery slope counts against the other and leaves us with a standoff situation, rather than a justification of torture. Incidentally, this kind of switching around and using an argument against itself is called sophistry if you don't understand it, or don't believe it, and clever, or devastating, if you do.

The important thing at this stage is to get a firm grip on some of these examples by discussing them carefully with your fellow students, instructor, or friends. They represent a very common type of argument with respect to many of the most important issues that face us. Think about the distinction between an abortion and infanticide. Think about the distinctions between tobacco, alcohol, marijuana, LSD, cocaine, and heroin. How often is the slippery slope argument used here? Think about issues where you've heard a regulatory board or an appeals board say, "If we made an exception here, we'd be making them all the time so we really have to draw the line." Many times—not every time—this is just a way of saying that the board members get nervous about being drawn anywhere into the gray area, and in order to make things easy on themselves, they will continue to make dinstinctions only between black and white, even though there are a serious cost and injustice that could be remedied if they were prepared to say that there is a difference in treatment.

5-6 Ambiguity and Its Exploitation

Vague or imprecise terms may be considered as terms which refer to a wide spectrum of possible interpretations. An extreme case of this is the ambiguous term, one which refers to two or more quite different meanings. The line between the two—that is, between vagueness and ambiguity—is not a sharp one, and you will often hear complaints made about terms like "democracy" in terms of their ambiguity, when in fact one might more precisely say that the problem with them is their vagueness.

But let's look at this in a little more detail. One might define "democracy" as a form of government in which the rulers are elected by public voting of all adults. Or one might define it as a form of government in which the government is subject to recall by a vote of the people. The term, if you're not clear which one of the two definitions it refers to, is certainly ambiguous. One could easily have an elected government which isn't subject to recall. The two concepts are logically distinct. However, even though many people have their own favorite definitions of democracy, and even though these definitions are logically distinct and not part of a continuous spectrum as most vague or imprecise notions are, the general truth is that the term "democracy" is a vague term rather than an ambiguous one, because its common meaning shifts along a complex spectrum, even though certain individuals have particular meanings for it that are conceptually distinct. The upshot of all this is that you don't want to be too rigid about whether the term is ambiguous or vague, until you've decided whether you're talking about its usage in a particular context or about its common meaning. In a really serious scholarly work on the nature and justification of democracy, for example, in C.B. Macpherson's *Democratic Theory,* one can indeed argue that it's used ambiguously, sometimes to refer to "one man (woman?), one vote" and sometimes to refer to "the maximization of personal freedom." But even that isn't a particularly serious criticism because Macpherson explains the ambiguity and operates with one or the other sense of the term at a time, fairly carefully. But in a general discussion, rather than in the context of a carefully structured book, the term is much more likely to be ambiguous in a bad sense (people disagreeing about it mainly because they mean different things by it) or just vague (people disagreeing about it because they haven't thought about where they'd draw the line between a democratic and an undemocratic society).

With these preliminary cautions, however, one can go ahead and talk briefly about the relatively rare case of plain ambiguity and the effects that it can have on argumentation.

The most important case of the exploitation or abuse of the ambiguity of a term occurs in arguments where there is a shifting of the meaning of a term during the course of the argument. The technical name of this error of reasoning or fallacy is the "fallacy of equivocation," a label which you do not have to remember. We'll normally refer to it as simply a shift of meaning. A typical case would be an argument which opens with one premise in which a term, let us say "criminally insane," is used in the premises with a certain meaning, in order to develop intermediate conclusions. Then, in reasoning from these intermediate conclusions, together with some extra facts, toward the final conclusion, the term is used in a slightly different way, and the argument wouldn't work if the same meaning had been used throughout. Either the first premises wouldn't have been true, or the inference from the intermediate conclusion to the final conclusion wouldn't have worked. That's a typical example of the "shift of meaning" fallacy, or the fallacy of equivocation. It's a fairly crude kind of affair, and you only have to keep your eyes and ears half open in order to pick it up. In *most* cases! But, like any logical fallacies, once in a while one comes across a case where it's pretty hard to spot the cause of trouble. These cases are nearly always very, very long ones—for example, a whole chapter, or a whole book, where the shift occurs gradually in midstream—and so they're not very easy to quote.

The ones that we can quote look pretty implausible, and you imagine that you couldn't possibly be taken in by anything so crude; but then once in a while you are. A crude example, involving the term "criminally insane," would look something like this:

> The crucial pragmatic significance of criminal insanity is that it absolves individuals so described from legal responsibility for their actions. The extent of true criminal insanity is probably something like 10 percent of the cases that are thus identified under the present inefficient system. However, there *are* certain clear cases of insanity, and we shouldn't allow our legitimate worries about overextension of the term to prevent us from treating these unfortunate creatures with justice. It would be ridiculous to act as if a paranoid schizophrenic was in full possession of his or her faculties and someone who should be held up for the full rigors of the maximum punishment afforded by the law. Yet this is exactly what has happened in the Manson case. A classical case of paranoid schizophrenia, diagnosed by several extremely competent psychiatrists, was treated as if it was a standard example of heinous crime. We have to be very careful not to let our nervousness about the excesses of psychiatry destroy our basic sense of justice.

What's happened in this argument is that we've shifted from the opening definition of criminal insanity, which ties it definitionally to the absence of responsibility, to a later definition which identifies paranoid schizophrenics in the psychiatric sense as being criminally insane, which isn't obvious at all. In fact, it's exactly what the debate is about in many court cases. The paranoid schizophrenic, operating within an elaborate delusional schema, may in fact, with respect to the act in question, be able to choose rationally, recognize right from wrong, and otherwise meet the standards for legal sanity. (Some more detailed discussion of particular cases will be found in *The Meaning of Criminal Insanity* by Herbert Fingarette, University of California Press, 1972.)

How should you tackle this type of fallacy when doing argument analysis? Look back if you don't remember.

5-7 Dictionary Definitions—Real and Ideal

We've been touring through the messy territory of troubles with meaning, and it's now time we started looking at ways of clarifying meaning. Traditionally, people think of the dictionary as the source of concise definitions. And so it is; but the kind of definition that you find there is not by any means the ideal kind that is so often discussed in logic texts. An ideal kind of definition would look something like this:

Triangle = three-sided geometrical figure

That's one of the kinds of definitions that you'll find in a dictionary; or, more likely, one piece of a definition that you'll find in a dictionary. It is a valuable ideal, and we want to begin by discussing its properties so that we have this ideal firmly fixed in mind before we start moving to the reality levels of the more frequently encountered definitions and to alternative procedures for specifying meaning. Notice that we sometimes call the whole "equation" the definition, whereas sometimes we call the right-hand side of it the "definition" of the left side, which is the term being defined. The key features of the ideal type of definition are as follows:

a   The meaning on each side of the equals sign is exactly the same: that is, one could replace either the term "triangle" or the above definition of it by the other, in (almost) any context, without loss of meaning. (The most obvious context where you could not do this is in the definition itself, since the definition clearly tells you something which could be quite informative, whereas, if you substitute the word "triangle" for the right-hand side of *it,* you'd get

Triangle = triangle

which is trivial and not informative at all.)

b   As a practical consequence of feature a, the consequence that is crucial for testing purposes, anything which is correctly described by the left-hand side of the equation must be something which is correctly described by the right-hand side, and vice versa. (That's just an unpacking of the phrase "has the same meaning.")

c   Another unpacking of the definition, which is useful in special cases, tells us that it would be a contradiction to describe anything by the term on the left-hand side and by the negation of the term on the right-hand side (or vice versa). That is, you couldn't say something was a triangle and didn't have three sides, or that it was a triangle and had four sides (which implies that it didn't have three sides).

Notice right away that the term "triangle" is also the name of a musical instrument, and it's also the name of a drawing device used in drafting, and it's also a term used to refer to the course that racing yachts sail, and so on. All these other meanings show us that the term, out of context, is ambiguous. Not that it's vague, which it might or might not be as well, but that it's ambiguous. It might be ambiguous and some of its meanings might be vague, or *all* of them might be vague. Or it might be ambiguous and precise in each of its meanings. What we have been looking at is a definition of one sense of the term "triangle." What you find in a dictionary is usually a listing of *all* the senses, and hence a whole series of definitions of a term which is, out of context, ambiguous. Terms that are ambiguous out of context are, however, rarely ambiguous in a given context. That's how we are able to understand the English language, nearly all of whose most common nouns are given multiple definitions in the dictionary. We understand which of the meanings is intended by contextual cues. This is perhaps the single most important feature of the real, as opposed to the ideal, language.

Now if somebody proposes a personal definition (of a particular sense) of the term, you may use any of the conditions *a, b* or *c* above to see whether the definition is, strictly speaking, correct. *Example:* If someone proposes to define "good teacher" as "someone who scores well above the average on student evaluation forms," you might go about scrutinizing this proposed definition by applying condition *b* above. Are there any cases of good teachers, in the popular sense of the term, who would not score high on student evaluation forms? And are there any cases of people who score high on student evaluation forms who are not good teachers? Before reading further, ask yourself if you can see any difficulties with, or answers to, these questions.

As we begin to reflect on them, we should immediately see that we're facing a problem of imprecision. There are many student evaluation forms, some of them hopelessly unreliable. If one were to use a student evaluation form which is essentially a rating of the extent to which the student *likes* the teacher (and there are such forms), one might easily find cases of rather strict, cold, and severe teachers who would score badly on these forms but who would nevertheless be very successful in teaching the students whatever they had enrolled in the class to learn.

You will notice that we have made two crucial moves as we get down to discussing this example in detail. First, we have started to talk about how there might be a good teacher who did badly on some such form, as if this was relevant to the accuracy of the definition. And second, we have started implicitly generating a more satisfactory or more basic definition of "good teacher" (in this case, as someone who succeeds in teaching whatever it is that the course is supposed to assist the student in learning). Each of these steps deserves a word of explanation, as it is extremely important.

First, it is crucial to understand that in order to criticize a definition, you need to think only of possible exceptions, not of actual ones. The reason for this is that the claim involved in the definition, and expressed as claim *a* above, is the claim that the two sides of the equation are *synonymous,* that is exactly the same in *meaning.* Hence, wherever either one could be applied correctly, the other one would have to be applied correctly; and that doesn't mean the same as "wherever one has already been or is now applied correctly, the other is now applied correctly." When we're talking about meaning we're talking about all possible (proper) applications of the term, not merely its present applications. You can see that this is crucial for a language because a language has to be usable to describe new phenomena, and of course it couldn't describe something new if the rules for its use tied it to only those cases that have existed until now. One couldn't write imaginative literature if one could not describe imaginary scenes. We can visualize and describe triangles which are tiger-striped, leopard-spotted, and polka-dotted, even though we may never have seen such a thing and may not even be at all confident that there is or will be such a thing. The meaning of the word "triangle" is just the same whether it's describing Δ or a triangle of immense dimensions which you have just visualized as part of a description of a spatial survey performed by a planetary exploration spaceship. Hence, if the definition above does correctly represent the exact meaning of the term, it will correctly translate the term in any reference to an imaginary object just as well as it will when referring to a real object. So, in order to criticize a definition, all you have to be able to do is to imagine a fair case of something which would be correctly described by one side of the definition, but would not be correctly described by the other side; such a case shows that the two sides do not have the same meaning. That's quite different from the issue of whether, as a matter of fact, all triangles happen to have three sides. For example, as a matter of fact, it might happen that the only featherless, tailless bipeds on the earth's surface were ourselves; but that wouldn't show that the term "human being" means the same as "featherless, tailless biped," since if we then encountered a plucked chicken running around, or a kangaroo with its tail amputated, we most certainly wouldn't refer to it as a member of the human race. This shows that we have in mind a meaning of "human being" that is not fully exhausted by "featherless, tailless biped." So there's no question that "featherless, tailless biped" does not cover the meaning of "human being" even though it may happen in fact to refer to the same group of individual entities at a particular moment in time.

In sum, then, the logical scrutiny of definitions must not be restricted to the mere question of whether the entities described by the left-hand side of the definition happen at the moment to be the same set of entities as those described by the right-hand side. The definition must go further, and answer the question of whether all entities that could be properly described by one side would have to be properly described by the other side. Hence, there is an exercise in imagination involved in the criticism of definitions. You have to try to imagine cases where it's perfectly clear that people who understand the language would immediately apply one side of the definition but not the other. When we apply this test to the above definition of "triangle" in the sense where it refers to a geometrical figure, we find that there really aren't any exceptions of this sort. Hence, we have succeeded in expressing the meaning of one sense of the term "triangle." But when we look at the definition of "good teacher" above, we can see that there could easily be good teachers who weren't rated well on a particular student evaluation form. We can also see that there might be teachers who are rated well on such a form who are not good teachers at all, but who are just popular, friendly, giving high grades, or saying something that seems to be true and interesting but is really false.

It might be a little unfair to be criticizing that definition simply by appealing to a case where a bad student evaluation form is used, which identifies good teaching with likeability, for example. It's true that the original definition is vulnerable to this type of criticism, but it is a relatively weak criticism, since the definition could be reformulated. Suppose we devise the best possible student evaluation form. It will still reflect the opinion of the students, and one distinguishing feature of students is that they are not so well informed about the subject matter as the most distinguished experts in that subject matter. It is therefore possible, though in practice not very likely, that the students might be greatly impressed by a teacher who had all the appropriate pedagogical skills and who appeared to be laying out for them a subject matter that made a great deal of sense, whereas, in fact, the information that was being offered was out of date and currently known to be incorrect. Hence, doing well on even the best student evaluation form cannot encapsulate the whole meaning of "good teacher," since that term certainly involves teaching what is true.

The second feature of this line of discussion is that, clearly, we're bringing in certain considerations that we implicitly think are part of the concept of "good teacher" but that aren't covered in the proposed definition. The two that we've mentioned so far are skill in producing learning on the part of the student in the appropriate area, and teaching what is in fact true or correct. These are, to use a terminology we have discussed earlier, necessary conditions for being a good teacher, but they're not sufficient conditions. An ideal dictionary definition of the type we've been talking about is supposed to provide conditions that are sufficient and necessary for the term that it defines. Since either side of the equation is supposed to be the same as the other in meaning, it follows that if either side can be applied, then the other can be applied; consequently, each side is a sufficient condition for the other; and hence (if you think about it), each is a necessary condition for the other. So the ideal dictionary definition is a classic example of a sufficient and necessary condition for the term defined. Here we run into another difference between the ideal and reality; for dictionary definitions in practice frequently provide us only with conditions that are usually or generally or probably sufficient and necessary for the use of the term, but not totally or logically or strictly or "definitionally" sufficient and necessary conditions for it.

So, as we criticize definitions, we do so by appealing to examples which people would instantly recognize and describe by the terms of either the left side or the right side of the equation, but not both; and we sometimes do so with some implicit reference to at least a part of a better definition; and, as we've seen from the preceding section, we may also do something that's very closely related to these, namely, look for contrasts that the term implies and see whether these contrasts are preserved by the proposed definition. Be systematic in criticizing definitions; be sure to cover all these points in your approach. One of the three may work if the others don't.

Notice that a proposed definition might provide a necessary condition for the use of the term being defined that isn't also a sufficient condition; or it might provide a sufficient condition that isn't also a necessary condition. Either would be a fault, and they are faults in different directions. But these faults are independent: a proposed definition can commit both of them simultaneously. There is another language for expressing this kind of deficiency in a proposed definition, and it may be a language that is more graphic for most readers. Suppose we define "triangle" as "any geometrical figure." This would obviously be too broad a definition; it includes too much: we might say it's too *inclusive* a definition. That's another way of saying that it states a necessary condition but not a sufficient condition. Something can't be a triangle without being a geometrical figure; hence it's a necessary condition for something to be a triangle that it be a geometrical figure. But something could be a geometrical figure without being a triangle (for example, by being a quadrilateral), and hence the proposed definition is not a sufficient condition for the term defined.

On the other hand, we might define a triangle as a geometrical figure with three sides, of which two are of the same length. That's an excellent definition of an isosceles triangle, which is a particular species of triangle. But it's too narrow a definition for the term "triangle" in general. You might also say it's too *restrictive*; this is the same as saying that it provides a sufficient condition for being a triangle but not a necessary condition.

It's quite easy to depict the relationship between the two sides of the proposed definition so as to reflect these various kinds of error. You can think of the territory to which each of the sides legitimately applies as represented by a circle. In a correct definition (Figure 1 below), the two circles coincide. In a definition which is too narrow, the circle represented by the definition (*Y*) falls entirely within the circle represented by the defined term (*X*) (Figure 2). In a definition which is too broad, the reverse is the case (Figure 3). In a definition which is both too broad and too narrow, or too inclusive and too restrictive, the corresponding picture would be of the two circles overlapping—some parts of each would fall within the other and some parts would fall outside (Figure 4). In such a case, we would say that the proposed definition is neither necessary nor sufficient for the use of the defined term: or that it is both too inclusive and too restrictive: or that it is both too broad and too narrow.

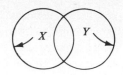

(Here the proposed definition is $X = Y$)

There you have the ingredients for the basic procedures for criticizing definitions. Once again, be systematic. Always look for the possibility that the proposed definition is too broad as well as too narrow; don't settle for finding just one kind of defect in it. Indeed, don't settle for finding just one kind of example to prove, say, that it's too broad; go ahead and find two or three if you can, since then you have several independent grounds for criticism in that direction, and will only have to renounce one of them if it turns out that you've made some slight error of interpretation. As practice, criticize this proposed definition: "college" = where you go to get educated after you leave high school (Quiz 5-A, question 1).

We've already indicated a number of ways in which real definitions tend to be less exact than the ideal ones we've been talking about. First of all, notice that the short formula we've used to represent a definition ($X = Y$) is in reality too simple. The Y part actually consists of several properties, Y_1, Y_2, Y_3, etc. So the definition usually looks more like this: $X = Y_1$ and Y_2 and Y_3. . . . The most extreme deviation from the ideal definition occurs when what you find in the dictionary is almost totally different from the ideal definition in that nothing in it (none of the Y's) is a necessary condition, although the total set is a sufficient condition for the defined term. In the ideal definition, each of the properties Y_1, Y_2, Y_3, is a necessary condition, and they are, taken together, a sufficient condition for the proper use of the defined term X. (And of course, taken together, they are also necessary, since if several things are necessary, putting "and" between them just makes the whole set of them necessary.)

Take a definition of a simple word like "apple." Using your imagination, we can readily think of counterexamples to the definitions that you find in Webster's Second, Webster's Third, the Oxford English Dictionary, the Random House Dictionary, and the other usual standards. That is, we can easily imagine growing apples in laboratory flasks, so that they're not the fruit of any tree; growing them from a skin cell from another apple, so that they are not grown from seeds; or that they do not have seeds from which something else could be grown. We can imagine them tasting quite unlike present apples but being so similar in every other respect that they would still naturally be called apples, and so on and so on. Every one of the "defining properties" mentioned in the dictionary can be shown not to be necessary; hence the sum of them all isn't necessary. And it is quite common for these everyday terms to be such that we can't specify any necessary conditions for them at all. All we can do is to give a set of conditions which is, as we say, jointly sufficient (that is, Y_1 plus Y_2 plus Y_3 implies X, but not vice versa). Or perhaps we can give several sets of conditions, each of which is jointly sufficient (that is, we can also find a set of Z's such that Z_1 plus Z_2 plus Z_3 also implies X—but not vice versa). Hence we learn that there are certain cases where the term can be properly applied (e.g., a case where Y_1 and Y_2 and Y_3 are all present); and we learn that there's a family of cases which are related in some not too precisely definable way, to all of which the term applies. (Y_1 plus Y_2 plus Y_3 is one case; Z_1 plus Z_2 plus Z_3 is another; and maybe there's a W_1 plus W_2 plus W_3 case too.) But our insight doesn't go beyond that: there isn't a buried secret formula which encapsulates the meaning in a more precise way. A famous example is the term "game." It's easy to list sets of sufficient conditions which amount to descriptions of football, hide-and-seek, pole vaulting, solitaire, each of which is therefore a description of a game and hence a sufficient condition for the use of the term "game," but it is hard to give necessary conditions. Try it! In situations like this, we sometimes refer to the indicators that are mentioned, the relevant components of any of these sets of sufficient conditions (in the case of, for example, "apple," things like being the fruit of a certain tree, being green in color at one stage of their development, or being crisp and white-fleshed) as being *criteria* for the use of the term, by contrast with *necessary conditions* for the use of the term. They are all we have, all that we can appeal to in explaining the meaning, but they're not necessary conditions. In a later section we'll have a look at the constructive use of this kind of fact in explaining meaning. What it really tells us is that when we can't find necessary conditions to make up a nice, ideal definition, we can still provide examples to illustrate and thus convey the meaning of the term, even if we're not providing a translation. Before we get to that, we'll look at some other very significant weaknesses of the "dictionary definition" approach to clarifying meaning. And before doing that, it may be useful to sum up what we have just been saying.

5-8   Necessary Conditions and Criteria

An ideal dictionary definition defines the term X by referring to a series of properties, Y_1, Y_2, and so on, in a formula like this:

$$X = Y_1 \text{ plus } Y_2 \text{ plus } Y_3 \ldots$$

To qualify as an X (a triangle, for example), something must then have all the properties Y_1, Y_2, etc. (having three sides, being a geometrical figure, for example). Having each of the defining properties is therefore necessary; they are *necessary conditions* for being an X. Having all of them is *sufficient.* The Y's are therefore described as individually necessary and jointly sufficient.

Now what we find in practice, in reality, is that such ideal definitions are usually possible only in mathematics—or when someone invents a new term and stipulates what it is to mean. Even in math, and soon after a new term has been introduced (if it "catches on"), we find the situation becoming cloudier, the connections looser than in the ideal definition. We find that we can still identify cases which seem to be clearly cases of X, but that the range of cases of X seems to expand as the concept X develops a life of its own, and we become unable to say that all such cases must contain certain common elements, the necessary conditions (Y) that were referred to in the original definition. This "degenerate" situation, it turns out, is the typical situation with essentially all the nouns, adjectives, verbs, and adverbs of the common language and of most of science. We can give rather imprecise general definitions of these terms ("apple," "estuary," "force"), or, sometimes, exact but abstract definitions which only pass the buck of comprehension along to another equally unclear term ("a force is whatever produces or could produce an acceleration"; "moral virtue" equals "the opposite of moral vice," and so on). But we cannot give adequate translations of these terms into a set of more specific, and hence usually (which is the point) more easily understandable, terms, each of which refers to a necessary condition for the application of the term. On the other hand, we can easily identify clear cases of X, which means that, if we can adequately describe such cases, we can give a number of sufficient conditions for the use of the term. For example, we can describe a Gravenstein apple from the tree in our own garden in sufficient detail so that one may be perfectly confident that anything which meets that description must be called an apple by anyone who understands the meaning of that term. That is, we have a case where having the properties W_1, W_2, W_3, etc. is a sufficient condition for being an apple, but no one of these conditions is necessary. We refer to properties like these as *criteria* for being an apple; that is, they are relevant components of a sufficient condition. They would be recognized as relevant by a fluent native speaker of the language (who would rule out the fact that a fly was sitting on this particular apple as irrelevant), and the whole set would be recognized as sufficient for the application of the term, but, unlike the criteria for "triangle," they aren't necessary.

There's no sharp line between criteria and properties which just happen to apply generally in practice. For example, being tailless just happens to be true of humans, but a native speaker would be unlikely to cite it as a criterion for being human, since someone whose coccyx happened to extend into a stubby caudal appendage (the anatomical jargon for a tail) would not for one moment be thought to be nonhuman. In looking for criteria, that is, while we know we can't expect them to be strictly necessary, we do look for properties whose absence would be felt to count a little toward weakening the claim of humanity. If an entity is neither a fruit, nor contains seeds, nor is crisp, nor is green when unripe, nor has the range of flavors of current varieties, nor falls into the size range at maturity from a golfball to a grapefruit, then one could hardly call it an apple, even though any one of these (perhaps any two) could be dropped and we could still be persuaded. No specific one is necessary, but the presence of some is necessary. It's necessary to have "representatives" of this group, but no particular member.

Pictorially, in the search for an ideal definition, we are looking for a set of properties Y, each of which is a necessary condition for X, that is, each of which is a broader or more inclusive concept than X:

but such that, when you take them all together, their only common ground is exactly X:

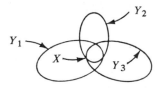

What we've been saying about real definitions of most terms is that the outlines of each property aren't nearly as sharp. You can think of them as fuzzy circles. So we finish up with a series of fuzzy circles that more or less enclose X:

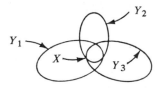

Here it's fuzzily clear that there are some points that fall within X but outside the range of any given Y, so no Y is a necessary condition for X. Yet the fact remains that the Y's are all that there is to the meaning of X: If we try to explain the meaning of X to a foreigner or to someone who had not previously encountered it, the Y's are what we'd mention and they're all that we could mention. (You have to employ some members of this club, but you don't have to employ all of them, or any particular ones.)

So, in the real world, there aren't many ideal definitions where the Y's are all necessary conditions for X. Mostly, the Y's that you'd use to explain the meaning of X (that is, to define X in the usual way) are only probably properties of a given X. They are not necessary conditions (nor probably necessary conditions) but just *criteria* for X which means (1) they are usually associated with X; (2) they are the properties a native speaker would mention or recognize as relevant to deciding the question of whether something is really an X or not. The one ghostly remnant of the necessary condition feature that still applies to these "critical definitions," namely that even though one can't claim that each of the criteria is necessary, one could claim that at least one of them (perhaps several) has to be present, can be expressed in terms of the abbreviations, as follows, Although it isn't true that:

Y_1 is a necessary condition for X

or that

Y_2 is a necessary condition for X

or that

Y_3 is a necessary condition for X

it is true that: either Y_1 or Y_2 or Y_3 is a necessary condition for X

or perhaps even that:

either Y_1 and Y_2, or Y_1 and Y_3, or Y_2 and Y_3 is a necessary condition for X. (That is, it might be true that you have to have two of them.)

Now go to your dictionary. How about its definition of "apple"? (Quiz 5-A, 2) Does it have any necessary conditions in it? Can you prove it?

What's the explanation of this "failure" of definitions? It's very simple. The "game" of language is not a game in the literal sense at all. It does have "rules" but not strict and fixed rules like chess. It is a pragmatic game like running or hunting, where the goal is success in a certain task—travel, or escape; a trophy, or food—and the "player" does whatever is most appropriate for that task. In a very complex world such as ours, the most useful functions of language, like, for example, communication of information or instructions, or requests for them, will be most efficiently served by using language to refer to the most commonly observed clusters of properties. When we refer to a "table" in our speech, we expect people to understand us to mean the kind of thing we are used to in the furnishings of our homes, offices, and institutions. Nobody could care less if there are a few bizarre objects around somewhere, or on the drawing boards somewhere, or conceivable, which do not look like these but which we'd still call tables. In explaining the meaning of the term, we wouldn't refer to them. They're not pragmatically important. *BUT. . .*

But they are sometimes extremely important in scientific theorizing; a precise analysis of what was meant by saying that two remote events are simultaneous led Einstein to the theory of relativity. And they are important in showing you something about the nature of meaning and definition, namely that the meaning of most terms involves a reference to a set of properties which cluster together even though a few cases of them scatter around elsewhere. The properties which normally cluster together are the *criteria.*

5-9 Fact and Fancy: Definitional Truth and Physical Truth

In these little diagrams that we've been drawing, with circles marking out the domain of X, Y_1, and so on, we need to be clear what the territory is on which we are setting out the boundaries. It is the realm of proper use (or the things to which that use refers), which of course includes actual use but also includes potential use. We've already stressed the fact that knowing the English language involves knowing how to apply it to many (though not all) new cases, situations, or entities that have never been seen before. You would have no problem in recognizing or describing something as a green rose, though in fact no such entity has ever existed. Hence, when we draw a circle to represent the range of proper use of the term "rose," it will cover many cases that we have not so far encountered in the real world. In a previous chapter, we have talked about necessary and sufficient conditions in the real world. Here we have been talking about necessary and sufficient conditions in all possible worlds. (There would be some which are undescribable in any language, and some which would require substantial additions to our language to describe at all thoroughly.)

If a condition is necessary in our world—as, for example, it's necessary for an adult human to have passed through a period of childhood—we say that it's *physically* necessary, *practically* or, more generally, *factually* or *empirically* necessary. If it's necessary in all the worlds to which our language can apply, as, for example, it's necessary for a parent to have had a child, we say it's *definitionally* necessary or *logically* necessary. Indeed, we usually make further distinctions under the first of these headings—and remember that none of them is a special technical term, that they're part of the logical vocabulary that already exists in, or is made up from, standard combinations of terms that already exist in English. These distinctions all exist just because they're very useful in argument or meaning analysis.

Under empirical or factual or practical necessity, we distinguish between cases where a law of nature "underwrites" the necessity—for example, it's physically necessary that solid iron sinks in water because of Archimedes' Law—and cases where we have arranged that something is necessary, but where it is within the power of people to arrange it otherwise. For example, it's necessary for you to pass a test in order to get a driving license in California. One might call these two subcases *physical* necessity (because physical law is the source of the necessity) and *legal* or *planned* necessity (for obvious reasons). Where the necessity is neither the result of natural law nor of planning, but has just grown up as a convention or habit-pattern, we talk of *social* or *cultural* necessity. And finally, where the necessity has ethical backing, e.g., is an obligation, something that we "have" to do in the sense of "ought," we call it a *moral* necessity. Remember that none of these distinctions is absolutely sharp, not even the distinction between logical and factual necessity. But they're extremely useful because most cases fall clearly into one category or the other.

Now what is the *contrast* dimension of the meaning of these terms, what's excluded by calling a relationship between two properties necessary? Necessary as opposed to what?

In the case of factual necessity, the contrast is with what happens to be true by accident. The classic example is that it may just happen to be true that all coins in my pocket are silver—but it's not necessarily true, either by virtue of a law of nature (physical necessity) or by deliberate plan or design. Incidentally, both "accidental" truths and physical necessities are to be contrasted with false claims, as are all necessary truths; but they are also to be contrasted with each other, since they are true for different reasons. Both, however, are factually true.

In the case of definitional or logical necessity, the contrasts are with factual truths and with *definitionally* false claims. So the set of distinctions looks like this:

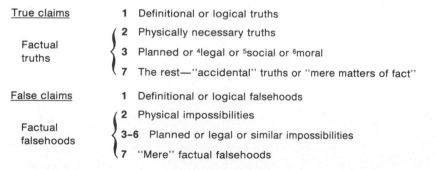

True claims		
	1	Definitional or logical truths
Factual truths	**2**	Physically necessary truths
	3	Planned or [4]legal or [5]social or [6]moral
	7	The rest—"accidental" truths or "mere matters of fact"

False claims		
	1	Definitional or logical falsehoods
Factual falsehoods	**2**	Physical impossibilities
	3-6	Planned or legal or similar impossibilities
	7	"Mere" factual falsehoods

As an exercise right now, classify the following examples as of types 1, 2, 3, 4, 5, 6, or 7, and as T or F. (See Quiz 5-A.) Add comments where necessary—and perhaps more than one label if necessary.

a You can't pass this course without reading this text.

b Sons have to have (or to have had) a father.

c Sons have to have a parent.

d It's impossible for a black woman to be elected President before 1984.

e Democracy cannot exist when there is no freedom of speech.

f The interior-angle sum of a triangle is 180°.

g You have to go through the hallway to get to the living room in most house designs.

h You absolutely have to repay that debt this week.

There is an important "pecking order" in these lists. The numerical order reflects a sequence of strength in the sense of the extent of the domain over which the truths hold sway.

1 Definitional truths hold in all worlds to which our language can be applied.

2 Physically necessary truths apply to all possible occurrences in the past, present, and future of our world. (If they didn't, the underlying law wouldn't be a law of nature.[1])

3 Social, legal, and planned necessities apply as long as the present social system applies (perhaps within a particular subculture).

4 Moral necessities are of the same strength as either 2 or 3 above, depending on whether morality is a kind of natural law or just a kind of social convention.

5 Accidental truths apply only until some circumstances which affect them change.

It follows that when you are criticizing a claim—for example, the premise of an argument—you are giving the strongest possible criticism if you show it's definitionally false, the next strongest if you show it contravenes a law of nature, the next if it contravenes a law of mankind or the arrangements of some subgroup thereof, and the weakest if you simply show it happens not to be true. (But even the weakest is strong enough to destroy the claim.)

This is just one of several aspects of the distinction between strong and weak criticism which is of such importance in argument analysis. But it's important elsewhere in the domain of reasoning, from the "propaganda analysis" end to the highest reaches of abstract reasoning. When an advertiser claims that a "properly tuned" engine using the water-injection apparatus being advertised can show gains of 50 percent in gas mileage, one should

---

[1] This is the usual convention, but, theoretically at least, physical laws might be location- or time-dependent.

immediately wonder whether this claim is true only when a special meaning is given to "properly tuned," or whether it's true as a simple, honest, factual claim in the ordinary meaning of "properly tuned." If "properly tuned" is being used to mean the tuning is done just so as to minimize gas consumption, the claim may well be true, but it won't be of much interest to the average user, because if you tune a car simply for maximum gas mileage, it becomes virtually impossible to start or accelerate. The claim has been made a planned or nearly definitional necessity at the expense of being a useful matter of fact. What "properly tuned" normally means is "tuned so as to best perform the usual functions of a car"; that's what you take your car in for when you ask for a tune-up. Now it really would be important if water-injection could give a 50 percent gain in mileage without loss of general drivability, power, and other desired capabilities. But it's totally uninteresting to hear such a claim if "properly tuned" is to mean "specially tuned for high mileage," since *any* car, without using a water-injector at all, can easily be tuned so as to give that much gain (e.g., by using a much smaller carburetor jet or advancing and jamming the ignition timing), if you don't mind loss of power, illegal emissions, and having to run it down a hill to start it.

The trained ear responds instantly to such slippery terms as "properly" or even "normally" or "generally," and begins to probe their meaning by asking questions or examining context. Is the claim going to be converted into a trival one, or even, in the limit, a merely definitional one, by using these terms in a special sense?

In the scientific domain, exactly similar problems of this type occur. The general principle of evolution is said to be "the survival of the fittest" or, in a fancier version, "the differential reproduction of the best adapted." Whether that's a trivial claim or an important one depends entirely on whether "the fittest" turns out to be defined as "those that survive," or in some independent way. If it is defined as "those that survive," the claim then reduces to "the survival of those that survive," which is totally trivial. There is a long history of attempts, beginning with those of Darwin and Wallace, to give some independent meaning to "the fittest" and hence make the principle of evolution enlightening. Exactly similar problems occur with respect to the gas laws in physics (which are said to apply to "an ideal gas") and the laws of elasticity (which apply to a "perfectly elastic substance"). What we discover is that the cash value of these laws lies beneath the surface—in the extent to which they approximate the behavior of real gases or substances, not in what they tell us about ideal or perfect substances, since such substances do not exist in the real world. The same is true in ethics: "Killing is wrong"—but not always. There is self-defense, just war, execution: the cash value is in the fine print, the application of the principle in practice.

Notice that we are here regarding it as grounds for complaint that such claims are "reduced to the status of definitions." That's not because there is anything absolutely inferior about definitions. Indeed, there is something absolutely superior about them, namely that they are necessarily true in all conceivable, or at least in all describable, worlds. But their truth is obtained at a price, namely that they cease to tell us about this particular world and start telling us about the meaning of words instead. When we want to know something about the particular world we inhabit, this switch is not useful to us, and it may be fraudulent. So definitional truths, despite their truth, may be "trivial" or "uninformative" about what we need to be informed about, though they're just what we need to explain the meaning of a term, and anything less would be unsatisfactory there.

And in mathematics or in the law or even in ordinary argument, it is sometimes a great triumph to be able to demonstrate that a particular claim is, or can be, reduced to a definitional truth or truths. For these may well be highly informative where they express the kind of information we are seeking; the fact that they are, when true at all, true with virtually complete certainty, becomes a matter to rejoice over, rather than to scorn because such truth was achieved via logic rather than observation or experiment. At the simplest end of the spectrum, the definition may be informative to someone who didn't know the meaning of the term defined. At the most complex end, a theorem of Euclidean geometry—say, Pythagoras's theorem—is informative to any student of geometry, even though it can be reduced (by several exceedingly ingenious constructions and proofs) to the definitional truths that constitute the Euclidean axioms.

So, whereas we will sometimes rightly scorn a claim when we show it to be definitionally true, we will in other situations be overjoyed to be able to prove it so. It's all a matter of what kind of truth or information we are seeking in the particular context. Earlier, we showed how increasing the precision of a claim increases its informativeness. But, we said (in fact, it's the other side of the same coin) making it more precise means that it will be harder to show that it's true (for example, more careful measurement will be required), and in the absence of evidence, it's less likely to be true. Hence, for both these reasons, the more precise a claim is, the less chance it has of being true. (Consider the following claims or bets in roulette; the next number to come up will be even, will be in the top third, will be one of four adjacent ones, will be 28.) Since information has to be both new (not previously known) and true, there's a crucial tension in the search for it. We can increase the precision of our claims, which makes it increasingly likely that people didn't know them to be true before—but it also makes them increasingly hard to prove. Or we can make them vaguer and vaguer, less and less precise, which makes them more and more likely to be true ("The weather tomorrow will be warmer or cooler"), but less and less likely to have been unknown beforehand. The ultimate reduction to triviality makes the claim definitionally true, and obviously so, in which case it's worth nothing to those who already know the language; on the other hand, you surely have made it true, which on other occasions is the big payoff. So the value (utility) of a claim varies with context, just as the meaning of a term does.

An extreme view, due to a school of philosophers called the positivists, held that when a claim was impossible[2] to disprove it became *meaningless*. What we've been saying is that it would be meaningless if it could not be *contrasted* with anything, and hence, that if one couldn't rule out (disprove) the contrasting state of affairs, one couldn't prove the claim to be true. It's a mistake to compress these two fairly plausible assertions into the positivists' slogan. For example, what are we to say about "There is no life after death"? It's pretty well impossible to prove or disprove it by any direct experiment that we can do here on earth, partly because if it's true, you'll never know it by direct experience, and it won't be testable at all if, as is quite possible (conceptually), the spirits of the dead cannot communicate with mortals in any way. But it surely isn't meaningless; for example, one knows quite well what it would be like to find out it's wrong, after dying. In short, it has contrast meaning though it may lack testability.

Here's an example that you should spend a little time on. An astrologer reads your horoscope and announces (amongst other things): "December 11th, in the afternoon, is a very risky time for you to make major decisions." Is this provable? Disprovable? How? Is it meaningless? (If not, what does it mean?)

These distinctions between types of truth can be applied to logic itself. Using p and q to stand for assertions, we can set out various "principles of logic" quite easily. As you look at them, you'll realize that they are themselves definitional truths, just truths about the meaning of the words that constitute the structure (rather than the content) of an argument. A really simple example would be: "It is false that p is false = p is true" (where we once again use the equals sign to convey "means (just about) the same as"). Another, less simple example (which even has a grand title, being one of DeMorgan's laws) is: It is false that p and q are both true = p is false or q is false. The other DeMorgan law is much the same, interchanging "and" with "or": It is false that either p or q is true = p is false and q is false.

If we use an arrow to stand for "implies," meaning here logically or definitionally implies, then we can (roughly) translate p = q as p $\rightarrow$ q *and* q $\rightarrow$ p. The equals sign is thus (at this simple level) about the same as a double-ended arrow.

---

[2] Meaning "impossible in principle"; that is, of such a kind that no conceivable evidence could count against it.

You can see that we're beginning to develop an elementary part of what's called symbolic or formal or mathematical logic. What we just said about the arrows and the equals sign can be put in these symbols as

$$(p = q) \quad = \quad (p \to q) \quad \text{and} \quad (q \to p)$$

Remember that "p is a sufficient condition for q" is $p \to q$; "p is a necessary condition for q" is $q \to p$. Notice that there's no great confusion resulting from using the $\to$ to refer to logically or definitionally necessary (or sufficient) conditions here, whereas, in the last chapter, we were using it to refer also to empirically or factually necessary or sufficient conditions. That's just one more example of how one symbol can be (1) ambiguous out of context, (2) perfectly clear in context.

A slightly more complex logical principle—the one that expresses a basic form of argument—is:

$$(p + (p \to q) \to q$$

The principle used in complex arguments with intermediate conclusions, sometimes called the "chaining" principle, is:

$$(p \to q) \text{ and } (q \to r) \text{ and } (r \to s) \qquad (p \to s)$$

An extremely important principle which can be used to found much of elementary logic and which should remind you of all the material about the relationship between the *truth* of premises and conclusions and the *soundness* of the inference from one to another is:

$$(p \to q) \text{ and } (q \text{ is false}) \to (p \text{ is false})$$

(This is the so-called principle of the antilogism.)

A typical fallacy, or false argument, is this one:

$$(p \to q) \text{ and } (p \text{ is false}) \to (q \text{ is false})$$

(That's called the fallacy of denying the antecedent.)

You will remember this form of argument being rejected in the last chapter by our pointing out that a false premise can easily imply a true conclusion (whereas the principle just quoted says that if a premise is false, anything it implies must also be false). To illustrate: If New York and Los Angeles are

10,000 miles apart (p), then they're more than 1,000 miles apart (q). Now, they are not 10,000 miles apart, so (p is false). Hence, if this form of argument was correct, you could conclude that they are *not* more than 1,000 miles apart: (q is false). But they *are* more than 1,000 miles apart. So this form of argument is fallacious.

There's an associated fallacy, called "affirming the consequent," which you'll also recognize.

$$(p \rightarrow q) \text{ and } (q \text{ is true}) \rightarrow (p \text{ is true})$$

Give an example which shows this a fallacy (Quiz 5-A, 6).

You can see how we could easily work up a book full of various theorems and fallacies expressed in these or more elaborate symbolisms. That's what the introductory logic course often does. The trouble is that it can become a complex game of its own and the messy business of dealing with the rhetoric and arguments of real life gets left behind. We just use the arrow symbol as an abbreviation for the word or words we could as well use instead, and we do not require you to remember the names of any of the fallacies we've just mentioned, although their two millennia of use by educated people has made them a part of the vocabulary of many thousands of literate individuals who never took a logic course. Your effort should go, rather, into using the points made and in practicing them on real arguments. When you're trying to clarify the structure or the defects in an argument, it may be useful to have one or two of these symbols up your sleeve because they can make the structure—or the fallacy—stand out more clearly than if you have to keep repeating whole sentences. So, in this chapter on the clarification of meaning, we've spent a little time on a procedure for clarifying the meaning of an argument. But now it's time to wrap the chapter up by looking at some other dimensions of the meaning of terms and at procedures for clarifying them.

5-10   The Other Dimensions of Meaning

A dictionary definition, especially the ideal version, focuses on what we sometimes call the literal meaning of a term. But that's only part of the story. We've already stressed the contextual considerations which enable one to identify which of the several possible meanings, or several ranges of meaning, the same set of letters or sounds can have. ("A very small elephant is larger than a very large mouse.") One way to put that point is to say that the context is one dimension of the meaning of a term, because it is a term-in-a-context that we normally have to interpret. But there are other dimensions, too.

The whole approach we've been taking so far is oriented toward the usual "referring expressions" like common nouns and verbs. It doesn't work at all easily with other terms in the language such as proper nouns, connectives (and, if . . . , then . . . , but, etc.) and participles. These can hardly be analyzed into sets of jointly sufficient and separately necessary properties. It's better to approach them by analyzing their function. (Look up "the" or "and" in the dictionary: does it offer a translation? What?) You can explain the function of many words that you can't translate. Even with some common nouns, such as the names of colors, you can't give real translations. What you do normally is to give or describe examples. And that's very like what you do with a proper name—you point to or describe what or whoever it labels or refers to. That description is not a translation of the name, but just a description of what happens to be the present location of the name's bearer. "Jacob Astor" does not *mean,* though it may happen to be *the name of,* the third man from the left in the old yachting photo on page 33 of *The Proper Yacht.* "Yellow" doesn't *mean,* though it happens to *be,* the color of ripe lemons. These aren't translations because, for example, a disease might strike lemons overnight which causes every lemon on earth to turn purple when ripe, but that wouldn't have the least effect on the meaning of the term "yellow."

Just as we sometimes exhibit examples to show or convey meaning, rather than offer translations into other words, so we may exhibit an example of the *use* of a term to achieve the same effect. We may explain the meaning of the word "not" by saying "not doing X" means the same as "doing something other than, or different from, X." In this case, we have actually offered a translation of one particular use of "not," namely, its use in the phrase, "not doing. . . ." But we may in fact have achieved our much more ambitious purpose, which is to convey the whole meaning of "not"; or it may take a few more examples like this to achieve that general purpose, depending on the linguistic insight of the listener. (This approach is sometimes called "implicit" definition.)

So there is a spectrum of procedures for clarifying meaning, from pointing to a particular representative of the class to which the term refers, through drawing or describing that class, through providing a translation of one particular use of the term, all the way to providing a completely general translation or synonymous expression, as the ideal dictionary definition does. And there are supplementary procedures such as describing the linguistic function of the term ("It's the preposition used to refer to . . ."), or describing the contrasts that the term is used to draw ("The nadir is the opposite of the zenith").

The message of this section, then, is that there are many ways of clarifying meaning and that they should be judged, not by the extent to which they conform to the standard of the idealized version of a dictionary definition which many logic texts treat as if it were the only proper model, but simply in terms of *the efficiency with which they succeed in making the listener able to make sense out of proper usages of the term.*

In particular, one must not regard the demand for a definition in the sense of a translation as always legitimate. With respect to a new or unusual term, by all means. With respect to an ambiguous term with several clear and distinct meanings, perhaps. But with respect to an abstract term in common language, a term like "justice" or "ethics," a term whose meaning is as hard to formulate as any theory about the nature of the abstraction itself, then the demand for an explicit translation is often a red herring in an argument, about as useful as calling for someone to prove everything she says all at once. Such terms can be clarified, if necessary, by illustrations, by giving an example of their use in the sense intended, or by explaining the contrast intended. But no language can be learned entirely from a dictionary, and no dispute over justice can be settled by appeal to one.

One last note must suffice. We have said little about the subtler flavors and dimensions of meaning, about what is sometimes called the *connotations* or the *associations* that a term may have. In the first place, these are not sharply distinct from the core or literal meaning, though it is worth distinguishing them for many purposes. Poetry and rhetoric exploit these rich fringes of meaning to good and bad effect. We know from metaphor and simile how, for example, color terms may come to be associated with certain moods or types of behavior (blue or white with coldness, red with anger and violence), and in some contexts a full analysis of meaning must go into such dimensions. We have already done this in examples of practical argumentation and will do it again.

In the second place, these connotations or associations cannot be regarded as illicit baggage to be cut out whenever we wish to speak rationally or argue logically. Such an excision is beyond our powers with respect to natural languages, but it is also beyond our mission or our rights. In reasoning, we must recognize such components of meaning, we must learn how to exhibit them, clarify them and work with them, not fight against them or seek to do without them. Emotional or poetic language is not just a part of language, but an important part of language. There are times when calling someone a bloody murderer is not a lapse into the language of the streets, an abandonment of the standards of impartial reason, but no more and no less than the truth, and the same with poetry.

QUIZ 5-A

The first few questions in Quiz 5-A are embedded in the text of the current chapter, since, as we get into heavier material, it seems important to give you a bit of a workout as you go along.

Answer

First you ask yourself whether it's too *inclusive,* that is, does "it" (the right-hand side of the definition) include some things that aren't included by the term "college"? Of course, it's obvious that you get educated, after leaving high school, in other places besides college; for example, the army, real life, or business school. Still, it might be said that although these are places where you do *get* educated, they aren't places where you *go to get* educated; that is, the principal reason for attending such institutions is not to acquire education but to do something else. This is a rather weak defense—at least some people join the armed services in order to get free training as a technician, or to get educated about the world (since the navy guarantees you traveling). But there are stronger counterexamples; to name one, people join traineeship and apprenticeship programs in order to get educated in particular crafts, skills, or professions, and these programs are not college. So the definition is too inclusive.

Now you ask whether the definition is too *restrictive,* that is, whether it excludes some things that are properly called "college." This is a little tougher. On the interpretation previously suggested, which takes "go to get educated" to mean "go with the intention of getting educated," one might well argue that a great many people don't go to college to get educated but to have a good time, avoid starting real work, meet a mate, or enjoy other side benefits. Hence, at least some colleges would be excluded because of the reasons for attendance of their enrollees. However, this is a pretty weak kind of counterexample, since as long as some people go there to get an education, and it would be hard to deny that some such people are on every campus, the place would qualify as a college under this definition, since the word "you" in it presumably refers to anybody, and not just to the person who happens to be reading this at this moment. The same kind of defense would apply to attempted counterexamples based on the fact that some people go to college without going through high school; either they have had correspondence or tutorial instruction, or they have educated themselves and take one of the "challenge" entry tests. One might say that the relative imprecision of this definition immunizes it against that type of example. However, there is a family of considerably more serious counterexamples. College is not just a place that one goes to, after finishing high school, in order to get an education, but it's also a place you go to after finishing college. So the definition is certainly too restrictive because it excludes graduate schools, and a good many colleges have *only* graduate schools.

So the definition is both too inclusive and too restrictive, with fairly clear and not nit-picking counterexamples to support both these defects. We may conclude that the definition is pretty unsatisfactory. There isn't any other type of error it could involve; but it could of course be even further from the truth if the counterexamples were even more extensive than the ones we've mentioned. Obviously, if you look at it, the definition does cover a good big slice of colleges; it isn't as far off the mark as it might be. (Compare it with "college equals a private high school"; in that case there'd be practically no overlap between the real range of reference of the term "college" and the range of reference of the proposed definition for it. The circles representing these would overlap only a little bit.)

2   When I looked up "evaluate," the only relevant definition of the common sense
of the term that occurs in the *Random House Dictionary of the English Language*
is: "to determine or set the value or amount of; appraise . . ." To define "evaluate" in terms of determining the value of something does suggest that we're pretty
close to a circular definition. Let's turn to the definition of "value" and see if it
gets us out of trouble. The first definition is: "relative worth, merit, or importance
. . ." That would be all right if we could get a definition of worth, merit, and
importance that doesn't involve the term "value" itself. Let's have a look. Turning to the word "worth," we find that it is defined in terms of either "goodness
and importance" or "having a value," so one of those tracks is completely circular, and the other leaves us with only the word "good" as a possible way out of
the circle. The word "good" is given fifty separate definitions. It would take us a
long time to track down the results of looking up every term referred to in these
definitions. Suffice it to say that a great many of them stray back into "value,"
e.g., through terms like "quality." It's fairly common to find that, in the dictionary, relatively abstract terms are defined in one of these "extended circles." It's
not necessarily bad, since somewhere around the circle you may encounter a term
that you already understand on independent grounds, and in that case the definition will serve the purpose of explaining the meaning of the word to you. It isn't
of very much use to define "good" as "the property possessed by things which
exhibit goodness," but if the circle gets a little more complicated, like the one
we've just followed around, then it may well reach out into some other part of
your understanding of the language and make a connection that will give meaning to the word that you're puzzled about.
It isn't often that you find crude errors of excessive inclusiveness or restrictiveness
in the dictionary, but you do find plenty of cases where what are provided as
defining properties are actually "only" criteria. For example, in the definition of
"apple" (in the *Random House Dictionary*), one finds "the usually round, red or
yellow, edible fruit of the tree *Malus pumila*."
Now you know as well as I do that there are a number of species of apple that are
green from first formation through full ripeness. You also know that to call these
fruits round is a little imprecise, especially given the extremely elongated shape of
certain species. And of course, there are certainly inedible apples like some of the
crabapples. What are we to do with the word "usually" in that definition? Upon
statistical grounds, it's probably true that the dictionary "definition" is correct.
But it really doesn't serve the function of a definition very well if there are clearly
cases of well-known apples that do not meet all these conditions or that indeed
meet only one, and that one only if it is construed very loosely. You and I clearly
have a better concept of apple in our head than that dictionary definition conveys. We have no difficulty in saying of a rather pear-shaped, green, and inedible
fruit that it's an apple, albeit it's an unripe apple, even if it was grown in a test-
tube (we'd use taste, texture, scent, and other characteristics as guides). But the
dictionary wouldn't enable you to identify it as such. That's one of the limitations
of dictionaries—they have to be concise. The extent of our knowledge of the
meaning of common nouns is so vast that we can handle dozens or hundreds of
cases that would not be covered by *any* short definition, with considerable agree-

ment between language users as to the correctness of our decisions. Dictionaries are just rough guides to the use of most terms, and very useful they are too; and, with some terms in mathematics, they can be precise and accurate. With most terms, however, they have to be either imprecise or inaccurate.

3   This question requires you to classify a series of claims as being true or false and, under each of these headings, as true (or false) by virtue of definition, physical necessity, plan or design, social or moral norms ("laws"), or as a mere matter of fact. (See Types 1–7, listed on p. 135.)

   a   You can't pass this course without reading the text.
       Not an easy one to classify. Since the skills we're talking about in this text are very closely tied to commonsense skills, though we're trying to add a considerable degree of refinement and improvement, and since we carefully avoid getting into too much jargon, it is just possible that somebody might pass the tests and hence get through the course without reading the text. Certainly this isn't a case of planned impossibility, because it isn't one of my goals to write a text that defines a new subject. The text is, for me, simply a means to improving a type of skill that can be recognized in the outside world anyway, and there are a number of other ways, and perhaps courses, which would make it possible for you to pass the exams in this course and hence pass the course. So this is either (merely) factually true or factually false, and we really don't have much evidence about which it is until a few people try to pass the course without reading the text. The chances are against them, but not so strongly that we'd have to say this claim is obviously or provably false at this point; although it is probably false as a matter of fact. (So its correct classification is F–7 or T–7, with the probabilities favoring F–7.)

   b   Sons have to have (or have had) fathers.
       The way the world is at the moment, the evidence strongly suggests that virgin birth in the human race is practically or completely nonoccurrent. (Even Christ had a father.) Since this is not a mere matter of fact, but a result of the nature of the conception and birth process as we now understand it, this is the case of a physically necessary truth, i.e., T–2. It isn't *logically* (or *definitionally*) necessary because of course, the idea of virgin birth makes perfectly good sense within the language, even if it doesn't happen to occur in fact.

   c   Sons have to have (or have had) a parent.
       Here we're up against something that looks more like a logical truth (T–1) because it's difficult to imagine what could be meant by referring to any entity as a "son" if he wasn't the son of somebody, i.e., of a parent. It might be a mother (in a case of parthenogenesis), but unless there was an identifiable person who stood in the parental relationship to an individual, one wouldn't concede that it was proper to refer to that individual as a son. And if there is such a person, then that person is a parent, so this is a *definitional* truth.

   d   No black woman could be elected President of the U.S. before 1984.
       This is certainly a true fact at the moment, and it isn't exactly a "mere" matter of fact. It is something which we have allowed to become the case through our

societal development, and it is certainly within the power of people to arrange it otherwise. That's what's meant by social necessity.

e   Democracy cannot exist when there is no freedom of speech.

Here the answer will depend on how we define democracy. There are some definitions of democracy—not too bad ones—which would build freedom of speech into the definition. In that case, this would be a definitional truth. There are some strong arguments—for example, those by John Stuart Mill—that it isn't possible for a democracy to exist without freedom of speech, although he didn't define democracy as involving freedom of speech. This would make it a matter of social necessity, or perhaps a matter of deep psychological necessity, in which case it would count as a subspecies of physical necessity. Or one might argue that the necessity is more a matter of planning or social mores than natural law, in which instance one would classify this statement as T-3 or T-4; and finally, if one wasn't persuaded by any of the previous arguments, one would probably have to accept the argument that in the absence of freedom of speech, one does not in fact have a democracy (which would mean this is a T-7 claim).

Of course, we're talking in a rather long-term sense about this example; it's clear that during wartime there are often curtailments on freedom of speech just for the duration of the emergency, in countries that call themselves democracies. One might be inclined to say that such a country is still a democracy even though there is no freedom of speech for the moment; hence T-1 is out. If one is very literal in interpreting the claim, one might just have to say that it is F-7, since there can be short periods of time when there is no freedom of speech and we still have a democracy. The argument isn't compelling, since one might also argue that, for the time being, the society has ceased to be a democracy, and will revert to being one when such restraints as this are eliminated.

f   The interior-angle sum of a triangle is 180°.

This is a definitional truth only with respect to Euclidean triangles. If you assume that the context is such that we are clearly talking about Euclidean triangles, although this isn't stated, then it's a definitional truth. If you take the sentence out of context, then it's definitionally false, or factually false depending on the geometry, since it is possible to prove from the definition of non-Euclidean triangles that they cannot or need not contain 180° of interior angles.

4   This question concerns the provability of an astrologer's assertion that "December 11th, in the afternoon, is a very risky time for you to make major decisions." Without going into it at great length, it's clear that this is a very difficult claim to prove or disprove. If you do make major decisions and they work out on that afternoon, it can still be the case that you are very lucky and that it is indeed a very risky time to make them. If you fail to make major decisions on that afternoon, perhaps because you believe the prediction, then you'll never know whether they would have worked out if you had made them. Nevertheless, the statement isn't meaningless, and what it means is much the same as what we

mean when we say that your chances are not very good of rolling a double six with a pair of dice. This isn't falsified by the fact that you do roll it, any more than it's proved to be correct by the fact that you don't. What would prove it to be true would be our running a very large number of trials with the dice and finding that it very rarely happened that you rolled a double six. Now the problem with using that line of proof on the present example is that it refers only to a single day, indeed a single afternoon, in a single year. Hence, we can't repeat a whole series of experiments that will be relevant. Nevertheless, we can have good general grounds for believing that this is true, and we may be able to get direct evidence in another way. For example, we might be able to use a very large number of people instead of a very large number of trials by the same person, and have those people—all of them under the same astrological sign—make or not make major decisions on that afternoon, and see whether they turned out badly; then we would have them make some other comparable decisions on an afternoon for which the prediction by the astrologer was favorable and see if we got a large difference. It's largely because experiments like these have never been done that the common remark by scientists that astrology is actually false is rather unscientific. We do have some significant general reasons for thinking that astrology is unlikely to be true, but they are essentially indirect reasons. Direct proof of the type I've been describing has never been attempted under careful scrutiny.

5   The question requests that an example be given which shows that "affirming the consequent" is a fallacy. "Affirming the consequent" simply means that you jump from the realizations that (*a*) one proposition implies another and (*b*) that the second proposition is true, to the conclusion (*c*) that the first one must be true. To believe this is really to believe that a false proposition couldn't have true consequences. But we know from examples that we've discussed before that it's easy for a false proposition to have true consequences. Any proposition that is false because it exaggerates the truth will imply more modest claims that may well be true. For example, the false proposition that all women are feminists implies the proposition that some women are feminists. But it doesn't follow that it's true that all women are feminists.

6   Set up and criticize a slippery slope argument aimed at proving that we should not legalize marijuana.
   a   "If we legalized marijuana, we could hardly avoid legalizing cocaine and then heroin, which are only different in degree with respect to severity of addictiveness and results of excess use."
   b   (The "fast switch" or "dose of your own medicine" move.) "If these differences of degree are not significant, as you argue, the differences between marijuana and the various legal drugs like alcohol or nicotine or Valium are not significant. Hence, marijuana should also be legal."
   c   (The "head-on" attack.) "You can die from an overdose of heroin, but not from an overdose of marijuana." Withdrawal from heroin has sometimes

proved fatal, and has usually been a major trauma; neither phenomenon is generally true of marijuana, possibly never true. These are not just differences of degree, but of kind, so the argument doesn't even get off the ground.

QUIZ 5-B

1 Women are not so strong, physically, as men. There are various ways in which this claim could be interpreted.
   a Give one interpretation—a plausible one, not an absurd one—that makes it true. (Do this by giving a "translation" that is more precise.)
   b Give a plausible interpretation (that is, one which could well be what a user of the sentence means by it) which could make it false.
   c Since the a and b interpretations are both possible, it follows that the claim is
      (1) False
      (2) True
      (3) Either true or false, depending on the interpretation
      (4) Imprecise
      (5) Ambiguous
   d In the absence of evidence to the contrary, the Principle of Charity would require you to adopt
      (1) Interpretation a
      (2) Interpretation b
      (3) Neither
      (4) Both

2 Reading Dynamics guarantees that you will triple your reading speed as a result of taking our course, with no loss of comprehension, or your money back.
   This statement is:
   a So vague as to be almost meaningless
   b Ambiguous
   c Imprecise
   d Clear enough to provide a reasonable basis for a legal contract, though you wouldn't want to pay the fee until you see how the instructor measures _____ (fill in).

3 If the function of the CIA is to further our foreign policy aims, and if the government in a given country always resorts to the killing of political prisoners, guerrillas, or police victims, it is a little hypocritical to act outraged about the CIA's planning to assassinate a single key person in that country in order to advance what our democratic government judges to be the cause of democracy.
   a What type of argument is this? Why?
   b State in one sentence the strongest possible counterargument.

4 Read the full-page advertisement quoted on page 150 very carefully:

DUNLOP HAS HIGHEST RATING IN
CAR & DRIVER RADIAL TIRE TEST

Car and Driver tested 15 different brands of radial tires for overall track performance. The results were published in September *Car and Driver*. All quotes are from that publication.

When all results were in, when all 15 brands were evaluated . . . the Dunlop SP-4 Radial was classified "Excellent" . . . the highest rating awarded in the test.

Tests were conducted at the Lime Rock road race course in Connecticut, "an uncommonly severe test of tire durability."

"We focused on dry road performance, which gets you down a race track (or down a country road) quickest."

One driver tested all tires. To keep results unbiased, he knew only the code number, not the brand, of the tires he was evaluating.

"We can't tell you which tire corners best or stops fastest, but we can tell you which offers the best combination of both. For track use and most road applications, this information is more valuable than the abstract results of skid-pad testing."

"Dunlop is a very easy tire to drive. It's quick, forgiving, and by far the most consistent tire we tested."

Car and Driver told their readers, "If you are looking for a showroom stock tire, our findings are as valid as a Supreme Court decision. The same applies if you are after a good handling street tire for your small sedan or super-coupe."

The Dunlop SP-4. Only one of the many Dunlop radial lines, all built to the same high standards of quality, performance, and durability. When you need tires, buy the ones the PROS recommend. DUNLOP.

a State in your own words the most natural, or one natural, interpretation of the heading at the top of the ad.

b Give a description, in a sentence or two, of how the *Car and Driver* tests might have looked, making it consistent with the details in the ad's fine print, and which makes the ad's heading extremely misleading.

c State an interpretation of the heading that is not misleading, if different from your interpretation in *a*.

d Is the ad misleading? Yes/no.

³ 5 "Chair" means "portable piece of furniture with a back, legs, and a seat for one person."

6 "Furniture" means "manufactured objects designed to provide surfaces for sitting, eating, and storage."

---

³ Remember that this book is trying to move you toward realistic examples, so it does not put detailed instructions before these questions. You wouldn't find any in real life. We could say, "Comment as seems appropriate," but that's trivial. Should you comment as seems inappropriate?

7 "Democracy" means "government of the many by the few, for the benefit of the many."

8 A sale ad says, "Save on broadloom carpet—list price $9.99 per sq. yd., sale $6.99, limited time only." What impression is conveyed, and what fact(s) might actually be very different from the impression?

9 Argue (*a*) for and then (*b*) against the view that "covert operations" (such as secret activism in politics through cash support and "dirty tricks") are a legitimate function of the FBI (at home) and the CIA (abroad). (*c*) What is your view, and why do you prefer it?

10 "Lease a new Cadillac, fully equipped, insurance and maintenance and loan car included, for only $115.90 a month, equity lease." What are the "catches" to look out for here?

QUIZ 5-C

1 Look up the definitions of "college" in your own dictionary and see whether they are immune to criticism.

2 Think of a concept that's particularly interesting to you at the moment, perhaps because of some current issue or course in which you're involved. Track down the chain of definitions in your dictionary by looking up the definitions of the terms used in the definitions of your term and then looking up the terms used in *those* definitions; and so on. Did you eventually get a circle? Does it matter? Could you avoid all circles in dictionary definitions? How? (Possible hares to chase through the dictionary are "equality," "pornography," "oppression," "power," "freedom," "insanity," "reason.")

3 **a** What does "democracy is the best form of government" mean? Use at least the contrast approach to answer.
   b Does that approach help clarify meaning here?
   c What else helps?

4 **a** What does "and" mean?
   b What does "true" mean?
   c What does "mean" mean?

Chapter 6

The Finer Points of Argument Analysis

6-1 IMPLICATIONS AND CONCLUSIONS

At the end of the last chapter we were talking about the subtler dimensions of meaning, and we argued that these, including the emotional and poetic dimensions, are sometimes crucial for understanding the meaning of statements, descriptions, or arguments. It follows that they will sometimes be crucial in argument analysis, because these dimensions of meaning may contain the *implicit* conclusions of an argument—the "implications" of an argument, as we often call them.

The line between the meaning of a statement and what it implies is not a sharp one. To properly understand the claim that the United States Air Force provided air support for a number of ground missions by the South Vietnamese army may require that you understand that "air support" is a euphemism for (that is, a sugar-coated way of saying) "bombing." That's a case of understanding the finer points of the meaning of a term that has crept into the language in a semitechnical way. "Military advisors" eventually turned out to "mean" combat troops. But, originally, there may well have been a distinction between "air support" and plain old bombing. For example, the spotting of targets and the relaying of information about their location to the ground gunnery-control centers was an example of air support. The use of planes to provide air cover for the infantry, that is, to provide protective forces that would respond only if enemy planes attempted to intervene, was another case of air support that was not bombing. But when the enemy has no air force and when conditions reach the state that they did in the last days of the war in Vietnam, where, on the one hand, the forces of the South were losing, and, on the other hand, the pressure of the media was becoming increasingly critical and powerful, we find an ideal situation for the term "air support" to become a polite label for bombing forces and positions on the ground, including of course, many civilians. Nevertheless, the Air Force found it attractive to be able to continue to use the euphemism instead of the proper name. Colonel Opfer of the U.S. Air Force, speaking at a news conference in Cambodia at that time, said to the reporters present, "You're always saying, it's bombing, bombing, bombing. It's *not* bombing! It's air support." (That remark was awarded the Annual Doublespeak Award by the Committee on Public Doublespeak, a committee of the National Council of Teachers of English.) It was once said that the Vietnamese war "was conducted not in secret but in jargon" (Henry Fairlie, "The Language of Politics," *Atlantic,* January 1975). Usually the sequence of events was that perfectly ordinary language was used in a perfectly open and proper way until something occurred that people were anxious to conceal or represent in a favorable but unjustified light. For example, in the early days of our involvement in Southeast Asia, we did indeed send in advisors to the agricultural, the educational, and the military arms of the government that we wished to support. Before long, however, it turned out that the advisors in the military dimension had suddenly become "advisors," that is, they were actually an army. One of the distinctions is, of course, that advisors don't actually pull triggers; it wasn't long before our men were pulling the triggers. Still, the Department of Defense continued to use the term "advisors"; and so did the State Department, and so did the White House. And it took a long time for most of the general public to catch on to this. So one has to be extremely cautious, in analyzing an argument, to determine the exact meaning of the terms and claims in it—a meaning which may change depending upon the month or year in which the argument was uttered or presented.

The situation on the domestic front is no better. In the huge computer storage system that records all education research (ERIC), the instructions to people who are summarizing their research articles include the instruction that one should not use the term "poverty," but "economic disadvantagement." That's a simple case of a euphemism, with even some kind thoughts behind it; the same could be said of the use of the term "exceptional children" to refer to children with physical or intellectual handicaps. But it's not clear that the saving is worth the misrepresentation. If you are searching for literature on the effect of federal intervention on extreme poverty, you're going to miss some of the research because the federally funded repository of all that research will not list the natural and correct term. And if you are looking for programs for exceptionally bright children, you may waste a lot of time looking through the programs until you realize that the correct euphemism is "gifted" rather than "exceptionally able" (or successful, intelligent, or similar designation).

There are many subtler examples that fall under the heading of "implications" of claims in our language. One to which a great deal of attention has been directed lately is the tendency to use "he" as the pronoun to refer to legislators, and "she" as the pronoun to refer to whoever is running a home. While there is a statistical basis for these pronouns in that more men than women are legislators, and the reverse for homemakers, the *implication* of using the single pronoun goes a little beyond mere generalization and into the realm of stereotyping. Where it is possible to avoid stereotyping by some relatively simple linguistic procedure, it's a good idea to do so since the effects of stereotyping are often morally unfortunate. (That is, stereotyping tends to make a woman company director or a male nurse into something weird or improper instead of merely infrequent.)

We're going through a period of reanalysis of the legitimacy of our public agencies, and this is an appropriate time to tighten up a little on our language. It's worth remembering the occasion on which Ron Ziegler, the press secretary to President Nixon, declared certain previous statements by the President on the subject of Watergate to be "inoperative," a brilliant example of an *original* euphemism. "False" is a nice old-fashioned word that does the same job, and it doesn't even have the implication that the individual who uttered the statement knew it to be false, in which case the correct word would be . . . what? (Quiz 6-A, 1)

In the past few years, a number of books have come out that focus directly on the use of language as an instrument of political power. Those of you who are interested in this dimension might want to follow up by reading some of them, for example:

The Language of Oppression, by Haig Bosmajian, Public Affairs Press, 1975
Power to Persuade: Mass Media and the News, by Robert Cirino, Bantam Books, 1974
Language and Public Policy, edited by Hugh Rank, National Council of Teachers of English, 1974
Politics of Lying: Government Deception, Secrecy and Power, Random House, 1973

Of course, the forerunners of these analyses are still worth looking at:

The Hidden Persuaders, by Vance Packard, Pocket Books, 1975
"Politics in the English Language," by George Orwell, reprinted in *A Collection of Essays by George Orwell,* Harcourt Brace, 1970

(Many of these references came from a special issue of *Looking At,* devoted to public doublespeak, April 1975.)

The other side of all this subtlety is that it's very easy to overreact to implications that you *think* are present in an argument, although it's not at all clear they're there. It's all right to raise an eyebrow, and sometimes to make quite a point, about a stereotyping assumption that is revealed by the use of the pronoun "he." But there are many contexts in which it will only count as a weak criticism of an argument which essentially centers on other issues. Remember to use your judgment about strong and weak criticism. There may be many implications in the way in which an argument is *phrased,* some of them quite objectionable; nevertheless, the argument may quite easily be tidied up by some rephrasing, without losing its main thrust. Be sure that the criticisms that you make bear on the main thrust, as well as on the incidental and objectionable implications.

In Chapter 5, we also looked at cases where the meaning really isn't clear, as opposed to cases where the meaning is not obvious on the surface. Sometimes language can hint at meaning when it has little or none. It's important not to assume that because there are some subtle hints or connotations associated with a certain type of language, it must really have a substantial meaning. A recent development in this area is what R. D. Rosen called "psychobabble" (in an article in *New Times*). Here are a couple of examples: "I've been keeping my head together by getting in touch with my body"; and "I'm into high energy. You know what I mean." The point is well illustrated in an anecdote that Rosen recalls about a patient undergoing psychoanalysis. The patient eagerly responded, at the beginning of therapy, to each interpretation his analyst made by saying, "I hear you, I hear you."

"I'm sorry," said the doctor, "I didn't know you were a little deaf."

"I'm not. I *hear* you. It means I comprehend."

"Well, *what* do you comprehend?"

The patient paused, "Jesus," he replied, "I don't know."

"Psychobabble," the psychoanalyst said, "is just a way of using candor in order not to be candid."

Most of us are still in a state where psychobabble looks pretty good to us. When people say, "You've got to go with your feelings. Let it all happen. It's all progress," one still feels that it's good advice. What does it mean? Ten years ago, people might have said "Stay cool." Ten years before that, they might have said "Take it easy," or "Relax." Well, sometimes that's good advice and sometimes it's not. Using it as a reflex comment on everything makes it meaningless—or false. Sometimes you have to *stop* its "all happening" and go with your judgment instead of your feelings, get to *work* instead of relaxing, and so on. Psychobabble language is different, and for a while it seemed to be saying something more interesting, and perhaps at the very beginning it was. But before very long, it lost almost all its real content, and today it is nothing more than an empty jargon, part of the performance of communication without the substance.

So, in argument analysis, the key is to look for the core, for the content, for the *main* meaning; then to look for any extra layers of meaning that may be important. Of course, in practice, the best way to go is to chase all the strands of meaning to begin with and then start to put them together and to work out what the main strand is and what the secondary strands are.

It's not hard to see from this section the extent to which *judgment* is a crucial part of argument analysis, indeed of understanding utterances in the English language. They are often rich in meaning or in the appearance of meaning, in connotations or associations or implications, and sometimes in resounding emptiness. Indeed, it isn't possible to condemn or praise much communication without taking account of the context; what may be subtle and sensitive in one context may be superficial and uninformative in another. Judgment enters here, and judgment isn't something that can be achieved by following a simple formula. Reflecting on the examples we've been discussing and the ones to come is the best way to develop judgment. Your judgment may not always finish up at exactly the same place as your instructor's or your peers' or mine, but at least you will be able to judge more quickly and more accurately once you've begun to see more clearly the types of abuse that are possible. For practical purposes of argument analysis, the implications (if you'll pardon the expression) of what we've been saying are that the second step of argument analysis—identifying the conclusions—will emerge from the first step (clarifying the meaning) quite gradually and subtly, and it is indeed just a part of understanding an argument that you're able to say what its conclusion is, whether explicit or implicit. The practical procedure you should use here is always the same: Write it out, get it down, spell it out. Try to formulate the main conclusion and then, later, the intermediate conclusions of an argument, not just in your head but on paper. The first try won't usually be right, but get it written down, look at it, and then reflect on the argument. Have you really expressed the main point that the arguer is trying to establish? If not, tidy it up or rephrase it completely. There is no better way of reasoning than with a pencil in one's hand—I say a pencil because it usually has an eraser on one end, and you are going to need both ends to get these things right.

The general advice that we've mentioned before is nowhere more applicable than here. Argument analysis is a long, hard business. Don't expect that you'll be able to do a good job—certainly not the best job of which you are capable—the first time you pick an argument to pieces as an assignment. Figure that the first time through is strictly for ideas, although you can set the task to yourself as getting the job done right right off. That'll make you work at it a little harder, but usually you won't get the job done right with that first try. Even this simple step in argument analysis, getting the conclusions correctly formulated, will often require several trials before you're convinced that you've done justice to the argument. And usually some more trials before somebody else is convinced.

6-2   COMPLEX STRUCTURES AND LONG ARGUMENTS

This business of getting yourself into the habit of writing and rewriting, as you do the argument analysis, requires that you use a set of abbreviations for your own convenience. You don't want to have to write out each sentence or claim to which you are referring every time you put it down in the structure diagram or refer to it in your criticism. This is particularly true with long and complicated arguments. In this section, we'll mention briefly a few ways in which one can cope with the "monsters."

As we've previously suggested, you can often mark up the original argument (preferably using a pencil, because you probably won't get the best breakdown the first time through) to indicate all the crucial claims in it that you want to link together in the structure diagram and comment on in the course of the criticism. In some assignments, where it's no use marking up the original text, since you're not planning to hand that in, and you can't make a photocopy, you may want to set out immediately, at the beginning of your answer, a little "dictionary" of the abbreviations that you're going to use. This might look something like the following:

> **1**   There is hardly any product that cannot be made more cheaply by somebody who does not care about quality.
> **2**   There is no getting away from the fact that quality takes more time and costs more money.
> **3**   People who believe that you can get quality for free are simply dreamers—or they've never tried to make something decent themselves.
> **4**   You get what you pay for.

In an argument that has a simple structure that involves using the first three of the above statements as premises, and then has a few connecting words which indicate that the arguer proposes to draw from those premises the conclusion listed above as the number **4,** you can easily set out a structure diagram as before, using just the numbers. It would look like this:

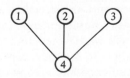

Or, depending on the connecting words, it might be this:

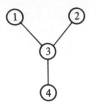

This is a simple way of conveying to the reader, as well as yourself, exactly what the structure is that you are taking to be the structure of the argument. You've worked out the meaning of the separate parts of the argument, which is, in this case, an easy task. You've completed the second step of identifying the conclusion, which is also easy, in this case. Now you've completed the third step, setting out the structure—that is, what premises are supposed to support which conclusion, with the help of what other premises. Again, this step was quite simple in the present case. But notice that you've already introduced a set of abbreviations that made it much quicker for you to complete the third step than it would have been if you'd had to rewrite all the sentences again. Of course, you had to set out your little "dictionary" so that the person who's reading your answer knows just what you are referring to. But you are going to save on the time that that took because, later on as you get down to criticizing the premises and conclusions or the inferences that connect them, you will be able to use the same numbers again. You'll be able to refer to the premises or the conclusion by a number, and to the inferences by an arrow connecting two numbers (e.g., 1→4).

It's quite simple to extend this procedure, which we've used as a standard one up until now, to handle very long arguments. Instead of using a number for each claim or assertion that's made, which can give you a pretty complicated structure after you get to about ten or twelve claims, you start using a larger "unit" than a single claim. Suppose we are talking about an argument that covers a number of pages in an article that you are reading. For example, it might be a long article which is attempting to summarize the case for and against school busing as it now stands. There are many issues involved in that by now, and an article that summarizes them is going to take a good many pages. You have the assignment of evaluating this article. How can you communicate to your teacher, or to another audience such as a study group or a parents group, the strengths and weaknesses of the article? If it is well written, a very natural step is to use numbers for the *paragraphs* because each one will be devoted to a separate point. Then your "index" will tie arabic numbers to the various paragraphs. (Of course, we're assuming here that your audience has a copy of the original materials; if they don't, you provide that copy, perhaps as a photostat, and you can attach the numbers directly to *it*. Or you make up a "dictionary" as before.)

Now, with the paragraphs numbered, you set out a structure diagram that shows the way in which they are related. Typically, in a well-set-out argument, each of the paragraphs will be aimed at establishing a point or further developing a point that's already been established. Set the argument out in terms of paragraphs; this will lead to a manageable and comprehensible structure. It would be tolerably long and difficult to comprehend if one had to do it in terms of sentences, and even longer if one had to do it in terms of claims, since there may be many claims in a particular sentence.

Now your criticisms of the article, if there are any, will certainly focus on some of these paragraphs and not on all of them to an equal degree. With respect to those paragraphs which you propose to criticize, you now "put them under the microscope," set them out with numbers for each of the claims that are involved, and carry on with argument analysis from there, as before.

All this effort goes back to the original mandate which we have stressed repeatedly: It's not enough that you develop a good instinct for what's a good argument or a bad one. You have to be able to *persuade others* of this. The function of reasoning is nearly always tied to communicating. Even when it isn't, setting out your argument analysis in full is really important in order to clear your own head about the strengths and weaknesses of the arguments. If you have to communicate with other people, you must use a system of abbreviations and labels that they can pick up very, very quickly, or they won't stay with you (or they'll make mistakes in understanding what you're trying to say). And even when the effort is purely a selfish one in order to see whether *you* have made slips, you yourself need a very simple and clear procedure for setting out structure and "backtracking" your criticism. One such structure is the use of numbered paragraphs, as just mentioned.

Another method that's sometimes important, especially where the material has not been broken down into paragraphs that correspond to points in an argument, consists in identifying the separate strands in the argument yourself, and providing a summary in a few words that will be clear enough to indicate the passage to which you are referring. Just as in writing out your original "dictionary" or index, when the claims get long and complicated, all you need do is give the first word or two and put in a series of dots followed by the concluding words of the claim, so you can summarize a whole subargument by giving just a few words. For example, suppose that in the discussion of busing, which goes on for several pages with hardly any paragraphing, one section covers the whole question of whether busing leads to academic gains by the previously less well performing students. You could display this in your index (as item **7,** say), which you are going to use in order to set out the structure of the whole argument, as follows:

> **7** "It's clear from the Coleman data that integration is beneficial . . . no alternative explanation."

Here we are assuming that the passage as it stands, even though it isn't presented separately as a distinct paragraph, is at least separated into a distinct set of sentences that follow one another. Sometimes even that won't be the case. Then you should use a summary of the line of argument, perhaps picked out from several different paragraphs or pages in the original:

> **7** The argument from the Coleman data that integration benefits the academically weakest of the populations that are integrated.

Here you've used a *description,* but you could have used a brief *summary* (sometimes called a synopsis or paraphrase or transliteration) of the original argument. In your structure diagram, you will show this as one of the premises from which some conclusion, perhaps only an intermediate conclusion, is drawn. Then it'll be easy for your reader, or for yourself when reflecting on the analysis, to see just what you are talking about. It won't be quite so easy to avoid making errors when you do it this way, because you've done a great deal of compression of your own already, and there may be errors in that. So you have to be particularly careful not to dismiss as satisfactory something that may conceal a number of buried errors, and not to complain about a line of argument which is, in fact, quite well presented in the original, although your summary doesn't do it justice.

There's no reason why this kind of procedure can't be extended to cover an evaluation of a whole book. It's just an extension of "outlining." One may use chapters as the "units" for the structure diagram; or one may use sections or parts of chapters, indicated either by their beginning and ending or, where the situation is more complicated, by your own summary of the substance of the argument that's being covered. Not all books are devoted to a series of arguments, but a number of the most important in the English language have that characteristic. It certainly applies to a great many, perhaps the great majority, of articles in professional journals, as well as articles in serious periodicals. So it's important to be very flexible about the way in which you set up the units for your structure analysis. Don't hesitate to use a mixture of the preceding devices. Don't hesitate to invent your own. But the test is always the same test; can the reader, someone who can't rely on telepathy to work out what you mean, tell quickly and precisely just what your labels refer to, and hence what your structure diagram says?

When we get into arguments which are not given in their entirety, that is, where we have to identify a whole series of assumptions and then tie them into the argument itself, these procedures will stand us in good stead. But they do need to be reconsidered in the light of that special situation. Should you perhaps distinguish the labels for assumptions or implications from the labels for what was present in the original argument? Often this is a good idea. One way to do it is to put parentheses around the numbers that you allot to material that you have inferred from the original writing or speech, and to use unparenthesized numerals for material that was present originally, or, as we've done earlier, to use letters for assumptions. Another procedure is to run through all the numbers that you need to label what was there in the first place before you start using numbers for assumptions and implications, so the higher numbers refer to "reconstructed" material. Yet another procedure is to use letters for both the assumptions and the implications, and arabic numbers for the material that was originally present. It's usually a good idea to employ and state one of these conventions, so that your reader or you yourself can more readily understand the structure diagram. When you are filling in implications and assumptions, you have to write them out *in full* in your "index" because every single word in them represents the results of quite a reasoning procedure on your own part, and they are very open to criticism as being too strong or too weak, not really built into the original argument at all, and so on.

Finally, it's worth commenting on certain peculiar forms of argument, ones that don't follow the natural kind of tree diagram we have been using so far. Sometimes, for example, arguers will produce an argument which they are not endorsing at all but wish to ridicule. They might be simply quoting an argument from a political opponent which they are going to refute, or they might be examining a speculation to see what difficulties it will run into after they have developed some of its conclusions. You have to watch how to fit these into a structure very carefully. You cannot do it by simply putting it in as part of the trunk of the tree in the tree diagram. You must set it off as a separate little tree on the side, leading to an implied conclusion which you usually have to add; then you can draw a line back to the main trunk from that implied conclusion. Here's an example:

> One of the most attractive lines of argument that the Democrats have used in order to justify support for a Democratic candidate for President in 1976 is the unfortunate affair of Watergate. But what guarantee do we have that such an event would not have occurred under a Democratic administration? Looking back over the track record of Democratic administrations of the past, it is easy to point to example after example of corruption, of political misjudgment, of impropriety and technical breach of the law. This, like other arguments that they have produced, can't really be regarded as having any real significance . . .

What's involved here is the *rejection* of an argument, not the direct addition of a further direct argument for the main conclusion (which is, of course, that we should vote for a non-Democrat for President in 1976).

One way of looking at this rather common kind of argument involves seeing that it consists in heading off an attack that we would normally take account of when we turn, in the later stages of argument analysis, to consider alternative arguments. That's the point where we stand back and look to see whether we have failed to consider some argument that points in exactly the opposite direction, or some argument that is even more powerful than the one we have rejected and which points in the same direction. The arguer in this particular case is *forestalling* such a step by considering in advance one of the apparent arguments in the other direction.

How can one handle this seemingly contradictory argument? From what we have just said, it is clear that there are two ways to handle it. You can either pull it out of the whole stream of argument and analyze the rest, turning to this only when you get to the point in your argument analysis when it's time to turn to other arguments that bear on the same conclusion; or you can treat it at more or less the time it comes up, but do so by setting it off to one side. It can have its own little tree structure, alongside the big tree of the main argument structure. And the conclusion to which the little tree leads is, "The Democrats are unlikely to be any better with respect to Watergate-type occurrences." With the addition of the obviously plausible assumption that either the Democrats or the Republicans are going to win, one can conclude, "Voting Republican should not be ruled out because of Watergate-type considerations," and that conclusion can be fed directly into the conclusion of the main argument, that one should vote Republican. In short, if you are very careful about how to phrase the "missing links," and very careful to separate the "apparent counterarguments" and their rebuttal from the main stream of an argument for a particular conclusion, they can be handled well enough. But you need to watch for them. Once you are used to spotting them, you'll see that what they really amount to is a kind of switch of roles by the arguer from the role of *arguing for* something to the role of *arguing against the arguments against* it. Both are perfectly legitimate ways to proceed toward a conclusion, but you must of course note that the negative approach doesn't leave you with any positive reasons for the conclusion—the argument will ultimately depend on whether there are independent positive reasons for voting Republican, since the counterargument shows only that you won't be any better off by voting Democratic (in this respect, at least).

6-3 SIGNIFICANT AND INSIGNIFICANT ASSUMPTIONS

You already know a good deal about how to identify assumptions. The crucial juggling act that you have to perform is to find something that's strong enough to patch up the holes in the argument, but not any stronger than it has to be, since otherwise it will be open to objections that the arguer isn't really saddled with. In the traditional kind of logic-book argument, where we give you an argument from the premise, "All warm-blooded Australian animals are marsupials," to the conclusion, "All warm-blooded Australian animals carry their young in a pouch," it's pretty easy for you to work out that the missing premise is the claim that "All marsupials carry their young in a pouch." But when we get to real-life arguments, the whole problem becomes a great deal trickier. In this section, we want to try to set out some of the traps to avoid, and to give you enough suggestions by means of going over several examples, so that you'll begin to get a pretty good start on refining your skills in "assumption hunting." It's helpful to begin by understanding that even the best analysts, people who are really experienced in the criticism of arguments—for example, lawyers with many years of experience, or philosophers or social scientists analyzing published articles—will often make errors in their identification of the assumptions that lie behind an argument they're criticizing. This is so even when they have as much time as they need in order to work the matter out and check it out. When they're under pressure, as in the courtroom or in the course of a debate at a professional society's convention, their frequency of error making goes up seriously. But it's also worth remembering that these people, when they get together in groups and jointly study an argument, can reach very good agreement about what the assumptions are. So identifying assumptions isn't really an arbitrary matter, it's just a difficult matter. And of course, it's a very important matter, since if you make a mistake, you finish up wasting many of your criticisms, because you're attacking a "straw man"; that is, either you are saddling the arguer with an assumption that he or she did not need and did not make, so can't be criticized for making it, or, alternatively, you are accepting an argument because the assumption that you think it rests on is beyond criticism, whereas in fact, the argument actually requires a further assumption that is very dubious. So the matter is one of the three most important steps in argument analysis (the others being the clarification of meaning and the overall assessment of the merits of the argument).

The first trap to avoid is that of quoting long lists of absolutely trivial assumptions. The title of this section is "Significant and Insignificant Assumptions." You have to learn not to bother to point out insignificant ones, but to focus only on the significant ones. There's no simple rule for making the distinction; once more, it's a matter of developing good judgment. But here are some specific types of triviality to avoid: First, it is entirely unhelpful to point out that a particular argument "assumes" that its premises imply its conclusion. Since the arguer is offering these very premises as support for this very conclusion, it's certainly true he or she believes that one implies the other: but it's so obvious that you're not doing argument *analysis* by mentioning this, you're only repeating the argument. Putting it another way, what kind of useful criticism could you possibly get from mentioning this assumption? Criticizing it is just the same as criticizing the argument itself, so you haven't done any clarification by bringing it in.

Another version of this trivial kind of assumption is often produced by beginners, particularly with respect to statistical arguments. "This argument assumes," they say, "that there's some kind of connection (or correlation) between the things the arguer is talking about in the premises and the things that are referred to in the conclusion." Well, you can certainly bet that the arguer is making that "assumption," but to say so does little more than repeat the fact that *these* premises were offered to support *this* conclusion, and hence obviously in the belief that there was some kind of connection between the two.

Another type of trivial assumption is the "assumption" that the words in the English language will be understood by the listener in the same way as they are understood by the arguer. For example, if someone argues from the fact that Jones is taller than Smith to the conclusion that Smith is shorter than Jones, one might point out that the arguer "is assuming that 'shorter' and 'taller' have their usual meanings," or, to bring in some jargon, "have such meanings that they function as converse relations." Certainly true, but about as interesting as pointing out that somebody who asks a desk clerk whether the hotel manager is in, is assuming that the desk clerk will not think the question means that the building is burning down. Your task in reasoning, and in particular in argument analysis, is to call attention to, and work on the analysis of, the *important,* the *debatable,* the *hazardous,* and the *hidden* points, not the ones that no one could possibly disagree with. An arguer, when pushing forward some premises for a conclusion, is usually assuming a great deal about the listener in terms of linguistic knowledge, capacity to reason, particular knowledge about the issue, and similar capabilities. General statements to this effect are of no value in argument analysis. Nor are particular ones about obviously unchallengeable assumptions. You can see from this discussion that assumption hunting consists mainly in looking for assumptions that are either *obviously assumed but of debatable truth,* or *not* obviously assumed and hence perhaps overlooked, and also debatable. In short, you're searching for a weak link in the chain, not trying to point out that there are lots of strong links that nobody actually put into words. Most communication operates on a carrier wave of unstated assumptions, contextual cues, and other things that it would be quite impossible to express in full.

Let us stress again that trivial assumptions are not confined to vague and general assertions about arguments; they can be very specific indeed. Suppose we have an argument about a particular robbery, the premises of which consist in a recitation of many details about the evidence, and the conclusion of which is the claim that a particular suspect was responsible. One might say of this argument that it assumes that one can infer from this *particular* long list of premises to this *particular* conclusion. It does indeed, and there's nothing very general about that assumption, but it's just as trivial as any of the ones we've discussed because it's just another way of saying that the arguer thinks this is a satisfactory argument, or at least one that ought to influence you.

Another trivial type of assumption that goes back to an earlier point in the argument being analyzed—to the premises instead of the inferences—is one that can be expressed by saying, "the arguer is assuming that there is *some* evidence for the premises being put forward." True enough, since otherwise there wouldn't be any point in offering them as "support" for the conclusion; but again, too trivial.

In general, there's not much value, except as a preliminary step in clarifying your thinking, to identifying assumptions of the form: "The arguer is assuming that there's some kind of connection between . . . and. . . ." The crucial question is, Exactly what kind of connection is being assumed? There are occasionally exceptions to this. If you can prove that there isn't any connection between A and B, it's enough to be able to show that an argument depends on the assumption that there is some kind of connection. For example, an argument may rest on the assumption that there's some kind of connection between ethnic classifications and honesty; as far as we know from the evidence available, there is no such connection. Hence, it was quite enough to be able to state the assumption in these very general terms, in order to be able to squash the argument. But usually what's at stake is the question of the exact kind of connection. For example, an argument may start with the premise that incidence of cancer in industrial towns is very much greater than it is in rural areas and move swiftly to the conclusion that we should crack down on emissions of waste materials by industrial plants. Such an argument is assuming that there's some connection between these emissions and the cancer, indeed, but what's more to the point is that it's assuming that the relation is a *causal connection* and not a *mere correlation*. For only if it's a causal connection would manipulating the emissions lead to (and cause) a change in the rate of cancer. Now the premises of course tell us only that there is a correlation between cancer rates and density of industrial emissions. In order to show that the connection is stronger than that—strong enough to uphold the argument—we have to produce a great many other kinds of evidence about experimental manipulation or controlled studies, etc. So the argument rests on the assumption of a *causal* connection between these two specific factors; not just on the existence of some relationship between the general conditions of cancer and industrialization. The latter claim is true enough, but it's so weak an assumption that it's an easy one to support, and it doesn't support the conclusion; whereas the real assumption behind the argument is a much "stronger" claim and one that is very difficult indeed to support.

The "Straw-Man" Problem—Being Fair to the Arguer   Remember that the other side of the problem of finding assumptions, besides finding connections that are strong enough to tie the premises to the conclusions, is that of avoiding the mistake of making them so strong that the arguer doesn't need them. Doing so is a typical form of the "straw-man fallacy."

If it is argued that a particular male candidate is better than a particular female candidate for a given job, one can't claim that the arguer is assuming that men are always better than women. Getting a fair or accurate version of the assumption is quite difficult for beginners, and leads to a great deal of ill feeling in arguments, as well as considerable wasted time.

Remember the argument discussed earlier, "She's red-haired, so she's probably bad-tempered." The argument consists of a single premise and a single conclusion—it could hardly be simpler. What is the missing premise? Let's review our discussion of it. The usual first reply from a class is, "Red-haired people are bad-tempered" or "All red-haired people are bad-tempered," which are intended to mean the same. That's quite incorrect, quite unfair to the argument; it sets up a "straw man." If the argument had the conclusion, "She *must* be bad-tempered," it would require something more like this premise. But the argument is much more cautious, and to draw the conclusion in which "must" is replaced by "probably," one only needs a premise referring to *most* red-haired people. Yet it is still incorrect to say that this argument assumes that most red-haired people are bad-tempered (or that a red-haired person is probably bad-tempered). The conclusion contains a further piece of information which narrows down the required assumptions; it is the reference to "she." The arguer may well believe that most red-haired *people* are not bad-tempered, only that most red-haired *women* are bad-tempered. Here's where we finally focus on the *minimum plausible* claim that's necessary to make the argument work, and that's (usually) what the assumption is.

The refinement in assumption hunting that we want to remind you of in this section is contained in that word "plausible" in the definition of an assumption in the last sentence. Sometimes the interest in plausibility will make it more sensible to identify a slightly stronger than necessary claim as the assumption in a particular argument in order to get the "minimum necessary" claim to connect premises with conclusions. For example, in the discussion of the red-headed woman, it might be argued that it's a little more plausible to suppose that the arguer believes that red-headed *people* are bad-tempered than that he or she believes that red-headed women are bad-tempered; roughly, because there seems to be no evidence about sex differentiation on this matter, and it might be thought there must be a gene combination that produces both a tendency to bad temper and redness of hair.

Suppose that we were to argue, "She's a homosexual and so she's probably a bad security risk." One could say that the minimum necessary connection between the premise and the conclusion in this tiny argument is, "Female homosexuals tend to be bad security risks." However, it might be more plausible to say that the missing premise is, "Homosexuals tend to be poor security risks," because whatever evidence there is about this matter almost certainly supports the more general claim. A matter of judgment is involved here. If you were trying to reconstruct the assumptions that the arguer probably made, you could bet heavily that they are proposing the broader claim to be true: that all homosexuals are poor security risks. That's the direction in which the argument from this point has always gone in the past, being based on the idea that homosexuals are liable to blackmail. It didn't make any difference whether they were male or female homosexuals. On the other hand, if you're analyzing the argument rather than the arguer, all that the argument requires in the way of an assumption is that female homosexuals are (tend to be) bad security risks. And it might just happen to be the case that, even though male homosexuals are no longer very good territory for blackmailers, lesbians are in fact still much less accepted and hence more susceptible to blackmail.

So in looking for significant assumptions, one sometimes, especially when dealing with the arguer in person, may want to look for the assumptions that were most likely made by the arguer, and these may turn out to be slightly stronger than the minimum necessary connecting claims. But when you're dealing with an argument "in the abstract," that is, out of context, you usually don't make these concessions, since what you gain from doing so—ease of communicating with the arguer who wishes to make a somewhat stronger claim than the minimum necessary one—is lost by the possibility that you will finish up creating a "straw man."

It's also worth reviewing the possibility of erring in the opposite direction in argument analysis. The "straw-man" fallacy involves ascribing a claim to somebody who doesn't in fact make that claim. The "iron-man fallacy," as we might call it, involves failing to see that someone is vulnerable, having made an assumption, when that is the case. For example, it's quite common in reading contributions to a discussion in the form of letters to the editor, whether in a professional genre or in a newspaper, to see a letter that ends triumphantly with a conclusion like this:

Mr. Jones is therefore quite wrong when he says that there were no aboveground nuclear tests during this period.

Here we look carefully at the line of argument, probably consisting of documentation from official announcements, or perhaps seismograph records, in order to see whether they support this conclusion. We need to notice very carefully that what this evidence will support, if the inferences involved are sound, is the conclusion that there were above-ground experiments during the period in question. It does not establish or support, by itself, that Mr. Jones was wrong about anything. For there is an additional assumption involved in this argument, namely, that Mr. Jones did indeed assert that there were no such tests. The iron-man fallacy is involved in omitting that further assumption when doing an analysis of the argument leading to the above conclusion. What Mr. Jones may have said was that there were said to have been no above-ground tests during this period, or he may have asserted that there were no *official* above-ground tests during this period, or made some other claim.

Suppose that the conclusion of the argument, instead of beginning "Mr. Jones is therefore wrong. . . ," had begun "*If* Mr. Jones believes. . . , he is wrong." Then we don't need to drag in the extra assumptions. This conclusion is only a hypothetical conclusion or a conditional conclusion, and it does not commit the arguer to the view that Mr. Jones did stick his neck out on this issue.

Now let's look at a completely different and very interesting range of cases that call on our judgment in determining what to call an "assumption" of an argument.

Suppose somebody needs some information about the properties of right-angled triangles. One way to provide the information is to quote the axioms of the geometry in question, normally Euclidean geometry, and say with a flourish, "These contain all the information that you need to know about right-angled triangles, and a good deal more." Of course, there is a sense in which they do, since all the theorems of geometry can be obtained from them by deduction, that is, are implied by them. Unfortunately, the knowledge is not being presented in a very useful way. We have not extracted or exhibited the relevent and important consequences of the axioms. They need to know Pythagoras's theorem, for example, not the basic assumptions of all geometry. And so it is with respect to the assumptions on which a particular argument rests. You have to find an illuminating version of them, and often this means mentioning facts about things not even mentioned in the argument, just as right-angled triangles aren't even mentioned in the axioms of Euclidean geometry, though those axioms nevertheless involve (imply, depend on) claims about right-angled triangles. Assumptions are one kind of implication of an argument: they are implied premises, not implied conclusions. Finding the interesting assumptions of an argument is thus partly a creative act, as is finding the consequence of the axioms of geometry. Of course, you can always say that the assumption on which an argument rests is that one can get this conclusion from these premises, and there's nothing false about that; it's just that it's supremely unhelpful. The successful argument analyst is the person who manages to uncover and present in an illuminating and relevant way the interesting and vulnerable assumptions that an argument makes. It may take a good deal of shuffling and rephrasing and a substantial slice of original thinking in order to see just what these are in a particular case. Take, for example, the argument that a particular candidate for appointment at a high level and in a politically sensitive branch of the government should be passed over because he is a homosexual and therefore overly prone to blackmail, and hence too much of a security risk for the job. This line of argument has been widely accepted in security work for a very long time in this country and many others. It could be formulated somewhat as follows:

> He is a homosexual.
> Hence, he is prone to blackmail.
> Hence, he is a security risk.
> And, this job requires security clearance.
> So, he should not be appointed.

This is an argument of a standard form, and relatively simple. It is really just a modest extension of an even simpler form, corresponding to the "She's red-haired and so she's probably bad-tempered" example; here, we could almost compress it to "He's a homosexual and so he shouldn't be appointed to this politically sensitive post."

Of course, one can say about this argument that "it assumes that homosexuals are poor security risks." But there are two things wrong with that analysis: In the first place, it's not quite accurate, and in the second place, it's trivial. It's inaccurate, at least for the reason which came up in the discussion about the assumptions in the red-haired girl case; that is, you have data here that clearly limit the assumed claim to male homosexuals, so you're not entitled to saddle the argument with a claim that refers to homosexuals in general. It's also inaccurate because there's another assumption involved, since we have an argument that has really two steps to it, rather than only one as in the case of the red-haired girl. Perhaps you can already see what the extra complication is in this case. Can you formulate one good reason that the argument in its compressed form (quoted in the last sentence of the previous paragraph) does not exactly depend upon the assumption that male homosexuals are poor security risks? (Treat this as question 2 in Quiz 6-A.) But let's get back to the argument as it was originally expressed and set out in indented form in the last paragraph. There's a second defect with the proposed kind of assumption that we're hunting at the moment. It's at too trivial a level. It does little more than repeat what the full form of the argument says. And that's not good enough. If somebody said to you that this argument assumed a certain geographic distribution of homosexuals in this country, you would at first sight be quite startled by the suggestion. The argument doesn't appear to be saying anything about the geographic distribution of anything. But remember that the axioms of Euclidean geometry can quite well be said to be "saying " something rather interesting about right-angled triangles, namely, that the square on the hypotenuse is equal in area to the sum of the two squares on the other two sides. At first sight, there doesn't seem to be anything in the axioms about right-angle triangles, but there are consequences in them for all kinds of triangles including right-angle triangles; they *imply* Pythagoras's theorem.

Similarly, the argument depends on certain rather interesting but nonobvious assumptions. But first let's pick up a couple of more obvious assumptions in order to show the difference between unilluminating and illuminating assumption finding. It is important to notice, in this example, the extent to which imagination and creativity come into the process of uncovering assumptions—that is, how different assumption finding is from some kind of routine calculation—just as they come into the discovery of new theorems "contained in" seemingly trivial axioms.

As we start picking at the argument we've just set out, we start asking ourselves exactly *how* and *why* the arguer thinks it works, making ourselves state this supposed thinking in detail, sniffing for the difficulties that are lurking in its structure and that are being successfully bridged—perhaps! This is particularly hard if we ourselves are somewhat inclined to think that the argument works. So first one tries to put oneself in the position of a person with a vested interest in proving the argument wrong, for example, the candidate who is to be rejected according to the conclusion of the argument. Suppose you are that candidate. What could you say against a line of argument that supposedly shows that you are unfit for the job?

The first thing to pick at is the connection between homosexuality and blackmail. How is this supposed to work? The idea is that anyone would be so afraid of being exposed as a homosexual that he or she would either pay blackmail or reveal secrets, with the first eventually, if not immediately, leading to the second. Why should someone be afraid of having his or her homosexual activities revealed? Presumably, there could be two reasons: First, that the person feels guilty about them, and would suffer humiliation or shame if others knew of them; and second, that the disapproval of others might be so severe that the homosexual would be fired if the matter was revealed.

One of the terms in the expansion of the argument is the word "reveal." The moment one begins thinking about the situation of many homosexuals in real-life positions, one realizes that, in many cases, there is no concealment of homosexual commitment. Hence, "revealing" this would not have any threatening force.

So the first serious problem with the argument is that it assumes the individual is not already known to be a homosexual. Isn't this assumption obviously true with respect to people in the kind of job category we're talking about? It's not entirely true, and (a quite different point) to the extent that it is true, it's true because we make it true; that is, as long as we refuse to give these jobs to homosexuals, we make it impossible for an overt homosexual to have such a job, which in turn increases the risk of blackmail with a covert homosexual who slips through the security check. So, in a way not unlike the way in which certain drug laws create crime, the ban on homosexuals on grounds of security risk helps create the security risk for homosexuals. In either case, there might also be some deep, underlying reasons that necessitate, on moral or other grounds, the prohibition of the behavior in question. But in the absence of these grounds, or as an offset to them, one must face the self-supporting nature of the combative procedures. To take another example, if one continues to refuse to appoint women to supervisory positions on the ground that men aren't used to taking, or won't take, orders for women on the job, one continues to perpetuate both the men's prejudice and the absence of women supervisors. So there is one general moral or "system-type" consideration that counts against accepting the line of argument we're studying. But to return to the more specific objection: It's clear than an acknowledged, known homosexual isn't subject to the force of this argument at all.

Nor, to be somewhat creative, should the covert homosexual be ruled out by it, or at least not completely. For it is clear that the person ought to be given the opportunity to acknowledge homosexuality openly (to "come out of the closet"), thereby removing the sting from the blackmail and getting the job (always assuming there are no other overriding reasons why homosexuals should not get such jobs). So the argument makes the weak assumption that everyone would rather pass up a job of this type than acknowledge homosexuality. And that's something that wasn't *obviously* assumed.

One practical procedure in argument analysis, of particular importance in moral contexts, consists in insisting that the argument be conducted in terms of *realistic alternatives* instead of on an abstract level of approval or condemnation. So the crucial question in the present argument is not whether homosexuals ever have some risk of being blackmailed, which is undoubtedly true in some circumstances, but whether they always (or nearly always) have a greater risk than heterosexuals. If not, you can't hold their sex preferences to be grounds for disbarring their candidacy. With respect to their nonsexual life, presumably the situation is comparable. With respect to their sexual life, it's clear that heterosexuals run certain special risks, albeit different ones from those of homosexuals. In particular, they run the risk of being exposed for the commission of adultery, "swinging," the use of prostitutes, and similar practices. Once one sees that the key question is whether this particular homosexual is a *worse* security risk than the competing heterosexual candidates, one begins to see some other assumptions that lie behind the argument we are considering. For there are some communities where exposure as a homosexual would have very little impact, whereas, in others, it would have considerable impact; and the same is true of exposure for heterosexual "sins." Remember that we're not talking about the question of whether exposure would destroy somebody's chances for being elected in a close political campaign, for there is probably a sufficiently large swinging vote in most communities to produce that effect. We're talking about whether there is such a powerful "straight" lobby and public attitude that a man who had a secure federal job could be removed from it for this reason. And that might be impossible even though a significant minority, or even a majority, of voters felt that he should be. The courts do offer significant defense in such cases.

As one comes to think in detail about the extent to which, and the way in which, the exposure of a homosexual constitutes a sufficiently threatening possibility so that the person would be willing to submit to blackmail rather than hazard it, one begins to see the sense in which the whole argument depends upon certain geographic assumptions. For it seems clear that the proportion of adult homosexuals who find their way to certain urban areas where there is a greater tolerance of a social life for homosexuals is larger than the proportion of the corresponding "risk" group of heterosexuals (actual or potential), namely, adulterers or those who (do or may) engage in premarital or purchased sex, who move to cities. So the argument will work, in general, only if the proportion of homosexuals in communities which would be powerful enough to have them removed from their jobs is greater than the proportion of heterosexuals in communities which would react just as unfavorably to heterosexual "misdemeanors." And it isn't at all clear that the reverse is not the case. So the argument, in its general form, does rest upon an assumption about the relative geographical concentration of homosexuals and those heterosexuals who are either engaged in, or likely to be engaged in, heterosexual "misdemeanors" (which covers a good proportion). That's an interesting discovery about the argument and a real weakness in it. To take a specific case, it's really absurd to suggest that the possibility of blackmailing even a covert homosexual in San Francisco is serious, and certainly it's much less serious than the threat of blackmail to a heterosexual having an interest in playing around and residing in an uptight rural community. Of course, as long as a federal agency continues to have rules against employing homosexuals, homosexuality will be a ground for exclusion; but those rules cannot themselves be justified by the kind of argument here.

The best way to understand what is happening when one is looking for assumptions is to ask why premises are provided when you're putting forward an argument. After all, in assumption hunting, you're trying to reconstruct the premises that someone would have put forward if stating the argument in full. The crucial point about an extra premise, one that we're going to add to the ones that are already visible, is that it should bring to bear *new, relevant,* and *convincing* evidence. As you look at those considerations, you can see the basis for the points we've been making, and for a slight extension of them. The requirement that the extra or "missing" premise (which is what an assumption is) be *new* immediately precludes a mere repetition of the supposed connection between the given premises and the required conclusion. There's nothing new about the statement that what is already being provided is supposed to give support to what is alleged to be the conclusion of the argument. So, typically, an assumption should be referring to something else that hasn't been directly mentioned in the given premises, and connecting it with some important concept that occurs in the conclusion. It may also refer to some of the concepts in the premises, but it can't (in general) refer only to those and the ones in the conclusion, or else it wouldn't bring in anything new.

Secondly, the assumption obviously must be relevant to the conclusion or it won't support it; and that's where the requirement of making it "strong enough" to do the job comes in. Finally, an assumption—indeed, any premise—ought to be persuasive or at least not objectionable in and of itself. Otherwise, it won't add any weight to the conclusion because it doesn't have any weight itself. And that is connected with the requirement that the assumption not be any stronger than necessary, since the stronger you make the claim, the less likely it is to be true, other things being equal. One might say that the further it reaches, the more likely it is to overreach itself.

As we've mentioned before, there are times when looking for an assumption that is convincing will lead the analyst to identify an assumption that is somewhat stronger than is otherwise necessary. For example, an argument may only require the assumption that women are incapable of jumping 32 feet in order to cross a crevice; but it would be a little peculiar to offer that generalization when it's well known that no one can jump 32 feet. So, in this case, offering the stronger generalization would make for a more plausible reconstruction of the particular argument.

You can see once more how the various considerations involve some tension with one another; the assumptions you identify mustn't be too strong or they will be an unfair reconstruction of the argument, since they will be fairly easily refuted even though the argument might still be perfectly sound. On the other hand, the assumptions mustn't be too weak, or they won't connect the stated premises to the conclusion. (Or they won't support an independent part of the conclusion that has so far received no support.) The assumption mustn't be a triviality of definition or fact—since it then isn't worth mentioning. Nor can it be a mere assertion of the fact that the arguer thinks this is a sound argument, since that's not worth mentioning. It must be something new, but on the other hand, it must still be true and relevant.

This all makes pretty good sense in the abstract; let's have a look at another example and see what it means in practice. Suppose somebody says:

> "The conclusive argument against nuclear power stations is simply that they might blow up. They should definitely be completely banned."

What is the speaker assuming? You might suggest that the assumption is:

> Everything that might blow up should be banned.

(One of my class students suggested that the assumption is, "Everything that blows up should be banned," but that's a little weak. It's a bit late to be banning things after they blow up!) The original assumption is too strong—it's unfair to the arguer to suppose he or she is committed to it. The way to see that it's too strong is by asking yourself what would be a good counterexample to the assumption suggested, and also whether somebody might not still be able to put forward the original argument without being committed to denying the counterexample. A counterexample to the proposed assumption would be a steam boiler, or a pressure cooker, or a gasoline tanker or truck. They all might and do blow up, but it's somewhat implausible to suppose that they should all be banned. At any rate, it's clear that a person who thinks nuclear power plants should be banned is not committed to thinking that all these things should be banned; hence the arguer can't be said to be assuming that *everything* that might blow up would be banned.

Now sit back and ask youself what reason somebody might have for thinking that nuclear power plants should be banned, other than the mere fact that they might explode. It's almost certain that what's disturbing the arguer is the *result*, not just the fact, of the explosion, so we might try something like this as the assumption:

> Any installation that might blow up and thereby release vast quantities of long-lasting atmospheric poison, especially if there might also be substantial loss of life incurred in the accident itself, should be banned.

Here we have an assumption that is considerably narrower than the original one and hence is considerably more plausible, because it isn't vulnerable to all those cases that constituted counterexamples to the original proposed assumption.

Although the new assumption is more plausible, it still contains serious difficulties. Can you see a new set of counterexamples? It comes awfully close to covering the manufacture of cigarettes, for example, and automobiles and gasoline. To make it more plausible, one should probably insert another qualifying phrase, something like "wherever there is a reasonable alternative." That makes the assumption more plausible; but it also means that you have to add another missing premise to the argument, namely, that there is a reasonable alternative to generating power by the use of atomic plants. So we made one premise more plausible, but at the expense of introducing another which is quite debatable. But we've got a much fairer reconstruction, a more plausible argument, and the Principle of Charity requires us to prefer it. Of course, we still have problems with the fact that there are reasonable alternatives to smoking cigarettes. Can you get around this?

There remains one further crucial source of difficulty for the argument, though discussing it is of no special relevance to the problem of assumption hunting. That is the problem of how you get from the danger to prohibition. It's not obvious that everything that's dangerous, even extremely dangerous, should be banned, even assuming that there is a reasonable alternative. We operate on a rather general commitment to the view that people should be able to go to the devil in their own way, and it's only in some cases that we intervene in the name of their own or others' welfare. That will be a topic for Section 8-2.

The example we've just discussed should show you how the tension between plausibility and overgenerality, between triviality and utility, works out in one particular case. But you need to work through many more examples than this to acquire the skill thoroughly. Here's one for you to try right away (Quiz 6-A, 3): Identify the assumptions in the following argument:

> The matter is quite simple. The United States government signed a treaty with the Apache nation, a treaty which has never been revoked, acknowledging their right to a huge tract of land in the Southwest known as the Chiricahua Reservation. They then shipped the surrendering tribals to Florida in cattle cars and opened half that land to white miners, ranchers and settlers. The Apache are now claiming what is theirs by right and they should receive the land, compound interest on its value, and damages for the suffering due to its loss.

6-4 COUNTERARGUMENTS AND COUNTEREXAMPLES

If you refer back to the outline of the procedure for argument analysis, given earlier in this text, you'll see that we've now covered it in some depth up to

Step 5, which involves criticism of the premises (including the missing premises or assumptions) and criticism of the inferences. We've already done a great deal of this, because many premises, whether explicit or implicit, are definitions or quasi-definitions, and we have spent a great deal of time on teaching you how to criticize them.

One generally doesn't do much about the large group of factual premises unless one has relevant, specific, factual information. Obviously, it isn't possible for a book on reasoning to impart all the factual information that you would need in order to criticize all the factual premises of all the arguments that you're going to encounter. We're focusing on the special kinds of premises that are open to logical criticism, of which the most obvious kinds are definitional premises or ones that assert an inference to be sound, and also on the criticism of inferences themselves, that is, the allegedly logical or reasonable steps from a premise to an intermediate or final conclusion.

It may be worth your while to reread the first pages where a brief outline of criticism strategy is given. You have, in the intervening pages, been provided with many further perspectives on the kind of criticism strategies that are possible—for example, through talking at length about the difference between sufficient and necessary conditions, and through using the technique of diagraming overlapping circles, etc., to illustrate overrestrictive and overinclusive claims. Here we want simply to pick up this general theme of the criticism procedures used in attacking premises and inferences and to tie it to Step 6 in the outline—the introduction of other relevant arguments.

The chief procedure for criticizing the kind of premises and inferences that we *can* criticize rests upon realizing that they are very commonly generalizations of one kind or another, or equivalent to such. The premises might, for example, say something about the morality of affirmative action quotas—that is, about the practice of requiring that a certain number of people from minority groups or women should be hired within a specified time. The assertion that affirmative action quotas are immoral is of course a generalization, indeed a universal, categorical, exceptionless generalization! That is, it denies the existence of *any* justification for such quotas. In order to criticize such a generalization, you naturally begin to think of possible special cases where such quotas would be justified—for example, where we're dealing with relatively unskilled labor, paid at very high rates, the skills being such that they could be acquired in a few weeks of on-the-job training, and we're looking at a labor union with many thousands of members and perhaps half a dozen blacks. In a situation like this, given a job market where there are a large number of people who are qualified, or could easily become qualified, for such a job, and who are very anxious to obtain it, one might well conclude that a good case could be made for requiring that certain modest quotas be met. If this is so, then one has attacked the universal generalization which was the premise under consideration. Notice that this isn't a case of attacking a definitional premise. There are a good many premises like this one which involve *analyses* or *interpretations* that can be attacked on philosophical or logical grounds, even though they're not simply definitional. We're all perfectly familiar with the procedure of criticizing generalizations by pointing out exceptions. That's the procedure of "counterexample." Of course, if the generalization is somewhat more guarded—if, for example, it refers to quotas being *generally* or *normally* or *usually* or *typically* improper—a single counterexample isn't going to refute it. We'll have to look at the question of whether there's a preponderance of counterexamples, or perhaps a very large number of important ones, even if not a majority. (Technically speaking, each one of these should not be called a counterexample individually; but they form a group which, if large enough, constitutes the evidence refuting the generalization, and we will sometimes refer to this group for convenience as a group of counterexamples.)

Another example of a similar kind of premise, in that it involves a philosophical analysis rather than a mere definition (which would be a *linguistic* analysis) or a purely factual claim, is, "The moment that the cells have united to form an embryo in the womb, at that moment an entity with moral rights is created." That is again a universal generalization, and one way to attack it is to look for a counterexample. There are other ways. One might look for arguments that point in the other direction. That procedure is what we call "counterarguing," as opposed to counterexampling. The quotation we've just given, which is, of course, a key premise in many of the arguments of the Right-to-Life advocates, i.e., those who oppose a woman's unrestricted right to abortion, is not easily refuted by counterexamples. The nature of the claim is really one that relates to a whole moral system; and one normally attempts to refute such claims by developing an alternative approach. In this particular case, for example, the usual line of opposition consists in arguing that moral rights are not inherent in biological entities as such, but only in people; and that the embryo at the time of conception is a long way from being a person. Indeed, so that argument would continue, personhood involves such things as having a self-concept, being aware of pain and pleasure, being capable of reflective action, and so on. It's clear that the entities that we normally refer to as people with moral rights do exhibit all these qualities. Are they defining properties or not? Here we're into the questions of the definition of the person and the definition of moral rights, and we may be able to appeal to counterexamples to refute certain oversimplified definitions of "person" or of "moral right." But we may also have to set out a substantial part of a moral theory to support our criticism.

So the procedure of criticism involves both counterexampling and counterarguing, and the procedure of criticizing a particular controversial claim may lead one quickly into both these approaches.

Let us look again at the procedure for criticizing inferences. An inference is a step from a premise or premises to a conclusion or conclusions. It is "represented by" the claim that the premises are sufficient conditions for the conclusion or conclusions. Let's take the case of an inference from a single premise to a single conclusion. If we represent the assertion made by the premise by the letter "p" and the conclusion by the letter "q," the claim that q follows from p, or can be concluded from p, is the same as the claim that p implies q or that q is a legitimate inference from p. All these claims amount to the claim that in all cases where p is true, q will also *have* to be true, or will *probably* be true. That can be seen as a variety of, or analogous to, a generalization.

Let's take an actual example. "If we postpone the presently scheduled 1978 emission requirements on automobiles, we'll save about 40 million gallons of gasoline per year." That's what we usually call a conditional statement, which asserts that it's legitimate to infer from the condition (or antecedent) stated in the first part of it to the conclusion (or consequent) stated in the last part. It can equally well be regarded as equivalent to a kind of generalization, one which asserts that relaxing emission controls will cause a reduction in gas usage, which is just the kind of generalization you might run into as a straight premise in an argument. As we've seen before, the inferences in an argument often can be reexpressed in a way that makes them equivalent to a premise, reducing the remaining inferences to very simple definitional ones. So inferences can often be criticized just like generalizations or just like definitions. In the automobile-emissions case, of course, the generalization that relaxing emission controls will reduce gasoline consumption is true only with respect to certain types of technology for meeting the emissions requirements. The use of stratified-charge engines, some types of Stirling closed-cycle engines, and a number of other technologies makes it possible for a manufacturer to meet the emissions requirement without any cost in gasoline consumption, and some already have. After all, one wants to remember the basic fact that burning up any components of a fuel generates more of the heat that you're trying to get out of the fuel, and thereby produces more energy from it, while at the same time leaving less in the way of residue, hence reducing emissions. Of course, it's a complex technological question whether you can do this efficiently. At the moment, many of the technologies use up more energy to burn up the residues that they produce in the way of heat while doing the burning; so it costs us gasoline to operate the emissions control systems. But it doesn't have to be that way. There are other weaknesses in the inference, that is, in the generalization; for example, the assumption is being made that people will not continue their present trend toward more and more economical cars in a way that is encouraged by the imposition of federal emission controls. Again, if the electorate feels that the avoidance of smog and conservation of oil are both desirable outcomes, and sees that these can best be facilitated by gradually shifting to increasingly economical automobiles, the relaxation of emission controls will not produce the kind of saving that is being mentioned here. And so on.

Take an inference which is supposed to be a strictly logical one, that is, one that follows directly from definitional considerations. For example, consider the inference from "Eureka is north of San Francisco, and Coos Bay is north of Eureka" to the conclusion "Coos Bay is north of San Francisco." If one want to attack an inference like this, one has to attack the definitional rules which are involved in the concepts of geographical direction. And that's simply a matter of attacking a definition, which one does by counter-exampling in the way discussed in the section on meaning.

So it's easy to see that the counterexampling and counterarguing procedures cover just about all the attacks one can make on an argument, whether on its premises, its inferences, its assumptions, or its conclusions.

We need say only a word or two more about counterarguing in order to have covered the next-to-last step in argument analysis, which is the *introduction of alternative arguments*. This last point to be considered in this section concerns the problem of drawing the line between *criticism of a given argument* and the *volunteering and weighing of further relevant arguments*. It's clear that if you're asked simply to criticize an argument, you can just point out whatever weaknesses in the premises and inferences that occur to you, and let it go at that. Supposing that you are able to find a number of such criticisms, you will certainly have shown that there are no good reasons for believing the conclusion of the argument is amongst those that have so far been mentioned. But, of course, there may be other reasons for believing it, or other reasons for disbelieving it, which you are aware of. Should you mention them? This is really a question of the situation that you are in, the role that you are playing. With respect to your own views, naturally you should take these other points into account. With respect to attempting to help others to formulate a correct view of the matter, you might or might not want to mention them. It might seem to be personally intrusive, it might be pedagogically bad (perhaps it's better to encourage students to discover these other arguments themselves), or you might be in a special role, such as that of a lawyer attempting to defend a client against certain charges. Here you are required to provide only the best defense, which usually means the best criticism of the prosecutor's argument, and it is not appropriate for you to volunteer further argument or interpretations (or even facts) which may tend to support the prosecutor's conclusions.

But I must confess that I think the limited role of "sniping" at arguments is one that should be accepted only when there are special reasons for doing so. In general, it seems to me that the criticism of arguments naturally and properly involves considering whether there are other arguments for and against the conclusion of the argument under consideration.

As a matter of fact, one can take all this a step further—bring it nearer to home, if you like—by suggesting that one should always conclude the evaluation of an argument with a period of reflection on your own position in the light of the argument. You may feel quite pleased with yourself for having identified some weaknesses in the argument. But does this lead you, personally, to reject its conclusion? If not, you are in possession, presumably, of some other argument for the conclusion. Bring it in, make it explicit; it's appropriate to do so as part of argument analysis. For example, the argument that you're criticizing has certain weaknesses, but you find yourself fully convinced that the conclusion is completely false even though you can demonstrate only that a particular argument for its truth doesn't work; then you probably have some other arguments in mind, consciously or unconsciously, which count against the conclusion. Pull them out and set them out, and look at them critically; subject them to the same scrutiny that you have turned on the argument under consideration initially.

So don't "let go" of an argument until you have forced yourself to decide what your own situation is with respect to the conclusion. Your feelings about that conclusion may indicate that you do have other relevant arguments in mind, and maybe you should mention them. If the argument fails and you finish up without anything supporting the conclusion, but, on the other hand, you have no very good reason for thinking the conclusion is false, you should end with a perfectly open mind about the conclusion. Are you truly doing that? Be sure you are really pulling out of your head all the relevant considerations that lie buried in it. Just as your knowledge of the meaning of terms is usually much more subtle than any simple formula that you can pull out to define them, so your knowledge of the probability of conclusions is often considerably more complicated that can be expressed in a single argument. Try to support your judgment, perhaps in a series of arguments, perhaps just by giving a series of generalizations that seem to you to have some bearing on the conclusion, though you're not quite certain how to construct an argument out of them. *Reasoning is very largely the conversion of unconscious judgments, feelings, and knowledge into something more explicit.* When these considerations are made more explicit, it's very much easier to analyze them or assess them and to decide on their true worth. That's why this process of role playing, of putting yourself in the position of having to decide whether you really and truly believe or reject (or are perfectly open-minded about) the conclusion, is worth doing: It helps to force you to make the implicit explicit, the unconscious conscious, and the covert overt.

Here's an example to test these skills on. Somebody puts forth the argument that giving people bad grades is a form of punishment, indeed sometimes quite a severe form of punishment as far as their career or scholarship plans are concerned, and that associating education with punishment is a surefire way to turn people off it. Therefore, the arguer concludes, grades should be abolished. Assess this argument. (Quiz 6-A, 4)

6-5   REFORMULATIONS OF CLAIMS AND ARGUMENTS

We've been talking about providing counterexamples to generalizations, and counterarguments to arguments. Now it's time to look at the defense against such approaches. Suppose that you give an argument for the evils of using gas-fired clothes dryers, using as your reason the fact that they consume on the average more natural resources than electric clothes dryers do. Of course, one of your assumptions is that it's desirable to slow down on consumption of fossil fuels, but then this isn't (it turns out) an assumption which your critic is challenging. Instead, your adversary points out that what you say applies to the average or typical gas dryer, but that it doesn't apply to all. In particular, the latest generation of gas dryers does not use a pilot light, and that it is the pilot light which accounts for the higher total cost in fuel of using gas dryers. The actual cost in fuel of doing one load of drying is considerably less with the gas dryer (or so your critic says).

If you have no reason to doubt your opponent's premises, then your best defense consists in reformulating your conclusion, and perhaps also your own premises. Instead of arguing that gas dryers should be banned or that they are bad, you simply circle around the counterexamples that have been pointed out and reformulate your conclusion so that it doesn't cover them. It will now read, "Gas dryers with pilot lights should be banned (or otherwise curtailed)." Your original generalization was a bit too sweeping, as the counterargument showed, so you narrow it down.

If you are attracted by the general moral argument that euthanasia is wrong because it involves the risk of depriving people of many years of life if a cure is discovered for their condition, somebody might point out that sometimes the person requesting euthanasia (or for whom euthanasia is requested) is so old that death would be certain to come very soon from one cause or another, even if a cure should be discovered for the condition—let us say cancer—which is the most immediate threat to the person's life. Of course, you might meet this argument by saying that even a slight saving of years of life is worthwhile; but that might be met by the further argument that some of these individuals are so unwell that life would not be a pleasure to them even if the cancer could be cured. A natural next move for you is to fall back to a slightly less strong claim and simply say that you believe euthanasia is not justified for people who would have a normal life expectancy of a good many years if the condition which is immediately threatening to life could be cured. That's a case of reformulating a generalization in order to take account of a counterexample to its initial form. The generalization is now a weaker one in the sense that it doesn't make such a strong claim; but, of course, it's a stronger one in the sense that it is now immune to a certain type of counterexample that was fatal to the original generalization.

In an analogous way to that just described, where we have been reformulating claims in the light of counterexamples, we can also reformulate arguments. Of course, reformulating claims means reformulating an argument. But there are a great many other ways. For example, one may add extra premises, delete some premises, get to the conclusion through a different intermediate conclusion, once it has been pointed out that the inference to the intermediate conclusion that was originally suggested is unsound, and so on.

In short, the first round of fighting in argument analysis is by no means the end of the story—at least in many cases. And the moral of that point is that you need to be very careful about the kind of criticisms you make when you are criticizing an argument, so that they won't be easily handled by some relatively trivial reformulation of a claim or of the argument. When you've made some critical comments on an argument, look ahead to ways in which they might be met by reformulation. *Role-play the arguer.* Try to imagine yourself defending the argument in the light of the critical points that you have raised. If this can be done, you should certainly take account of the defensive moves you have just thought up when you're trying to decide how to sum up your assessment of the argument.

One of the most important types of reformulation involves clarifying and sometimes even slightly shifting the meaning of a term. An argument may begin about whether childbirth at home is as safe as it is in the hospital. Various considerations are raised, such as the increased probability of picking up an infection in the hospital and the increased risk that an emergency in the home couldn't be coped with because of the absence of a specialist or some special drug. At this point, the person who's arguing for the superiority of home childbirth says, "Of course, if it wasn't for the absurd prejudice of doctors against attending child delivery in the home, one could have a specialist (instead of a midwife) present, with most of the necessary drugs and apparatus." This is an immediate shift in the nature of the argument. It is a case of reformulating the claim that is at stake. The argument began by being an argument about the relative safety of home childbirth and hospital childbirth, but now it's become an argument about the possible relative safety of the two approaches if doctors worked in a way different from the way in which they do currently work. This is a reformulation of the conclusion, and it might be argued that it really amounts to *clarification of what is meant* by the conclusion, rather than an *alteration* of the claim itself. It isn't really worth a big fight to decide which of these is the case: that would be an ego trip. The main thing is for you to be on guard against the possibility that you are interpreting some term, or some phrase, or even a whole sentence, in the argument in a way different from the way the arguer now interprets it.

Suppose the argument is about whether it's sexist for schools to have different schedules of required exercises in the physical education classes for girls and boys. The counterargument is produced that girls aren't as strong as boys, and it would be unreasonable to set them exercises which demand equal physical strength. The reply to this is that the only reason why girls aren't as strong as boys is continuing discrimination, beginning in very early childhood, of which this discrimination in physical exercise tasks is just one example. All such discrimination is sexist, it is said, part of the sexist culture, and hence, it is certainly true that discrimination between the required exercises is sexist.

Notice what has happened here. The argument has shifted from what one might call the question of whether any "added sexism" is involved in setting different exercises to the question of whether setting different exercises is "part of" the general sexist pattern. There's been a shift of meaning, at least as far as the critic of the argument is concerned. It may be that the critic misunderstood the arguer; or it may be that the arguer, faced with a certain type of counterargument, reformulated the conclusion in order to withstand the threat better. The main function of an argument should be to arrive at the truth, and not so much to score points along the way; so it's often best to adjust to the new sense, to treat it as a clarification of the original position, rather than to claim a partial victory through having forced a withdrawal from the original position.

It's pretty clear that arguments about sexism or racism, or the causes of crime, or artistic brilliance, and so on, are likely to involve some skirmishing about the exact meaning of these terms, and the skirmishing is likely to result in at least clarification, but possibly also reformulations. Simply calling for an explicit definition of the key term is not a particularly helpful procedure in most cases. It will be useful where the term is a technical one that admits of a precise definition, but it generally won't be useful where the term is a crucial theoretical, philosophical, or ethical term, because its full meaning is not easily set out in a definition. It will be better to use the methods of examples and contrasts (discussed earlier) to clarify meaning, in the course of an exchange between two people. When you yourself are under attack, it will seem to you that clarification of your original intentions is taking place; when you are the attacker, it will seem to you that the arguer is reformulating (evading) rather than clarifying. Whichever it is, the decision isn't very important except perhaps in a debating society. The main point to remember is that in formulating as well as in reformulating arguments, a great deal can often be saved even when an important point has been made against the original form of the argument. One frequently sees people giving up on an argument because somebody has pointed out a very serious weakness in it, when what they should be doing is making quite sure that their instincts have nothing more to be said for them. There may perhaps be a way to reformulate the argument that salvages an important form of it. One of the real signs of maturity in people engaging in argument, or in reasoning in general, is their willingness to offer reformulations to their opponents when they can see that such reformulations would save an important point for "the other side."

6-6   STRONG AND WEAK CRITICISM

We have referred throughout this book to the difference between strong and weak criticism, and to the desirability of ensuring that one learns how to make that distinction both in the role of defending an argument and in the role of criticizing it. We have illustrated, on a number of occasions, particular ways in which one can distinguish between strong and weak criticisms. And we have stressed that the idea of a "strong" argument or claim is confusingly ambiguous. A strong claim may mean one which sticks its neck out a long way like the claim that white males are more aggressive than Asian-American males. Or it may mean a claim for which the evidence is strong, in which sense "strong" could be fairly well translated as "well supported." The stronger a claim is in the first sense, the less likely it is to be strong in a second sense, other things being equal. You will remember that one example of this came up in connection with the discussion of precision. As we make a claim more and more precise, it becomes increasingly informative, *if true;* but it also becomes increasingly difficult to support, requiring more and more refined methods of measurement. So as it becomes stronger in one sense, it becomes *less likely to be true,* other things being equal. That is, it is less strong in the other sense.

When we talk about strong and weak criticism, the same ambiguity is present. It's a strong criticism of an argument to say that it's "entirely hopeless"—much stronger criticism than to say that it "doesn't seem to be quite satisfactory." But this is the sort of strength that refers to the strength of the *claim,* rather than the strength of its *support.* One might equally well say, in the other sense of "strong," that a strong criticism of an argument is one that really turns out to be well supported, and that the second one just quoted is much more likely to be well supported, since it takes much less to support it. So *it* is stronger.

Given the ambiguity in the terms strong and weak, let's focus on the type of criticism that is desirable, that is, well supported and incisive criticism. To use other terms, we want to be careful to produce criticism that "goes to the heart of the argument" and that succeeds in showing that it failed there, not in some peripheral way. We're not particularly interested in criticism that is strong only in the sense of merely *claiming* to utterly destroy an argument. We need criticism that really undermines it completely. Or, to be more precise, we need to distinguish carefully between criticism which is really serious for the argument and criticism which requires only a reformulation to be taken care of. In short, we want criticism that is as strong as possible both in the sense of making a strong *claim* and in the sense of having strong *support*.

One of the most common faults in people beginning argument analysis, or reasoning in general, is a tendency to throw in the weak comments with the strong ones. Your instructor will frequently remark, perhaps verbally or perhaps in the margin of your assignment, that a particular criticism or line of argument is weak, or perhaps that another is strong or very strong. Make sure that you understand thoroughly the basis for these assessments. They constitute one of the most valuable kinds of judgment that your instructor can provide for you because they gradually teach you to discriminate between the most useful and the most trivial types of argument, criticism, or reasoning.

6-7 OVERALL JUDGMENT

The last stage in the procedure that we outlined for argument analysis consists in tying together everything that has gone before, and summing it up (if at all possible) with an overall judgment, assessment, or evaluation of the argument. Just as in grading student work, it's often much better to point out that there are certain good features and certain other bad features in a complicated argument, rather than just assign an overall grade. But this business of "fractionating" an evaluation can also be used as a cop-out. That is, a teacher who doesn't like to be critical will search for "something nice to say" to a student, and then say that, giving it about as much force as some rather mildly expressed criticism. The overall impression that this creates in the student's mind, when reading (or hearing) these comments, is that he or she has made some errors but has also done some good things, and that these more or less balance out. The real situation may be entirely different. The good point may be a finer point; the weakness may be very serious. It's extremely important that instructors call a spade a spade in the evaluation of reasoning, because the procedure of evaluating reasoning itself exemplifies reasoning, and if it is done in a misleading way, it *commits* one of the faults that it is supposed to *correct* in the student, a hypocritical situation. Sometimes one hears that there is no way to compare apples and oranges, and hence that it's impossible to give an overall single grade to work which exemplifies, on the one hand, considerable creativity, but, on the other hand, significant defects in the validity of the arguments provided. But the process of overall judgment requires you to weigh apples against oranges. (So does ordinary practical shopping.) Make no mistake about it, that's exactly the game that reasoning is obliged to play for excellent practical reasons on many occasions. When you go out to make a major purchase, perhaps of a television set, you will have to weigh apples against oranges: you will have to weigh the fact that a certain set is easier to carry around against the fact that it has a somewhat less satisfactory picture. You'll have to weigh the fact that it's considerably cheaper against the fact that the place where you're buying it is unlikely to provide service if it breaks down. Of course, these are all apples, oranges, peaches, and pears, incomparable in some sense. But there's such a thing as putting them all together in a rational way, rather than in a stupid or irrational way. If you let price be the absolute determiner of what you purchase, you will finish up making some very foolish purchases. If you ignore price entirely, you will finish up being unable to make many purchases that you would very much like to make solely because you don't have any money left, when you could easily have bought what you wanted and still had money left. Both errors are errors of reasoning.

The process of evaluation is, on the one hand, the most elusive and difficult of all reasoning activities and, on the other hand, the most important. It is the most important because it is the most closely tied to action. When we have found out that there are certain weaknesses in a certain argument, that some of them can be met by reformulation and that some of them can't, that some criticisms of some parts are strong and some criticisms of other parts are weak, we have found out all that we can about the basis for our final evaluation. But we haven't made it yet. In order to make it, we need to "weigh up" all these considerations. That means we have to decide, and have good reasons for deciding, how much is left after the demolition work is finished and what it's worth. Why do we have to make such decisions? Why can't we just leave the list of established criticisms and refuted criticisms as they lie? Simply because we're going to have to perform actions on the basis of this argument; risk our money on the basis of this other argument; risk our reputation on the basis of yet other arguments. When these things are at stake, you have to decide whether to go with the argument on balance, or against it. Merely listing pros and cons doesn't get you to "the bottom line," the real pay off.

The argument may be one about the superiority of a particular life insurance policy over another, and on your decision hinges the future welfare and happiness of your children or other relatives. You look carefully into a number of competing policies and rapidly discover that each of them has certain advantages and certain disadvantages. You must now go about the process of weighing these advantages and drawbacks in terms of their relative importance to you, and then, of course, adding up the "scores" that each of the policies merit in each of these respects, in order to arrive at a final conclusion. You go through exactly the same kind of consideration in an informal way in making decisions about what to do with a free evening, or whether to get married or to have kids, or where to go to school or what courses to take. Making the considerations *explicit* is a way to make the whole procedure more reliable, because the apparatus of criticism comes into play much more easily with respect to explicit argumentation.

You want to buy an automobile? There will be arguments for buying one of a certain size, type, price, maker and importer, dealer, guarantee, and performance; and there'll be arguments for another or for several others, along these dimensions as well as other dimensions. Then you have to get down to the business of deciding how important to you the various dimensions are; then you can combine the factual data with your carefully justified estimates of importance into an overall judgment. And you can't avoid combining them into an overall judgment if you're finally going to have to pick one or the other alternative. It's no good complaining that you had to weigh seating capacity against reliable service and that these aren't really comparable qualities.

In the same way, an instructor, when providing an overall grade for a student, will have to combine a number of different considerations in order to provide that single letter grade. It isn't perfect; it doesn't tell the student as much, in some ways, as a more detailed description would. But it does give an overall estimate of quality that is often highly useful, and it tells you a great deal more than mere fractionated grades would (that is, grades on each of the dimensions of performance). Similarly, when you evaluate an argument, in the end you will have to decide whether or not it affects your degree of belief in the conclusion; and the extent to which it does that is really the grade that you are giving it. Don't shirk that obligation, as long as there is any point to it at all. *Make an overall judgment* of the worth of an argument when you finish all your considerations and analysis. Remember that, even if it doesn't direct you toward a particular action, it does direct or redirect you toward a particular belief, and that later actions may depend on that belief. Reasoning is not just an abstract matter, like analyzing chess positions; it is the skill that lies behind making good decisions, performing sensible actions; that is the skill that leads to developing sane and humane attitudes.

QUIZ 6-A

1 Press Secretary Ziegler once declared certain previous statements by President Nixon on the subject of Watergate to be "inoperative." This is a nice example of an original _____. "False" is a nice old-fashioned word that does the same job and doesn't even have the implication that the individual who uttered the statements knew them to be false, in which case the correct word would be _____.

Answer

Of course the answer here is "lie," and the distinction between lies and false statements is often a crucial one in arguments. Fundamentalist Christians sometimes argue that one must believe either that Jesus was a liar, or that He was the Son of God. This is an example of a *false dilemma,* that is, a pair of possibilities that do not exhaust the alternatives. The third possibility is of course that Jesus was *mistaken,* but not lying.

2 Consider the argument, "He's a homosexual so he shouldn't be appointed to this politically sensitive post." Does this argument assume that "homosexuals are poor security risks"?

Answer

No. Although the arguer might well be making this assumption, you can't infer that from the argument. You can infer only that the arguer is making *some* assumption about the connection between homosexuality and ineligibility for a politically sensitive post. And that is not an illuminating assumption. What's the most likely missing premise? Perhaps it would be something like, "It would be politically embarrassing to have it discovered later that he was a homosexual"; together with some other assumption like, "The degree to which his performance would be superior in this post would far offset the costs to the party or the country of the embarrassment that disclosure of his homosexuality would produce." Probably the next most likely assumptions would be ones that refer to the possibility of blackmail of homosexuals and the consequent possibility of a security leak through this individual. If you are obliged to attempt a serious evaluation of the brief argument quoted out of context here, you would undertake to create several of these possible lines of defense and to critique each of them, as we can easily do here. If you can ask the arguer what assumptions he or she is making, the answer will simplify the analysis considerably. But, in any case, you must be clear that you cannot make a reliable inference here as to what the assumptions were in the abstract; the best you can do is to cover some of the most likely combinations of assumptions.

3 What are the assumptions in the following argument?

The matter is quite simple. The United States government signed a treaty with the Apache nation which has never been revoked, acknowledging their right to a huge tract of land in the Southwest known as the Chiricahua reservation. They then shipped the surrendering tribals to Florida in cattle cars and opened half that land to white miners, ranchers and settlers. The Apache are now claiming what is theirs by right and they should receive the land, compound interest on its value, and damages for the suffering due to its loss.

Answer

The basic point of the argument is simple; a broken contract should be remedied by (*a*) restoration of the property which the contract called for turning over, (*b*) compound interest on its value for the time that the Apache did not receive benefits from it, and (c) damages for the suffering due to its loss. The land in question appears to be half the Chiricahua reservation, rather than all of it. The damages claimed are all that might be reasonably argued for, since the claims involve no reference to damages for inhumane treatment above and beyond deprivation of the reservation. That part we will put on one side, not even considering it among "other relevant arguments" since it is not relevant to the conclusions of this argument. (But it is relevant to action on the general question of damages. If that general question is not going to be taken up, the damage done by inhumane treatment provides us with another reason for paying *these* damages, namely, that they are property compensations for something else for which no damages are to be paid.)

One of the important facts about this argument is that it's a highly plausible one. Indeed, it has achieved a great deal of political support in Native American circles, so that it must be completed or rebutted in order to avoid political repercussions that, in some areas particularly, are becoming pretty serious.

It is interesting to note that the law does not accept this argument as it stands, and the law developed that position without prejudice toward minorities. The law rejects this kind of approach for the calculation of very old debts due to breach of contract, and there is some good common sense behind it on this point. (Here we're considering other relevant arguments in order to set up a kind of perspective on this one, and perhaps to help us improve on assessment of the assumptions which we are about to dig up.) The reason the law doesn't accept this line of argument is very simple: The amount of recompense, computed in terms of compound interest, is certainly disproportionate to the way in which assets appreciate. If a deposit in a bank, not land, had been stolen from the Apache, and if the thief had been allowing that deposit to accumulate interest in his or her own name, the court would unhesitatingly transfer ownership of the bank account to the Apache, when it had judged the treaty to have been valid and breached invalidly. But the fact is that land cannot be treated as equivalent to its then cash value in a bank account. It does not appreciate over long periods at the rate that compound interest increases the size of a bank deposit.

Now let's look carefully at the argument for assumptions. There are three components in the conclusion which we should separate. First, there is the claim that the Apache should receive the land. Second, there is the claim that they should receive compound interest on its value. And third, there is the claim that they should receive damages for the suffering due to its loss. Different assumptions are required in order to reach each of these conclusions. The first assumption is that an initially illegal transfer should be revoked, no matter what other innocent parties will suffer and no matter how long it is since the original breach of contract occurred. Notice that we have introduced a reference to other interested parties, although no such reference occurs in the original argument. This is an instance of bringing in insights that illuminate the assumptions. It doesn't require any specialized knowledge of the history of the Southwest to see that the argument has already mentioned white miners, ranchers, and settlers, and that these individuals took up the land by government authorization; that much is present in the argument. One might adopt a fairly tough line and argue that they should have seen that the government authorization was illegal, and that they should have been held responsible as cocriminals. However, whatever one says about them, it is very difficult to argue that their grandchildren, inheriting established ranches in that area, should be treated as having no right to be considered because of *their* criminality. In short, other people who had operated in what seemed clearly to be a perfectly legal way have developed interest in the land. One might still argue that *they* should be recompensed by the government which originally led them into this situation. But then, of course, that government isn't around any more. Should the present government accept all responsibility for the actions of its predecessors? The argument assumes that it should, or else that the interests of the present tenants should not be considered. The latter assumption would be about as cruel as the original deprivation.

Now, should a government be responsible for all the consequences of errors by its predecessors? One of the reasons that we elect new government officers regularly is so that each one can make a fresh start. Our government officials are not automatically entitled to abrogate treaties, but, on the other hand, they're not automatically to be saddled with all the sins of their predecessors. Perhaps some compromise is appropriate, from this point of view.

But, whereas the previous argument is a highly debatable one, there is a serious assumption present in the passage that we're analyzing, about which we haven't spoken so far. That is the assumption that the Apache have received nothing at all in the intervening period from the government. But they have of course enjoyed a slice (though not all) of the so-called advantages of citizenship. They have received protection of the defense forces of the nation, some of the protection of the police forces of the nation (and some of the repression from that source), and, perhaps most significantly, they have received very substantial support in the dimensions of welfare and education from the federal government. While it is quite inappropriate to suggest that these perquisites offset the massive rip-off completely, they do require some adjustment in the rather simple formula proposed in the argument as compensation to the tribals for their land.

The assumption that they should receive compound interest on its value has already been criticized; a more appropriate formula would involve reference to the present value of the land involved, which would be considerably less. However, the land as it stands has been substantially improved by fertilization, irrigation, and other processes, and the value due to those improvements needs to be deducted from the appreciated value. However, again, the income taken out of the land over a long period of time, where it was not turned into land improvement, needs to be added back in, and it may well be appropriate to add interest on that.

The assumption that people who are compensated by transfer of the property that should originally have been theirs, plus compound interest on its value (even with the adjustments just suggested), should in addition receive damages for the suffering due to its loss is a little more complex. Most of the suffering due to its loss presumably arises from deprivation of income, etc. that would not have existed had they not been deprived of it. However, that loss has been covered by the preceding reimbursements. Are there further "damages from the suffering" over and above that deprivation? One would need to argue rather carefully for this.

The question requests only the identification of assumptions; as usual, only by looking a little bit ahead of that, to the justification of those assumptions, or their refutation, are we able to get a fairly clear formulation of the assumptions themselves. In the process of doing this, we have anticipated some but not all of the final evaluations of premises and the argument as a whole. One special feature deserves comment: When three conclusions are drawn, as here, it is important to set the assumptions out so that they represent the fact that the conclusions are not wholly isolated. You notice that our assumption for the third conclusion (or the third component of the one conclusion) has to be formulated as "It's appropriate to compensate people for suffering due to the loss of property through breach of contract, over and above return of the land and (adjusted) return of the equivalent of the income from the land." Otherwise, we would have an assumption which would support the obviously appropriate conclusion that some kind of damages were due, but it would not reflect the missing link in an argument where other components have already afforded claims for substantial reparations.

Still interested in the argument as a whole, and where one should finish up on it? Do question 3 in Quiz 6-C.

4   Giving people grades is a form of punishment, indeed sometimes quite a severe form of punishment as far as their career or scholarship plans are concerned, and associating education with punishment is a surefire way to turn people off to it. Therefore grades should be abolished.

Answer

Let's do this one briskly in order to show that it isn't always necessary to get into the more elaborate forms of structure analysis. The meaning of the terms in the argument is pretty clear, given that one understands that "punishment" is being used to cover disappointment. The structure is simple: Bad grades are punishment; punishing turns people off; hence grades should be abolished.

The first assumption that's going to cause trouble is the one that bad grades are the only kind of grades. Since they obviously aren't, the most that can be said for the argument is that it would support the conclusion that bad grades should be abolished. Clearly, the current phenomenon of "grade inflation" shows that a great many instructors have accepted the conclusion that bad grades should be more or less abolished, without accepting the conclusion that all grades should be abolished. So the argument is crucially defective in that respect.

The second point of attack is simply to register a complaint about the premise which asserts that giving people bad grades is a form of punishment. In a technical sense that identifies punishment with negative reinforcement, that is, with any stimulus that tends to diminish the frequency of the response to which the reinforcement was applied, bad grades certainly have that effect. And it is on the basis of that technical sense that the argument proceeds to infer that people will be turned off as a result of getting bad grades. But that involves an oversimplifying assumption, namely, that getting a bad grade in one particular course will (a) turn people off the whole educational system of which that course is only a small part, and (b) not be accompanied by other reinforcers, such as positive vocational guidance suggesting a constructive alternative path to the present career goals or alternative attractive career goals that will "take the sting out of" the "punishment" of the bad grades. Since the influence of one bad grade obviously is quite easily overcome by getting good grades in a number of other courses, to the point where people are not turned off the whole system, the first part of this assumption is unsound, and the second—though less obviously—is certainly unsound in particular cases. For example, somebody may get bad grades in a course which she doesn't like and wanted to drop, and be able to persuade her counselor or parents that dropping plans for a medical career is now necessary; she may therefore see the bad grade as a blessing in disguise, and not as a punishment at all.

Hence the premises and the assumptions lead to some very serious criticisms of the argument. Moreover, there is another argument that bears on the same conclusion which has to be considered. That is the argument that the function of grading is to inform people, not to provide them with enjoyment, and that education can hardly produce socially and individually good results if it doesn't combine an adequate system of information about the success of students on various subject matters with the provision of good training in the subject matter. Without the discriminatory procedure of differential grading, students have no basis for making a discrimination between more or less promising areas for concentrating their time. Hence, a system of education which does not provide bad grades where bad grades are appropriate will not serve the individual or society well. Providing enjoyment does involve eliminating or reducing punishment; but providing enjoyment is not the principal task of the system of education. Hence the line of argument presented rests on a further assumption, which we hadn't previously noticed, namely, the assumption that the maximum yields of a system of education will be achieved by abandoning honest and skilled feedback to the students as to their performance, if that feedback will prove to be disappointing. That assumption is obviously unsound, and the other relevant argument that we're now considering shows it to be unsound; so we have to abandon the line of argument presented entirely.

QUIZ 6-B

1 "The mere fact that anything exists at all would be inexplicable unless there were a Creator. No more compelling proof of the existence of God is required than this, the hallowed cosmological argument."
Criticize this argument, paying particular attention to Steps 6 and 7 of the procedure.

2 "No one should blame the 'addict' for his or her addictive behavior. For everyone alive has bad habits—eats too much, watches the Late Show too often, is a fingernail biter, avoids exercise—and these are just as irrational and as persistent as those labeled "addictions," for example, drinking or smoking too much. In fact, the relatively recent identification of gambling addicts and "workaholics" just shows how arbitrary the distinction is. These behavior rigidities are just part of the human condition, not "sins." They require understanding, not sitting in judgment."

3 **a** Is there an afterlife? List some facts that seem to support your answer to this question. Can you construct a strong argument for your position?
   b Construct the best argument you can for *the* (or **a**) position you do not agree with as to the existence of an afterlife.

    c Give one strong criticism of the argument you have just constructed.
    d Reformulate the argument to handle the criticism, conceding as little as possible.

4 Why do you think the questions in this quiz, near the end of the text, are not multiple choice?

5 At the end of each description of a tour in a current American Airlines travel ad, there's a sentence much like this: "For further information, call your travel agent (or us) and ask for details on tour 637AA721WAD28704."
    a In terms of what we have said in the scope of this book, can any criticism be made of the quoted sentence?
    b What criticism?
    c How can it be justified?
    d Is it an example of strong or weak criticism?
    e Is your answer to **d** a strong or a weak evaluation?

6 Give the best arguments you can for getting a college education and for not doing so. Evaluate them and justify your evaluation. Are you biased on this issue? *Might* you be? Should that affect your evaluation of the arguments? How?

7

CHARLES McCABE
HIMSELF
RETHINKING RAPE

The thing to do about rape, in my opinion, is to take the sex out of it.

I am not being frivolous. The crime that we call rape—having sexual intercourse with a woman forcibly and without her consent—would be much better handled by society if it was treated, not as a sex offense, but as what it truly is—a heinous and aggravated form of personal assault.

As such, the punishment should be properly grave for the convicted, like maybe 15 years in the cooler.

Thanks to the feminist movement, rape is a big thing these days. The recent trial of Inez Garcia brought out some pretty weird feelings about the whole subject.

Rape is said to be the country's fastest growing violent crime. Convictions for it are rising about 15 per cent each year, due largely to the fact that women are more willing to report the crime than formerly, and to take the police hassling that often goes with it.

Police understandably don't like rape cases. One of the reasons is the woman scorned. She will, and far too often does, report a rape when the truth is that she was more than willing. She is advancing the charge as a kind of revenge.

Then, too, the rape case too often resolves itself into a case of one man's word against one woman's word, and is thus ultimately unresolvable.

But what is really wrong with our rape laws, from the point of view of the victim as well as that of law enforcement, is that they are all tied up with sex, and our curious way of handling sex crimes under the criminal sanction.

Morals and shame and all kinds of irrelevant nonsense are contained in the word rape. If a raped woman were to come to the police with a complaint for aggravated personal assault, the matter could be seen as straight police work. It would be handled like other cases of personal assault which are also usually not easy to prosecute.

If, however, the rape should be followed by an unwanted pregnancy, and perhaps an equally unwanted abortion, the crime would be treated with all the more gravity.

Inez Garcia went to trial for shooting to death a 300-pound man who held her down while, she charged, another raped her. Her defense was based on the fact that a woman should have the same right as a man to resort to violence to protect her honor.

She blew her case in mid-trial when she rushed to the bench and shouted to the judge, "I killed that mother f-----, so why don't you just find me guilty and put me in jail, you lousy pig." She was later sentenced to life imprisonment for murder.

Charles Garry, Mrs. Garcia's lawyer, later told columnist Shana Alexander: "I've never seen a woman turn on her own case like that. She scared that jury silly. At first I didn't understand why she wouldn't tell the court she was sorry, since she'd already told the prosecution psychiatrist God would punish her. Now I realize she was playing to the gallery. She didn't want to let her supporters down."

Rape is too important a thing to be left to the extreme feminists. For them it is just another weapon in the war between the sexes which is their stock in trade.

If instead of taking to her gun Mrs. Garcia had complained of grievous personal assault, and if, and this is the really big if, police attitudes on the subject had been de-sexualized, justice might have been served, and served fully, without the murder for which she was convicted.

I realize that this is rather Utopian thinking. But if you think the unthinkable long enough it often becomes thinkable, like the near-impeachment of Mr. Nixon. Our rape laws just don't work, like nearly all of our sex laws. This is one case where we might solve a problem, merely by changing its name.

QUIZ 6-C

1 Is there a "reasonable alternative" to smoking, and what is it?
   a For adolescents
   b For smokers
      What is your definition of "reasonable alternative" as revealed in your answers to **a** and **b**? Does it imply that you should give up driving a car? Having sex? Why not?

2 "The very notion that it's appropriate to apply one single letter, a grade, on the end of a 30-page term paper, representing perhaps 120 hours of work, is *absurd.* And that's what grading is, *absurd.*" Comment.

3 What reparations are due the Apache? (Complete the analysis of question 6-A, 3.)

Special Types of Argument

We have now covered, first briefly and then in considerable detail, the basic procedures of argument analysis and their ramifications into the criticism of functional prose and, in general, all prose when the perspective of appraisal is other than aesthetic. We conclude the book with two chapters in which we indicate some of the ways in which the basic material applies to some special cases (Chapter 7) and ties into certain other subjects that should be thought of as natural continuations of one's thinking about the processes and applications of reasoning (Chapter 8).

7-1 SAMPLES AND GENERALIZATIONS: SCIENCE

Reasoning in science is in fact of a great many kinds. If you read through a textbook on theoretical physics, you will find most of the reasoning to be of the same kind as that in any mathematics text; that is, it exemplifies what is technically called deductive argument, argument in which each step follows from the previous one by the application either of definitions or rules, or of more complex principles that have themselves been developed from definitional rules.

Then again, another substantial part of scientific reasoning in almost any field involves the evaluation of competing hypotheses. This is done by a complex process of reasoning, one that involves the derivation of consequences of the hypotheses and the comparison of these consequences with known facts (or, first, the investigation of reality to discover the relevant facts); the reformulation of the hypotheses in order to generate more nearly exact consequences (if this is necessary); the rejection of the hypotheses if the consequences are too grossly incompatible with the facts; attempts to refine, by simplification and by relating to other areas of scientific knowledge, the basic tenets of the hypotheses, and so on and so on. Certain aspects of this process have been called "hypothetico-deductive" reasoning. But the process as a whole is a good deal more complicated than that particular view of it suggests. Notice that it includes the "reformulation in order to bypass counterexamples" step that we've already covered; and the identification of implications and assumptions also comes in. Scientific reasoning involves many of the same elements that come into argument analysis. There is, however, another extremely important type of inference which does characterize science, the details of which have been developed in the present century to a degree of refinement never previously attained, one which is of particular importance in the social sciences, which are themselves essentially a product of the twentieth century. This is the process of reasoning to a generalization from observations of a limited number of particular cases. The semitechnical phrase for it is reasoning from "characteristics of a sample" to the "characteristics of the population" from which the sample is drawn. Some of the governing principles of this type of inference are covered in a branch of statistics known as *inferential* statistics. (The contrasting branch of statistics is *descriptive* statistics, which concerns the representation of facts by means of the use of such types of "summarizing statistic" as the mean, median, and standard deviation.) We're concerned here, not with the mathematical discipline of statistics, but with the basic reasoning steps that underlie it. Even with respect to these, we will be covering a very limited part of them in this section, but it is close to being the heart of inferential statistics.

The fundamental type of inference here is well exemplified in the standard opinion poll. When the Gallup poll, for example, is to determine the opinion of the country about a particular candidate for President, it does so by interviewing between 1,000 and 2,000 citizens. From this sample of the population, it is possible to draw extremely reliable and rather precise conclusions about the opinion of the population as a whole. It is possible only because the sample is very carefully chosen. About 200 million Americans are not interviewed at all, yet we can conclude reliably what their opinions are from the few interviews that we do make. This is a remarkable achievement of applied social science, and it is one that, though open to abuse, can also keep lawmakers more closely in touch with public opinion in a way that makes possible the better functioning of a democracy. But of course the opinion poll has immense significance outside the political domain. It can tell us about the probable success of a new product, when it is used in market research; it can tell us about the extent of knowledge of basic facts needed to survive in a modern society, as when it is used in large-scale educational testing; and so on.

The sample is itself still quite a substantial group of individuals. When we have finished the interviewing of the sample, we have to boil down the results so as to obtain a useful description of the opinion of the sample. This process is part of *descriptive statistics;* it involves only *deductive reasoning*. For example, we may discover that 54.6 percent of those interviewed favor candidate A over candidate B. Reaching this conclusion is no more than a merely arithmetical step, though it is part of the process of reasoning. But now we come to the procedure of generalizing to the population. There is no trick to this if certain conditions are met about the typicality of the sample. One simply asserts that approximately 54.6 percent of the population as a whole prefers candidate A. All the skill here lies in the process of picking the right sample in order to get the desired degree of approximation. And that is what we need to look at briefly.

It is convenient to think about the process of identifying a sample which will enable one to generalize to the population as a whole as involving two basic requirements. The first requirement is that the sample be *representative*. The second requirement is that sample be adequate, i.e., large enough.

The requirement of having an adequately large sample is obvious enough. A sample of one, in a political opinion poll, would clearly not yield a basis from which one could generalize to the voting behavior of the population of the United States as a whole, since a single person would presumably be voting either for candidate A or for candidate B, and you can be sure that 100 percent of the population will not be voting for one of these candidates. A sample of two or three or four is going to be just about as unsatisfactory. A sample of 100 percent of the population will of course give us the right answer, but it will destroy the whole value of surveys, namely, that they cost less than the election itself. Do we need a 50 percent sample? Without previous knowledge, one would guess that a 50 percent sample would be pretty safe. Could we get away with a 25 percent sample? Here is where one's intuition about the matter begins to weaken. The suggestion that we could do a good job with a sample of only 1 percent of the population would be pretty implausible if we didn't have the enormous body of successful predictions behind us that have resulted from modern survey techniques. Still, 1 percent of a population of 200 million is still 2 million people, and interviewing that many is going to be a highly expensive business. The situation today is that very good, although not the best possible, results can be obtained with a sample representing $\frac{1}{1000}$ of 1 percent of the population. It's obvious enough that the whole trick lies in the procedure whereby the sample is picked, and we'll turn to that in a moment. First let's get an idea of the general level of accuracy (or approximation) that we're talking about. This will depend upon a great many factors, but, roughly speaking, if we go from a sample of 2,000 to a sample of 4,000, we will not be more than a very few percentage points more accurate (that is, if we predict 54.6 percent will vote for candidate A from a sample of 2,000, we might, although it's quite unlikely, find that the sample of 4,000, equally carefully chosen, would lead us to correct this to 56.8 percent). It would be more typical for the change to be only a few fractions of 1 percent. If we go to a sample of 6,000 or 8,000 or 10,000, we'll virtually never pick up an improvement as large as 1 percent, more usually, it will be 0.1 percent, and obviously this is very rarely worthwhile. So it's a measure of the extreme efficiency of the sample selection procedures that they will get us so close with such a tiny sample, and we have to bear in mind that even if we took a sample 10 times as large, we could still be off substantially as far as predicting an election is concerned because of events that occur between the time of the polling and the election. Notice that there is a two-stage inference involved in political polls. First, there's the inference from the sample to a conclusion about which candidates people in general prefer at the time the sample is taken. Then, there's the prediction that that percentage of preference will hold up until the election. The second prediction is much chancier, and errors in it are really not something one can blame on the polling organization when, for example, a late-entering candidate begins to catch up very fast, or a scandal breaks. In any case, the kind of bet that's involved there is not the type of inference that we're concerned with at the moment; it's not an inference from a sample to a population, but an inference from the population's preferences at one time to its preferences at another time, which obviously doesn't depend on statistical considerations alone but on political stability and the emergence of new factors.

How do we go about selecting a sample in such a way that a size of $\frac{1}{1000}$ of 1 percent of the population is adequate? This is where we get to the question of the *representativeness* of the sample. There's no abstract rule that will answer this question for us. A sample may be representative with respect to political behavior, but completely unrepresentative with respect to marketing behavior. This is why George Gallup can command a rather substantial fee for his services: he knows what principles to use in selecting a sample for particular types of generalizations.

Basically, you have to start off by determining what factors affect political preferences. For example, it's well known that people with very large incomes tend to vote Republican rather than Democratic, so it's clear that your sample will have to include a proportion of upper-income people as well as lower-income people, or else it will be subject to what's called *bias* for picking from a group which doesn't have typical political preferences. Similarly, it's known that many more union members will tend to vote Democratic than nonunion members. So you have to be sure that your sample contains some of both. How many of each? The same proportion of each as the population contains. If 35 percent of the population (in this case, the population of voting adults is the one that you're concerned with) are union members, you take care that 35 percent of your sample will contain union members. Since men and women will quite often have different response patterns, especially but not only if a woman candidate is running, it's important to ensure that each 50 percent of your sample represents one or the other sex. Actually, it would be more precise to ensure that your sample has about the same proportion of each sex in it as *actually vote;* this might turn out to be a larger proportion of men than women in some cases, and possibly the reverse in other cases. Again, where issues that affect children are at stake, as is often true, a sample which represents the population's distribution between parents and nonparents is likely to be required.

Now you can begin to see that the selection of the sample will be very severely constrained, if it is to be a representative, yet small, sample. To tell if it is of adequate size, one will need other information of a purely empirical kind about the accuracy that can be achieved with samples of a certain size. If we have to meet twenty or thirty requirements on the sample in order for it to be representative with respect to the differences among people that affect their voting behavior, we may well have to go to a sample of 1,000 or so in order to meet all these conditions. (Obviously, you can't have a sample of ten people that will meet even the conditions that we've already described.) So the pressure of your knowledge about the number of (independent) factors that influence voting preferences will drive the sample size upward, and your interest in accuracy will of course also tend in the same direction. The great compromise that has to be made by the pollster is to decide on the point of diminishing returns, that is, the point at which further increases in the sample size will only produce improvements in accuracy that are insignificant for the purposes of the poll. If the poll is done (as many are) in secret, to advise a candidate of his or her chances, the results need be accurate only to within about 5 percent, or perhaps, at the beginning of a campaign, even 10 percent, since a serious effort in the campaign can swing the results that far without too much difficulty. If the poll is for national publication, and if the reputation of the pollster is at stake, it will be necessary to go to a rather larger sample, since a swing of only 1 percent or so will quite often decide a major election.

The Nielsen ratings, which determine the fate of most of the shows on television, at least the shows which represent the most substantial investment by the networks, are based upon the reactions of a very small sample of families; but, once again, we have empirical evidence that using a larger sample doesn't lead to significant changes in the results. Of course, it's another question entirely whether one should let the fate of a television show be determined by the number of families that are watching it. Since one is attempting to advise the advertisers who foot the bill for the show, the crucial relevant information would be the number of people who are led to purchase products by the advertising that occurs in the commercial breaks during the show. But we have so little empirical evidence about this that we fall back on the very crude measure of "total number of *viewers*," on the assumption that any viewer is equally likely to make a purchase of whatever is being advertised. That assumption is surely incorrect, but we don't know the direction in which it's incorrect. Sometimes people make guesses that certain types of product would be more appropriately sold to some types of viewer, the ones who are viewing a show of a particular kind, such as the broadcast of a football game, and they operate on these assumptions. But these are not really well based empirically. They are simply plausible bets. The television rating game is much more seldom based on scientific evidence than is the public opinion poll.

How does one tell whether a sample is representative? Obviously, from the preceding discussion, one needs to know a great deal about factors that influence whatever it is that one's trying to generalize about (which is normally called the *criterion variable*). We all have a great deal of knowledge of a general kind about what kinds of factors affect what kinds of behavior, and consequently, if we use our imagination, we're usually in a position to apply at least some basic tests to the sample that's being used in order to see whether it meets the standard of being *representative*. It's more difficult to judge whether it's *adequate;* there are technical statistical considerations that come into this, as well as a great deal of empirical knowledge. About all one can do here is to be very suspicious of very small numbers, unless one has prior "track record" evidence that suggests that the pollster has the required skill and evidence to make generalizations from very small samples.

An early disaster in the history of political surveys was the *Literary Digest* poll. This was a poll done to predict the outcome of a presidential election, and it was done by taking a substantial random sample of the names from telephone directories across the country, conducting the interview by telephone, and summing up the results in the usual way. Before reading any further, ask yourself whether that sample was a representative sample for the purpose. If you think it was not, write down, as precisely as you can, your reason for thinking that it wasn't representative.

The reason that it was not a representative sample is that, particularly at that time, people who owned telephones were not a representative sample of the economic strata of the voting population. They tended to be wealthier than people without telephones, and political voting is significantly affected by economic classification. As a result, the poll was excessively optimistic about the fate of the Republican candidate, so much so that its forecast was entirely wrong, and the failure was so widely known that the *Literary Digest* ceased to exist as a magazine.

Let's take a slightly more subtle case. One of the major polling organizations determines the sample of people that it wants to interview and then sends its interviewers out to find these people at their home addresses. If nobody is home when the pollster calls, the interviewer moves to an alternate name on the list, the name of somebody drawn from the subpopulation who has the same general characteristics as the person who's not at home. A rival organization has a slightly different approach. If the person selected is not at home, the interviewer is required to go back twice, at different times, in order to see if the person may then be home, before moving to an alternate name. Can you see what the reason might be for adopting the second procedure, by comparison with the first? If so, write it down before proceeding any further. (Forcing yourself to write down your reasons here is very important since it requires you to express them carefully and correctly. It may well be that you have a vague sense of what's wrong, but that if you were to try to express your feeling exactly, you would make a claim that wasn't correct. If you had tried to express it, you would notice this; and you would be forced to think the matter through a little further before settling on an answer.)

You have to ask yourself, What could explain the fact that somebody is not at home when the pollster calls? Well, during what hours is the pollster most likely to call? Interviewers normally work during the daytime, although they also work during the evenings. People who are most likely to be away from the house include all the adults in the family who hold jobs. Although it's also possible that people are away from the house because they're shopping or at a doctor's or dentist's office, it is virtually certain that they will be away if they hold a regular job. If you immediately move to an alternate choice, you will tend to be picking up an unrepresentatively small portion of families where both husband and wife hold jobs. Does that matter? It does matter, because such families have a stronger tendency to vote Democratic than other families. You might not know that fact directly, but you might be able to reason that it's rather likely, since, for example, the chances are greater that both members of the family will belong to a union, and you know that union membership is tied to a tendency to vote Democratic. Hence the "return visit" procedure, though more expensive, is likely to give better results.

Suppose that we want to take a poll on the subject of student opinion toward having campus security guards carry firearms, and we set ourselves up to interview people at a convenient campus location, let us say near the entrance to the campus cafeteria. Now we interview every tenth person who comes through the door. That looks like a pretty unbiased approach; but is it? (Treat this as question 7-A, 1.)

In talking about sampling procedures, one will often hear reference to the desirability of using a "random" sample. We'll conclude this section by saying a word or two about the concept of the random sample. If you want to make a generalization about a whole population, and it might be a population of insects or birds or trees, rather than the population of the United States, and you don't know anything about what characteristics of the population affect the property about which you want to generalize, your best bet is to take a purely random sample. This kind of sample we've been talking about is a hybrid between a purely random sample and an entirely specific, or nonrandom, sample. Suppose you are going to make a generalization about the purity of aspirins that are produced by commercial manufacturers. You are going to pull a sample of the pills from the various production lines and give these samples a complete chemical analysis. How should you pick the sample that you pull? A few obvious facts would occur to you; for example, you might suspect that the first few pills produced when the machines start up in the morning may not be very typical, since the chemicals may tend to concentrate or evaporate overnight, so you'd want to pick your sample from the main body of the day's production run (or to pick only a few from the early part of the morning run). Suppose that you decide, on statistical grounds, that you ought to look at perhaps one pill in four or five hundred. Suppose the day's production is 100,000 pills. That means you ought to pull a sample of about 200 pills. Should you step in in the middle of the run and take 200 pills off the moving belt all at once? No, because you know very little about what affects the purity of the pills. There may be various factors that depend on the time of day, the operating temperature of the machinery, the addition of new loads of chemical, shifts in the machine supervisors and operators, and so on. It will clearly be much better to space out your sample collection across a day's production run. It may be better still to space it out across several days. A good strategy might seem to be to pick out every five-hundredth pill that comes down the line, since whatever factors are affecting production, they are unlikely to be precisely timed so that every five-hundredth pill will have characteristics different from the rest of the production run. Still, the machinery may make changes every 500 or 5,000 pills. So you will get an even more random sample by using a table of random numbers to determine time intervals or pill numbers, and then pick whatever pill happens to be passing down the production belt as your timer or counter indicates the next random number from the table of random numbers.

If you're interested in the details of how this might work on a time basis, you would use a clock that registers in hours, tenths of hours, and hundredths of hours (instead of the usual hours, minutes, and seconds). Then you'd pick three digits from your random-number table, say 391, and you'd pick a sample at hour 3.91—whatever pill was passing by a certain point on the belt at that moment. Now you pick a second three-digit number from your random number table, or perhaps just use the next three digits from the table, and pick a pill from the production line corresponding to that time, and so on until you have your sample of 200 pills for the day. This system will certainly give you a sample that is not correlated with any systematic defects in the equipment.

If you want to do an experiment on the relative benefits obtained from the use of different reading programs, you normally have to compare the achievements of a group of pupils that uses one of these against the achievements of a group of pupils that uses another. How do you tell which students should go into which group? A good procedure is to "randomly assign" pupils to the two groups. How do you do this? A common procedure is to alphabetize the names of the pupils and then allocate alternate names to each of the groups. This assumes, and it's a very plausible assumption, that there is unlikely to be any correlation between natural talent for learning reading and a person's numerical position on an alphabetized class-order sheet.

Using a more selective procedure than pure randomization, as done in the Gallup poll, increases the "efficiency" of the sampling; that is, it means that you can achieve a generalization with the same degree of reliability from a smaller sample. The technical name for the procedure of placing certain constraints on your sample—for example, that it contain about the same proportion of men and women as the population that you want to generalize about—is *stratification*. We talk about stratifying a sample with reference to sex, socioeconomic status, age, IQ, and other characteristics. In the experiment on the relative effectiveness of two reading programs, we would normally stratify the sample by requiring that each group contain an equal number of boys and girls, roughly an equal number of high, middle, and low IQ pupils, and so on. The way we would do this in practice would involve grouping the students under these headings—e.g., group the names of all the boys together, and the names of all the girls, and then we would randomly select half the boys to go into the experimental group and half the girls to go into the same group. We could make this random selection by the procedure of taking alternate names from the alphabetized list that we've already talked about, or by various other procedures including the use of random-number tables. If we carefully "match" the two groups in terms of these variables (sex, IQ, etc.) that definitely do affect ability to learn from certain reading materials, we can attach greater reliability to our generalization about the population from which we took the sample; or we can use a smaller sample and achieve the same degree of reliability in the generalization. This is the use of "stratified random samples" and "control groups," two of the most important procedures in scientific method.

We've been talking about inferential statistics; there are also interesting problems about reasoning with descriptive statistics. Everybody knows that talking about the "average American" or the "average woman" can conceal a multitude of misleading conclusions. A more careful study of descriptive statistics leads us to distinguish between three or four quite different senses of the term "average," for example, the types of average that are described as the *mean,* the *median,* and the *mode.* We won't go into detail about these matters here, since most of you will have had some elementary statistics in one or another social science course, or can achieve a very good understanding of these points by reading the first chapter in any statistics text. The discussion of inferential statistics above is somewhat unlike that normally provided in a statistics text, and it stresses certain similarities to other types of reasoning that we've discussed elsewhere in the book, rather than treat it all as a mysterious new subject. In particular, we had to set up the discussion of samples in order that, in Section 7-4, we can talk about causation a little more adequately. Section 7-4, as well as 7-2 and 7-3, also involves a discussion of types of reasoning that are very important in science, so we don't want to suggest that inference from and to populations is the one key scientific type of reasoning. But it is a very important type of scientific reasoning.

7-2 INDIVIDUALS AND GENERALIZATIONS: ETHICS, BIAS, AND PREJUDICE

We have been talking in the previous section about the inference from facts about individuals to facts about the population of which they are parts. In this section we're going to talk about reasoning from facts about a whole population to conclusions about the individual members of the population. This type of reasoning has about the same kind of status in ethics as the previous type of reasoning has in science. That is, it is one important type of reasoning, and it raises a number of crucial ethical questions; but it isn't by any means the only kind of reasoning in ethics, and indeed it represents a type of reasoning that is very important in science, too.

Suppose you know that women are, in general, less strong physically than men (taking up again an example we discussed earlier). Suppose that you are in charge of the selection of drivers for a taxicab company. You know that there are occasions when some physical strength is required in the performance of the tasks of changing a wheel and moving fairly heavy luggage for people who can't lift it themselves, and perhaps, in some cases, resisting physical assault. Are you entitled to place an advertisement for applicants in which you require that only men apply? That's an ethical question,[1] but of course it's also partly a question about the reverse type of reasoning from the kind we discussed in the last section. Given the truth of the generalization about women, what do you really know about the individuals? Of course, the answer is that you know very little. The ethical point arises because you really don't know very much about the individuals. It stresses the fact that since your action will affect individuals, you must not, morally or ethically speaking, act in a way that condemns individuals as a result of their membership in a population which can have certain general characteristics that they, as individuals, may not share at all. To put the matter more tangibly, you are certainly not entitled to restrict applicants to men, since there may well be, and often are, women who are just as capable in performing the whole range of tasks involved as men, and may indeed be far more capable than most men. And, more to the point, more capable than many or all of the male applicants.

It's important to realize that there are conceivable circumstances where a generalization about a certain group may be a satisfactory basis for action, indeed may be a morally sound basis for action. For example, when calling for volunteers for an especially hazardous mission, the commanding officer may restrict the volunteers to people with no dependents. Obviously, he's working off the generalization that people with no dependents typically have fewer responsibilities, or fewer serious responsibilities, to other human beings than those with a family. However, this may not be true in all cases. The excuse for using it as the basis for action is the lack of time to go into a detailed history to decide which single people support aged parents or young siblings, and as a generalization, it's probably true that people with families do have slightly more "lives at stake" than single people do. That is the crucial feature of this situation. First, there is a true and relevant generalization, and it isn't offset by any other equally probable generalization that points in some other direction. Second, there isn't time to get down to the details of the particular cases.

It's because the second of these conditions is not met in the usual employment situation that restrictive advertising or recruiting is usually not justified. Of course, one might try to justify it on purely practical grounds. It's more likely that a male applicant will pass the minimum tests for physical strength that the Detroit police department uses, hence it saves money to restrict applicants to males. And this is quite certainly true, but it's not

---

[1] And also, thanks to recent legislation, a legal question.

enough to offset the very serious general consequences of accepting the argument. The general or system consequences of accepting the argument are that we exclude all women from police forces, even those who have the necessary physical strength. As a result, a certain point of view on crimes that affect women—especially rape—and a crucial dimension of representativeness, which can strongly affect the rapport with and faith in the police force, are lost.

These general consequences are often overlooked by employers making a choice that is, in the short run, advantageous for them. And it is for this reason that the state argues it should step in and enforce laws about affirmative action and other fair employment practices.

It's undoubtedly true that there are a great many white men in the country who would not enjoy taking orders from a black supervisor or office manager. And, although the reverse is certainly true in some cases, the generalization that "blacks will tend to encounter more resistance in getting their orders carried out" is true. If we use it as a basis for restricting applications for senior positions to whites, we will of course be preserving the status quo, and ensuring that the prejudice that presently exists is not overcome. These general effects we are very anxious to avoid in the name of justice, and it is because these effects follow that we argue against the legitimacy of using the generalization as a justification for action in individual cases—except for emergency situations.

You can see how this ties into the type of issue mentioned at the end of the preceding section: descriptive statistics tells us something about the whole population, but it does it by condensing the information about individuals, and usually by representing the population in terms of its average, its range, or other classification. Such general descriptions of a population are extraordinarily useful for many decision purposes, for example, they may help us decide where we should put our effort in changing the school system. But they must be regarded as items of information to be used with very great care when we wish to take action on the fate of an individual person.

The tendency to act improperly from generalizations of this kind is part, though not the worst part, of what is referred to as racist or sexist behavior. The worst type of racist or sexist behavior, or prejudiced or biased behavior in general, occurs when the action is based on a false generalization that should be known to be false. The generalization may be false because it is expressed in terms of all members of the given group having a certain characteristic, whereas only some or perhaps most of the group have that characteristic. If all members of the group had the characteristic, and if that characteristic is relevant to appointing, promoting, selecting, and rewarding employees, it would be appropriate to use the generalization. But very few generalizations about human beings fall into this category, and to act as if they do, when such action may adversely affect the interests of the people to whom the generalization refers, is to act from bias or prejudice, which in particular cases is called sexism or racism.

Just as descriptive statistics provides extremely useful ways to interpret or understand huge bodies of data that would otherwise be quite unintelligible, so the procedure of *stereotyping* is a very natural and useful type of human thinking. It amounts to representing groups of things or people by a single, allegedly typical, example. But the "fallacy of stereotyping" consists in treating this stereotype as if it represents all the individuals in the group of which it may be a fairly typical example. So the stereotypes of the campus radical, or of the hippie, or of the businessperson or of the surgeon or lawyer or Mexican or professor, are all useful devices, in a rough-and-ready kind of way, for certain types of thinking. They may represent the general characteristics of a population quite well and may be useful for contrasting one population with another. (Think of the "typical" Republican versus the "typical" Democrat, for example.) But when it comes down to cases, you have to be willing to face the fact that an individual may, as we say, shatter the stereotype. The extent to which human beings are capable of reacting flexibly, openly, and rationally to a person who is very unlike the stereotype of the population from which he or she comes is a measure of their reasonableness and of their capacity for justice.

It's unwise to act as if all stereotyping is always fallacious. It is sometimes used as a shorthand for the "fallacy of stereotyping," in which case it does mean something fallacious or morally improper. But, to be precise about the term, we have to recognize that it's no more fallacious than talking about ideal types (the ideal manager or parent) or typical Catholics, atheists, and Baptists. There is scientific information which entitles one to make claims about typical people from certain groups; but it in no way legitimates drawing conclusions about a given individual with a membership in that group unless absolutely nothing else is known about the individual, and then only a probable conclusion. It doesn't justify action with respect to that individual, unless no other information about that individual can be discovered, say during a job interview.

Bias and prejudice, then, are to be seen as conclusions or actions based upon either false generalizations or generalizations improperly applied to an individual case. Notice that there is an error in either the premises or the inference of an argument in each of these cases. It's crucial to realize that bias and prejudice are forms of error. This seems obvious enough, but if you listen to the way the words are used today, you'll notice that we have drifted toward calling people who have definite views on a particular subject "biased" with respect to that subject, regardless of whether their views are right or wrong. This is a particularly unfortunate position, since it implicitly assumes that people can't be correctly convinced about any issue on which somebody else is convinced to the contrary. If this were true, it would be prejudiced to regard the earth as being round rather than flat. There are still some enthusiastic members of Flat-Earth Societies around the globe.

Let's be clear about what we're saying. Suppose that we're going to appoint a new commission to investigate the legitimacy of the death penalty in the state of Idaho, where the matter has recently become a controversial one. A particular man is proposed. Someone says that he's biased because he is well known for his strong commitment to the necessity of the death penalty. It's of course a general truth that we don't want to entrust a matter of importance to biased people, because "biased" carries the implication of falsehood. In this case, however, we're not entitled to that implication unless we've already settled the issue of which position is false, but that's why we're setting up the commission. You're not entitled to call a man biased because he supports the death penalty vehemently, or because he opposes it vehemently. You're entitled to call him biased only if his reasons for supporting or opposing it are mere matters of prejudice—that is, if they involve demonstrably incorrect inferences or correct inferences from premises that are demonstrably false. You might think that at least somebody with a very strong prior commitment on an issue like this is incapable of understanding the alternative point of view and hence would not be a proper person to appoint to a group that will have to discuss the issue. But you have no idea whether that's true. These are separate dimensions of ability, and, although there's no doubt as to the statistical connection between them in that some, perhaps most, people who have strong views on one side of a matter are incapable of listening to the other side, the best people in the field are often not thus prejudiced. They hold a view which, although strong, cannot be faulted in terms of reasoning except by extremely sophisticated means, which have not yet been uncovered. They have, in short, an argument which appears to them, as rational people, to be a conclusive argument for their position. They recognize that there are arguments on the other side, but they believe they can identify weaknesses in those arguments. It's a fallacy and indeed a slur to identify such people as biased or prejudiced. The only respect in which they're like someone who is prejudiced is that they have a strong view on the subject. Unlike identifying somebody who obviously is biased and prejudiced, it isn't possible to show—certainly not easily—that they are reasoning erroneously. Hence, it isn't possible to tell whether people who maintain a certain position vigorously are biased or prejudiced. It's a matter of *what their reasons are,* and *what their knowledge of and capacity for assessing the reasons of the opposition are,* and *what their reaction would be to new evidence.* If they are immune to new evidence, if they dismiss the arguments of their opposition with trivial counterarguments or misrepresent these arguments, if they draw their own conclusions in a way which suggests that they are only providing rationalizations rather than good reasons for their opposition, they are biased or prejudiced. They may still be biased or prejudiced at some unconscious or not easily detectable level, but you can't hang somebody for that kind of possibility. If you could, suspicion would be grounds for imprisonment.

In the light of this discussion, you should answer one of the following questions and regard the one you pick as question 7-A, 2. Is a Women's Studies department entitled to restrict applicants for its faculty to women? Is a Black Studies department entitled to restrict its applicants to blacks? Is a department of religion entitled to regard an atheist as an ineligible applicant for a position? Is a department of political science entitled to regard a member of the Communist party as ineligible? Is a department of political science entitled to regard a committed Fascist and racist, for example, a neo-Nazi, as an ineligible applicant?

7-3 PROPERTIES AND GENERALIZATIONS: ANALOGY

Argument from analogy is a vitally important and extremely tricky type of argument. On the one hand, in science or ethics or the law, it is often the only type of argument that can be developed on an important issue. And, even where other arguments can be developed, argument by analogy is often the most powerful and compelling type of argument we can use. On the other hand, it is elusive in the sense that it's very hard to give its precise structure or to spell it out in full detail; and it is often double-edged in the sense that an analogy can be turned against the arguer to point to the opposite conclusion from the one which was proposed.

One of the reasons why analogies are difficult to handle is that they are a more abstract type of argument than the two kinds that we have been considering in the preceding sections. Just how much trickier they are is perhaps best demonstrated by saying that argument by analogy is identified as a *fallacy* in at least one widely used elementary logic textbook. What the author really means is that it's a fallacy to suppose that arguments by analogy give you as much certainty as deductive arguments—that is, those in which the steps depend only on the meaning of the terms. But it's not likely that anyone has ever really thought that argument by analogy provides one with that degree of certainty. Analogies supply us with what are sometimes called "plausibility arguments": Sometimes they provide us with a kind of grasp or understanding that persuades us of something, but their strong point is not the capacity for conferring absolute certainty upon the conclusions which they are used to support, or even a certainty as high as that of the premises from which the conclusion is inferred. Analogy is just a more explicit kind of reasoning than the simile or the metaphor, to which it is a natural cousin. Similes and metaphors are often used to convey implicitly some suggestion—some implied conclusion—which the analogy makes more explicit. They are legitimate *inductive* or probabilistic arguments, and are of central importance in science and law.

"Banning the possession of handguns is like shackling everybody except criminals." As expressed, this could well be described as a simile; but, because of the implicit implications, it can also be regarded as a condensed form of an analogy, which is really just an extended or complex simile—a claim about the similarity of two things. Now a simile can be used to suggest, as in this statement, that a certain conclusion should be accepted. It then becomes a compressed argument from analogy. In the example given, the implied conclusion in most contexts is that it would be wrong to ban the possession of handguns (since it's obviously wrong to shackle the innocent and let the guilty go free). Hence, argument by analogy consists of arguing from certain similarities between two things that are said to be analogous, to a conclusion (or conclusions) about one of them which is said to follow since the corresponding assertion holds about the other. Thus, if the things that are said to be analogous are X and Y, the analogy is supported by certain similarities (A,B,C) which may be left unspecified since they are thought to be so obvious. Our attention is then drawn to the fact that X or Y has the property p; hence, it is suggested, since X and Y are analogous, the other (Y or X) has the "corresponding" property q (the analogous property).

Running through the handgun example, we have an analogy between banning the possession of handguns (X), and shackling the innocent (Y); this would be supported by pointing to the fact that in both cases, people who are unwilling to defy the law will be handicapped (this is the similarity A). Now, since it clearly is morally wrong to shackle the innocent (this is the property p), it follows by analogy (so it is suggested) that it is morally wrong to ban the possession of handguns (this is the property q that corresponds in the case of X to the property p in the case of Y).

The logical structure of this argument is essentially that of reasoning from the existence of some similarities to the presence of another similarity. It could be described as reasoning from a sample of properties, which turn out to be common to two systems, to the conclusion that another property is also probably common to both systems. If you think back to the type of inference that's involved in going from a sample to properties of a population, you can see that this is a case of inferring from samples of the properties of two objects to a generalization about most of their properties, and hence to the conclusion that a particular one of interest will be shared by both of them.

Notice that it would be quite wrong to say that arguments from analogy involve jumping to the conclusion that all properties of the analogous objects are the same, since if all properties were the same, the objects would obviously be identical rather than merely analogous. One of the old favorites in discussing arguments by analogy is the ancient analogy between the state

and the human body, with the head of the state (notice the metaphor) representing the head (of the body), the police and army and the other branches
of the executive representing the arms and legs, the consumption of goods by
the state being represented by the consumption of food and other things by
the individual, and so on. Now it's clear that nobody putting forward this
analogy thought that there were no important differences between the human body and the state. For example, it's obvious that the separate limbs
cannot survive independently of the body, whereas the individuals in the
state, or groups of them, can survive, at least for long periods of time, and
often long enough to form a separate state, without connection to the rest of
the state. Hence, argument by analogy cannot be thought to be an argument
to the conclusion that all the properties of the two analogous systems are
held in common, although it would certainly follow from that, that the one
the conclusion refers to is held in common. Such arguments are, by their
very nature, arguments to the probable sharing of a certain property, based
upon the substantial extent to which other properties are shared.

Once we have this general picture of argument by analogy, it's obvious
how to go about criticizing it, though it's not at all obvious what constitutes
a *definitive refutation* of an argument by analogy. One criticizes such an
argument by pointing to what are called dysanalogies between the two systems, that is, properties which they do not share. An example is the capacity
for independent survival, just mentioned, in the analogy between the parts of
the body and the parts of the state.

Given that the argument is not intended to involve, as an intermediate
conclusion, the assertion that all the properties are the same, then what one
has to refute is the claim that most of the properties are the same, or that
properties of the type to which the conclusion refers are the same or mostly
the same. It's much harder to refute these "weak" generalizations involving
terms like "most" than it is to refute categorical generalizations referring to
"all" properties or objects. But the line of attack is clear enough; one has to
go about the process of looking at the properties of the two things being
compared, and see whether one can't make a case that they are mostly
different or that the particular type of property to which the conclusion
refers is, in fact, usually different in these two types of things.

A neat and powerful, but rather different, move consists in using the
very same analogy to argue for the opposite conclusion. In the case of the
analogy about the handgun laws, one can argue that shackling innocent
people makes it harder for them to move into the path of crime. The implied
conclusion is that the handgun law at least prevents, or tries to prevent,
people who are not already gun-wielding criminals from joining that group.
Some restrictions on freedom, it might be added in a conciliatory footnote,
are necessary in order to preserve the freedom of all.

The direct attack on the analogy, by listing the differences between the things that are being compared in order to undermine the plausibility of the suggestion that there's a crucial similarity, can also be illustrated in the case we've been discussing. Here we would say that banning handguns is not like manacling the innocents since it puts exactly the same manacles on the criminals, i.e., their possession of a gun now becomes grounds for prosecution, and we're thereby able to imprison many of them before violence is done to others. This is not paralleled by any feature of the alleged analogy of manacling the innocents. Moreover, it might be argued that possession of handguns results in a great many unintentional, serious, or fatal accidents, because most people who have guns are not experienced in taking the care necessary to use them properly and safely. Hence, there's a bonus for the innocent in the handgun legislation which doesn't correspond to any bonus in shackling the innocent.

In the course of the Watergate hearings before the Senate investigating committee, the second-in-command of the White House staff, John Ehrlichman, was asked if he could explain why the White House had thought it appropriate to hire burglars to break into the office of the psychiatrist who had been treating Daniel Ellsberg, the Pentagon consultant who released the Pentagon Papers to the press. It was clear that the White House hoped to get some "dirt" on Ellsberg, which could be used in a direct blackmailing procedure, or in a discrediting procedure with the press. Why was this thought to be an appropriate kind of procedure for the White House to engage in? Ehrlichman replied with an analogy, and you should treat it as an exercise to assess it, criticizing it if you feel that that's appropriate (Quiz 7-A, 3). Ehrlichman said that the situation was like the following: Suppose that you learned that in a safe deposit box in a bank vault in Washington, D.C., there was a map showing the location of an atomic bomb that was timed to go off the next day and blow up a large part of Washington. Breaking into that bank vault would, he suggested, be like breaking into Ellsberg's psychiatrist's office—what else could one reasonably do? It may be relevant to add a word or two about an exchange that followed immediately between one of the senators and Ehrlichman. The senator said that it occurred to him that the appropriate thing to do would be to call up the president of the bank and ask for the keys, explaining one's reasons. Ehrlichman replied that they had done the equivalent of that; they had attempted to bribe one of the nurses in the doctor's office to get them the file.

The final comment on analogy is to mention that the next step beyond it, in the sequence from metaphor through simile to analogy, is the concept of a *model*. Models, which are crucial in scientific thinking but also in political and business planning, are really elaborate analogies, sometimes of a highly formal kind (mathematical models, computer models) and sometimes of a vague and an almost poetic kind (the free enterprise model). One of the classic models in the history of science is the so-called planetary model of atomic structure. This was the view that the atom could be conceived of rather as a miniature solar system, with a nucleus that was extremely heavy compared with the "planets" swinging around it (which correspond to the electrons). These planetary electrons would be in relatively stable orbits, at distances from the nucleus which were very, very great compared with the diameter of the nucleus, which was, in turn, very great compared to the diameter of the planets. Now it turned out that this way of thinking about the structure of the atom was able to account for a great many of the phenomena that were known to physics at the time it was most popular. Notice that nobody was suggesting that all the properties of the solar system were shared by the atom. For example, there was no suggestion that the planetary electrons had satellites. A nice feature of models, and of analogies in general, is that they often suggest further similarities which, on investigation, turn out not only to hold but also to explain some puzzling phenomenon. In this particular case, an experiment, known as the Stern-Gerlach experiment, produced results quite impossible to explain on any known model of the atom, including the simple planetary model. Then somebody thought of the fact that in the solar system, the planets not only revolve around the sun, but they also rotate about their own axes. Suppose that one was to postulate the same in the atom, that is, suppose that each electron had some spin as well as a rate of revolution about the central nucleus. This would clearly give the system dynamic properties different from one in which the electrons had no significant spin; for example, they would have a store of energy over and above the kinetic energy due to the rotation in orbit. Hence, the results of interactions between streams of bombarding particles—or strong magnetic fields—and atoms would be different. It turned out that this difference was just about right to explain the results of the Stern-Gerlach experiment.

This kind of example has often been taken to show that the role of models in science is essentially *psychological,* that is, it assists the scientist in thinking up new hypotheses, but it has no real explanatory power in itself. The scientist uses the model to generate the new hypotheses, which he or she tests explicitly and if they turn out to be confirmed, adds them to the body of knowledge on the subject. While this is partially true, it involves a mistake about the nature of explanation, and to that topic we will turn in the next section. But, as a final example for this section, to link it to the next, you might discuss the widely held idea that scientific theories are analogous to scientific instruments, i.e., they serve to achieve an important end, but they do not have any intrinsic, true scientific content. Specifically, we invent notions like the electron and photon, the relativistic increase of mass with velocity, the gene, and so on, in order to enable us to generate predictions and assertions, but we should not conclude that these "hypothetical entities" have any real existence, any more than we should think that a surgeon's scalpel contains life-generating properties just because it can be used to save lives. Do you agree? (Quiz 7-C, 1)

7-4 EXPLANATIONS AND JUSTIFICATIONS: CAUSES AND REASONS

The topic of explanations and their nature is a vast one, and it is extensively discussed in the philosophy of science, as well as in the philosophy of history and elsewhere. We will not attempt here to elaborate on it at any length, but we will try to draw one important contrast, that between explanations and justifications, and to stress once more the creative-imaginative element that is involved in explanation hunting and so important in providing and criticizing powerful arguments.

You will recall our stressing that the process of criticism of argument characteristically involves the testing of inferences, and that the testing of inferences characteristically involves trying to think of circumstances in which the conclusion could be false even though the premises were true. Thinking of just one such case destroys a deductive argument completely (although it might be reformulable as a probabilistic argument); thinking of important *families* of such cases undermines and can eventually destroy even a probabilistic (inductive) argument. We stressed that there isn't any rule for thinking up such explanations, and one's ability to do it is improved by two activities. The first is a steady increase in one's general knowledge of what causes what, what sometimes affects what, and so on—knowledge that leads one to think of alternative explanations, by analogy if not from direct acquaintance. The second source of improvement lies in the skills gained through extensive practice in the criticism of arguments and in the setting forth of good arguments in the face of criticism.

What we call "imagination" is to a large extent the ability to draw on a very wide range of knowledge—of models, if you like—which illustrate some of the pitfalls that other proposed models may fall into. For example, in much of the research on extrasensory perception, the investigators have been quite inexperienced, and as a result have been all too easily persuaded that some extraordinary ability, such as telepathy, is being demonstrated, when in fact there are other possible explanations. If one has had considerable experience, both in reading the literature of previous investigations and in performing some oneself, and if one has acquaintances in the illusionist or "stage mentalist" guilds, one goes into such an investigation armed with a dozen or more alternative explanations that have to be ruled out before a persuasive case for telepathy can be made. The fact that there are a number of experiments where such alternative explanations do appear to have been refuted is what makes the field truly interesting. The fact that the casual kind of "parapsychological experience" such as a foreboding that turned out to be correct (or a dozen of them), or a dream which involved an event happening somewhere else (or a dozen of these), is of no interest to somebody who is familiar with the serious investigation of alternative, naturalistic explanations of these reports. The same applies to water-divining ("dowsing," "water witching"), fire-walking, psychic surgery, and like feats. One of the reasons people are so gullible about these areas is that organized science has reacted to them in a totally unscientific way, for the most part. Naturally enough, people whose common sense enables them to see that scientists can be, and frequently are, prejudiced along with everybody else suspect that the dismissal of such areas is just a sign of that prejudice. Sometimes it is, and sometimes it isn't. If one wishes to take these investigations seriously, one has to commit oneself to a very substantial course of study. It is now more than thirty years since I founded the first university-based research group for the investigation of parapsychological phenomena in the Southern Hemisphere, and the chain of investigations and discussion that has followed since has been amongst the most intellectually stimulating experiences of my life; not surprisingly, it has also led to a considerably expanded knowledge of ingenious ways of faking—consciously or unconsciously—supernatural phenomena. Let's see how ingenious you are at providing possible explanations of some of the phenomena that have recently been exhibited by the Israeli "psychic," Uri Geller (quiz 7-A, 3). One of his performances consists of asking the audience to pass up to him any wristwatches or pocket watches that have stopped working. After holding them in his hands for some time and attempting to "infuse them with psychic energy," they quite often start running again. What alternative explanations (to the psychic one) can you think of for this? How would you go about deciding whether the psychic explanation was correct?

Remember that, in Section 7-1, where we were talking about criticizing inferences from sample characteristics to "population characteristics," that is, to generalizations about the population, we stressed the fact that a major thrust in the criticism of such inferences consists in trying to think of explanations of why the sample would exhibit a certain characteristic although the population as a whole might not. For instance, a sample of names drawn from the telephone book, however randomly, will not be a politically representative sample of the population as a whole if people who get their names into telephone books have any characteristic that is politically different from characteristics of the population as a whole. Obviously, there is an economic nonrepresentativeness about telephone owners which invalidates the inference. Similarly, in Section 7-2, where we were thinking about inferences in the opposite direction, from characteristics of the population to characteristics of individuals, clearly we were trying to think of ways in which the assertions about the population could be true, but corresponding assertions about individuals false; that is, we were trying to think of alternatives to the view that the population had that property because each member or most of them, had the property, i.e., alternative explanations. If the generalization about the population is universal and exceptionless and categorical, and *only* then, one can proceed immediately to conclusions about the individuals. If the generalization about the population says something about what it *tends* to do, or what it *typically* does, or what its *average* member does, one can't draw any definite conclusions about the individual, only probabilistic conclusions that will be open to complete refutation by direct investigation of the particular individual. So the process of attempting to think of counterexplanations is central to the whole business of criticizing, and thus to the business of providing arguments. The very testing of an inference itself involves trying to think of a counterexplanation of the facts put forward as premises, other than the claim presented as the conclusion. (Usually; give an exception for Quiz 7-C, 7).

So much for connecting the discussion of explanations with what has gone before. Just a word or two about the nature of explanation itself, and then we can turn to the distinction between explanation and justification. Explanation is one of the most controversial concepts in logic and the philosophy of science. There are many people—probably the predominant school at the moment—who believe that explanations are just psychological devices of no intrinsic logical or scientific force. There are others who believe that explanations are both psychological devices *and* a key, possibly even *the* key, logical and scientific device. There are yet others who believe that the psychological content is merely incidental, but that a purely formal analysis of the concept can be provided which shows that it has a basic and important logical structure independent of the psychological aspects of it. It is certainly true in the history of science that particular models of explanation, notably the animistic and anthropomorphic models of explanation, have infused our thinking well beyond the range of their legitimate application. No doubt the reason why we like to explain phenomena in terms of animistic and anthropomorphic concepts is that they are so easy for us to understand because of our familiarity with animals and humans. Nevertheless, the fact that on occasions our psychological preferences and rigidities have tended to distort our patterns of scientific explanation is no ground for supposing that we can dispense with the psychological element in explanations. (That might simply be throwing out the baby with the bathwater.) Acquiring understanding, which is what one gets as a result of accumulating explanations, is the highest goal of learning, and it isn't just an old myth that suggests that's so. Understanding involves obtaining a "mental grasp" of a subject matter or a phenomenon, the capacity to apply it to new problems, for example. Explanations are much more than mere mnemonic devices (that is, memory-jogging devices, such as rhymes that give you the names of the American Presidents); they are richer and deeper than such devices. Like analogies, they generate much more than they start off with. When you are provided with a thorough explanation of electromagnetism or of the disease transmission cycle in the case of malaria, you are put in possession of a kind of framework for your knowledge in that area that spins off practical suggestions, theoretical conceptions, and marriages between the two.

Just because of this elusive semipsychological component in explanation, this requirement that the explanation convey understanding and not the mere ability to recite a few facts that are contained in the words used for the explanation, it is very difficult to pin down the difference between a satisfactory and an unsatisfactory explanation. Astrology offers an excellent example. Many people believe that they obtain real understanding of the character of somebody when they learn the sign under which that person was born. It is a belief which has been with us for thousands of years, and it is probably more popular now in Western cultures than it has been for hundreds of years. A group of distinguished scientists recently published a letter in the *Humanist* denouncing the resurgence of belief in astrology, but the letter exhibited very little more than prejudice, as far as an independent observer is concerned. As mentioned before, no careful, critical experiment has been performed in which astrological predictions have been matched against predictions made on other grounds. If one starts discussion of astrology at the general level, of course it's obvious that the configurations of the heavenly bodies have very marked effects on earthly phenomena, as tides and crops show. So, one is left to fall back on the fact that these distinguished scientists, none of whom has studied the subject directly, think there's nothing to it. That is hardly a persuasive or indeed a proper line of approach to the subject. One would have to argue that our knowledge of the general influences that do exist suggests very strongly that they would not extend to the formation of character or to a direct control of the particular kind of events on the earth's surface that are referred to in horoscopes, etc. However, one would also have to agree that we simply lack serious experimental investigations of the validity of astrological predictions.

There have been a great many occasions on which folk wisdom has turned out to be false, but there have also been a *very* large number of occasions when folk wisdom has turned out to be true or to contain part of the truth, after it had been scoffed at by organized science for a long time. The most obvious examples of this come from folk medicine, but there are others, including graphology, weather prediction, agriculture, and innumerable examples in the areas of crafts and athletics. An extremely healthy dose of skepticism about the reliability of science is an absolutely inevitable consequence of any scientific study of its track record. Not surprisingly, this is not a popular subject amongst scientists. People don't like to be shown to be inadequate according to their own standards, whether the standards are those of ethics or those of science. One of the most interesting borderline cases has been that of psychoanalytic theories, the validation or invalidation of which has been a bone of contention in psychology for more than half a century. At the other extreme, the Skinnerian version of behaviorism is equally controversial. In the political domain, the question of whether the Marxist dialectic provides genuine understanding is of the same kind.

All these "models" (or theories or conceptual schemes) provide the practitioners with a special language, a jargon of their own, and a large number of alleged explanations and predictions. How reliable are these explanations and predictions? How much *real* understanding, as opposed to *feeling* of understanding, do these approaches provide? How much better are the predictions that they yield than those of an intelligent observer not using these theories but using all the other background knowledge that we have about psychological or socioeconomic events? It's not easy to answer that because, in the first place, the experts from any one of these groups do not agree with one another to a very large extent. A rational approach requires very careful investigation of the theory for its internal clarity and coherence before one can even decide what "it" implies. Reason then requires that one compare its predictions with those based on other general knowledge, rather than with the mere standard of truth and falsity. It's easy to produce true predictions. For example, it'll surely be true that six years from now you'll either be married or not; but of course the value of that as a prediction is totally trivial. When we start looking for the *scientific* value of the predictions, retrodictions, and explanations generated by these theories, we have a very much harder standard to meet than if we're simply looking for truth. We have to find *new* and *valuable,* as well as true, predictions.

We now turn to the distinction between explanations and justifications—between causes and reasons, as it is sometimes put. The search for explanations, of which causes are a particular case, is the search for a framework into which one can fit a phenomenon in such a way that one can answer a whole series of questions about it, relate it to other phenomena in the same field, and so on. One is seeking to achieve understanding of the phenomenon. But the search for justifications, for good reasons for something, is conducted in a different framework, a framework with some, but not very much, overlap with the former. A justification has to be a good reason for a belief or an action; a *moral* justification has to be a set of reasons that are morally adequate to support a certain conclusion or action. The fact that the *cause* of your crashing into the plate glass door was your not seeing it in no way constitutes a good reason for crashing into the plate glass door. The fact that the *explanation* of your lying to a congressional investigating committee was that your job was at stake in no way provides a *moral justification* for the lying. All this seems obvious enough, but there is a philosophical position which has attempted to confound the two questions, the search for explanations and the search for justifications. This position, which is technically called "hard determinism," argues that first, on scientific grounds, we have to believe that there is an explanation of every event even if we don't have it at the moment; and second, that if there is an explanation of an event, the event had to occur in the way in which it did—could not have occurred in any other way—and hence any discussion of justification, or praise or blame or evaluation, is as inappropriate as talking about justifying the path of the planets in their orbits. What cannot be other than it is can scarcely be blamed for not being other than it is. Once one understands fully why something occurred, so the hard determinist argues, one can no longer see any point to the question of whether it *should* have occurred or *should* have been done, or whether it is or was right or wrong. Similarly with beliefs; since what we believe is determined by our hereditary composition and the environment to which we've been exposed, we cannot believe other than we do believe, and hence it is pointless to criticize our beliefs as if they could somehow have been different.

Without getting into the entire argument about free will and determinism, of which this discussion is part, it is important to understand the difficulty that the hard determinist is up against. When one says that a justification, like a proof, has to meet certain standards of evidence, or standards of moral probity if it's a moral justification, one is saying nothing more or less controversial than is involved in saying that in order to be considered for the Olympic trials, a miler has to have a best time that's under four minutes. We're not judging whether somebody should be blamed or praised in some peculiar sense in setting these standards; we only wish to assert that this kind of performance is what it takes to be eligible; and we may also wish to admire people who can run a mile in four minutes, just as we might also admire people who can wiggle their ears, or dance gracefully, or reach the rim of a basketball net without leaving the floor. In the same way, we may admire a sunset or a glider in flight. Arguments have to meet certain standards in order to be acceptable, standards that vary depending upon whether actions that risk life and death are at stake, whether a scientific reputation is in jeopardy, whether moral assessment is involved, and so on. If the standards of good argument are met, the argument in question gives a justification for the conclusion. If they're not met, it doesn't. The success of a particular individual in providing an adequate justification for an action may or may not be completely determined by his or her environment and heredity. But even if it is, it is still entirely appropriate to judge the person's performance in terms of the standards of merit that identify adequate justifications, just as it is with the mile runner. An argument that is less sound, or a moral justification that is less than adequate, can't be made to work any better by pointing out that it was produced by an illiterate. Of course such considerations may affect the extent to which you praise or blame the person for producing a substandard argument, but they don't have any effect at all on the standards of merit for the argument.

The French have a saying, *"Tout comprendre c'est tout pardonner"*—"To understand everything is to forgive everything." The suggestion is that once one has a full explanation of somebody's behavior, one must forgive it. That's not to be confused with the idea that once you understand somebody's behavior, you have to *approve* it. Approval requires justification, and causes don't produce justifications. Indeed, they don't produce arguments at all. In point of fact, it's not clear that to understand something, even completely, should lead one to forgive it. If one understands that it was an act of deliberate choice, made in self-interest, that led some man, after collecting a reward, to kill a kidnap victim so that he couldn't be recognized by the victim later, one may still feel totally unable to forgive the action and, indeed, one—in my view—*should* not forgive the action. However, that's an issue for the free will and determinism discussion in a Problems of Philosophy, or an Ethics course, and we'll pass by it for now. What we have to cling to firmly is the distinction between causes and reasons, between explanations and justifications, and the legitimacy of having standards for *evaluating* arguments, whether or not one has the theories and data required for *explaining* arguers.

It may seem like a rather abstract point. Why is it important at the practical level? Perhaps the most important practical connection lies through the concept of bias or prejudice, which we discussed in Section 7-2. Biases and prejudices are often causes of beliefs. Sometimes people get hung up on the fact that biases and prejudices are not always easy to detect, and conclude that perhaps they are always present and they are what always determine *all* our beliefs, the "arguments" that we put forward being essentially smoke screens, or "rationalizations," as they are sometimes called. One needs to keep a firm grip on reality here, and not be misled by an abstract philosophical argument. No secret bias or prejudice is forcing you to the belief that 2 and 2 are 4 or that siblings are brothers or sisters, or that triangles have three sides. These are matters of definition, and the whole realm of deductive argument is founded on inference according to such definitional rules. Of course, one can sometimes make errors in very complicated deductive arguments, and bias may lead us to make such errors. We should take care to scrutinize deductive arguments very carefully when they bear on an issue where we have strong feelings. But when all is said and done, and when several independent experts, with different biases and prejudices in the field, have all carefully checked out a fairly straightforward deductive argument, one is entitled to say that one has extremely strong grounds for supposing it to be a sound argument. The remote possibility does remain that there's an error there which is due to bias, but it is simply a remote possibility. When you see a car crossing the dividing line of the highway and heading straight toward you, the remote possibility exists that it's a hallucination, but you'd better not act on the basis of that remote possibility. You'd better get off the highway just as fast as you can and as safely as you can, and if you can't do all that, get off the highway unsafely. Remote possibilities are not what you should guide your life by. The same applies to the hypothesis of universal bias and prejudice as the "real" determiner of all our conclusions. If I set out to decide whether it's better to invest my savings in a savings account or in tax-free bonds, there's a procedure for doing this rationally. It involves calculating the extent to which the difference in taxation balances off against the difference in safety, and if a few certified public accountants specializing in tax advising all agree that my conclusions are correctly drawn, then I can forget about the possibility of bias and prejudice. It's there, but it's too small to take seriously in an action context.

When we get into the area of race relations or ethics or international politics, of course it's much easier for bias and prejudice to operate without being detectable. But that's no more interesting than saying that theoretical physics is much harder to understand than elementary chemistry, and hence we have to look more carefully at what appear to be good arguments, and be willing to recognize that a greater degree of skepticism about the conclusions is appropriate. It doesn't follow that nothing can ever be established beyond reasonable doubt in the area, or that bias and prejudice are determining most, or even a significant part, of the conclusions that are drawn. We have a long history of these subjects to guide us, and it shows that mistakes do occasionally occur and are sometimes serious, even when careful tests of the argument have been made, but not often. So first we look for counterexplanations of the data that haven't been considered in arriving at the conclusion that is put forward as the underlying explanation. We look for counterarguments. We look for technical flaws in the premises and inferences. We use subject-matter experts and logical experts of different viewpoints and backgrounds to do the looking. At that point, we're in a position to make a judgment with considerable confidence. We can still be wrong, but that possibility is no longer very likely. You may get run over when crossing the street, but the chances are negligible if you look both ways.

Consider one practical application of these considerations to the role of the teacher of a controversial subject. Some people have argued that a teacher of philosophy, say, who is about to embark on a discussion of the problem of the existence of God should begin by laying out his or her "prejudices" on the table. This is thought to be "honest" and to show a willingness to recognize the fallibility of (even) professors. As exercise 7-A, 5, discuss the following reaction to that position.

> Far from being honest and helpful, this is a crowd-pleasing confession of incompetence. If what is being laid out are simply one's positions on the issues about to be discussed, then—since these issues are within one's field of professional competence—one presumably has what one takes to be good arguments for them. Hence they're *not* known to be prejudices and should not be described as such, since prejudices definitionally involve identifiable errors. If these conclusions are conclusions that *can't* be reached by good reasoning, then it's professionally inappropriate to hold them as conclusions, and it is a concession of gross incompetence to maintain them as positions at all. If one isn't quite sure whether the arguments one has establish one's conclusions, then the time to mention *that* is when you get to laying them out, at which point you can indicate that you're not convinced that they really establish the conclusions. After all, it's a professional judgment that an argument is not decisive. Again, there is no justification for the advance announcements. These advance announcements may be crowd-pleasing, but they concede the *propriety of prejudice* in the expert. A professor should restrict himself or herself to making clear how frequently the alleged experts turn out to be wrong or in conflict on subjects about which they're quite dogmatic, and add to this—if it's felt to be necessary—the fact that it's clear that this will apply to the present speaker or writer as well as to most other people. But the one thing that can't be done is for somebody to identify the prejudices that are *unconsciously* affecting them—that's a contradiction in terms—and the one thing that's inconsistent with professional standards is to identify prejudices that are consciously recognized as such, and still wish to maintain the conclusions they affect as sound professional judgments.

The last topic in this section concerns causation itself. Everyone knows that one has to distinguish causal connections from mere correlations. The Bureau of Statistics tells us that there was a steady rise in real family income through the 1960s at the same time as there was a steady decline in the birthrate. By applying statistical tests, we can discover whether this correlation is truly significant or a mere coincidence—like a tricky run of five successive throws of "doubles" with a pair of dice (where the two dice come up with the same number on each throw). But that doesn't tell us whether increased wealth causes reduced childbearing, or whether something else (e.g., better technology) produces both effects. The early days of investigation into the relationship between smoking and lung cancer mostly involved reports of high positive correlations, but nobody could be sure that there was a causal connection. It's generally much harder to establish causation than correlation. As usual, the trick is mainly that of trying to find alternative explanations, and then ruling them out by direct experiments and observations. For example, the smoking/cancer correlation might reflect the fact that heavy smokers tend to be city dwellers and that either the stress or the atmosphere of cities tends to produce lung cancer. To rule out this hypothesis, we'd look deeper into the statistics to see whether we found a big difference in cancer rates amongst city dwellers, depending on their smoking level; and the same for country dwellers.

But what about the possibility that there is some genetic predisposition in some people that tends to lead them to smoke and *also* tends to give them lung cancer? If this were true, the smoking wouldn't be causing the lung cancer but of course there would still be a high correlation between the two. Here we can easily design, in the abstract, an experiment that will decide the issue: We would simply pick a large random sample of children, divide them (randomly) into two groups, and ensure, by bribes or coercion, that one of these groups did not smoke, and that the other did smoke heavily.[2] Fifty years later, we'd know the answer. This type of design, the so-called fully-controlled, fully-experimental study is always the best design for identifying causes; but, as here, it frequently involves completely immoral manipulation of human beings. And it's just a little slow in getting results.

A number of other very clever insights were required to establish beyond reasonable doubt that smoking really does cause lung cancer. For example, a study of adult converts to Mormonism (which prohibits smoking) who previously smoked showed that the younger they were when they gave up smoking, the better their chances of not getting cancer. Making the rather plausible assumption that conversion to Mormonism is not controlled by any (hypothetical) genetic factor that produces smoking and cancer, we have here a sample of people in which circumstances have almost acted like an experimenter in "manipulating" the amount of smoking people do, and we find that it does "control" lung cancer. There were also experiments with mice which showed that skin cancers could be induced by painting their skins with the tars and nicotine from cigarettes. This web of indirect evidence gradually built up the strength of the causal conclusion beyond reasonable doubt.

Suppose that we discover there's a very much higher incidence of cancer of the uterus among women who are using birth-control pills than among those who are not (that is, we have a high *correlation*). Do we have good grounds for inferring a causal connection? If not, exactly why not, and how could we settle the issue? (Quiz 7-A, 6)

The importance of causes is their connection with *control*. Correlations as such give us no basis for control, though they may be useful for *prediction*. It used to be thought that there was a significant correlation between the sunspot cycle and business prosperity. If true, it would hardly help control

[2] Except for one possibility—what is it? (Quiz 7-C, 8)

the latter; but since sunspots are semipredictable, we would have had a useful predictor nonetheless. The early symptoms of a disease are another example of something which is a useful predictor but useless for manipulation.

Suppose there are two or three small towns in the United States with a high degree of fluoridation of the water, and two or three with essentially zero fluorides in the water supply. If there is a very large difference in the incidence of dental cavities between the two groups, favoring the first, do you have persuasive evidence for fluoridating the water of cities with less than the fluoride level of the low-cavity towns? Spell out your reasons in full. (Quiz 7-B, 5)

The governor of Connecticut once introduced mandatory suspension of licenses for speeding. There was a 30 percent (or thereabouts) decline in highway fatalities in the first year of the mandate. He was very proud of this. Before you joined in the congratulations, what would you have wanted to know that you (and he) could know there and then? (7-B, 6)

7-5 DIALOGUES AND DEBATES

Although dialogues and debates do represent special types of argument, and a little can be said about them under that heading, they also represent something more crucial to the process of reasoning than that comment suggests. One can illustrate this by mentioning that one of the most original and influential philosophers of the twentieth century, Ludwig Wittgenstein, used to claim that there was really no point at all in philosophical writing, only in philosophical discussions (dialogues). What he had in mind was something like this: On very important issues that involve really complex and abstract ideas, as do philosophical—and ethical and political—issues, there's no way in which all the possible lines of support and defense can be set out within the available period of time, even if somebody could or would read or listen to them all. Hence, the only sensible procedure is to begin by indicating a general line of thought in order to get the immediate reactions of those with whom one is interacting, to focus on the worries that they have (rather than all possible worries), to produce one's argument for handling those worries, and to go on from there. Thus the dialogue proceeds along the lines where the needs of the parties involved turn out to be greatest, rather than attempt to cope with all needs of all possible parties to such discussion or disputes. There is a long tradition behind this approach, beginning in Western history with the Platonic dialogues, and in Eastern philosophy long before that. It's thus not an accident that the dialogue is the chosen method for dealing with these complicated issues; it is probably the best.

There have been philosophers who even made a philosophy out of the structure of dialogue: the so-called Hegelian synthesis was achieved as a result of the process of putting forward a position, called the *thesis,* followed by the counterpresentation of an "anti-thesis," the emergence of a "synthesis" from these, and then of an antithesis to the synthesis, and so on.

So one extremely important feature of dialogue is that it provides one with an opportunity to get early reactions to a line of argument. Therefore it is more appropriate in dialogue to begin by presenting the main thread, or the first steps of an argument, and then encouraging a response. Long speeches for openers leave too little possibility for adequate interaction. (These conclusions might well be applied to most meetings and many lecture-courses, as is done in the "Personalized System of Instruction" or the Keller plan, now quite widely used at the college level, emphasizing individual interactions and eliminating most lecturing.) It is important to distinguish between serious dialogue or discussion and a certain type of debate, where the "game" is to "score points," rather than to reach the best solution. One of the drawbacks about the "debating team" approach as a way of instructing people in reasoning techniques (which is not its only purpose) is that it tends to make too much of a fetish out of point-scoring, rather than, for example, willingness to compromise when one is convinced that the opponents have a better argument, and so on. In short, its risk is that it may lead one to trade in truth for competitive superiority. On the other hand, it has some excellent virtues; for example, it requires that one fight as hard as possible, dig as deep as possible, for defenses which at first sight one might not have supposed existed for the position which one is allocated or adopts at the beginning. This is an excellent exercise in that it teaches you that one's first picture of a position is often very misleading as to the extent of its rather readily available support. Again, debate format encourages you to try to anticipate the objections that will be made by the opponent. This is excellent practice for the step in argument analysis of introducing other relevant arguments (and counterarguments). It makes straw-man arguments suicidal. It is also excellent practice for trying to distinguish between strong and weak criticisms of the opponents' arguments, since the limitations on time, and the need to appeal to an audience that will judge the issue, make it necessary to focus on a relatively small proportion of the possible points that one could make. Again, public speaking skills can be improved enormously with debate experience. But there is no substitute for systematic written analysis, repeated until one has a concise and potent presentation. It is the best basis for debate—and for all serious thinking.

Dialogue and debate stress the importance of *communication,* as opposed to mere exposition, a stress that has characterized this text throughout. Rhetoric does the same; and many of the skills discussed and presumably communicated in this book are often covered in courses in a department of rhetoric, or speech, or communication. This fact illustrates the growing emphasis in recent decades on the communication aspect of reasoning. It isn't a new tradition, since it is to be found not only in Plato but also in the Sophists of ancient Greece, and again in the Paris schools of the Middle Ages. But it is very much more practical than the preoccupation with symbolic logic that has become the domain of the philosophy department in present-day universities. Although we have not brought into this text many of the technical concepts and historical schools in rhetoric (or in jurisprudence, for that matter, where there are other equally relevant traditions), this omission is mainly from a desire to avoid greater length, not from a belief in their lack of relevance.

One of the issues that comes up in the course of dialogue and debate concerns the credibility of authorities, including sometimes the authority of the person with whom the debate or dialogue is being conducted. There are no really useful general rules for determining who is to count as a reliable authority, except by referring to their track record in relevant cases. It's very little use to quote physicists on political issues or politicians on issues in physics. Nevertheless, there is a tendency to quote scientists outside their specialty fields as if their scientific approach could be relied on to transfer across the boundary of their specialty. Although there are some outstanding examples of scientists with this kind of general rational approach, there are a tremendous number of them who are in absolutely no way superior to any other functioning adult with respect to topics outside their fields of expertise: they are just as subject to prejudice, to lack of relevant knowledge, and to overestimates of their own acuity. (This, by the way, is certainly a self-referential statement.) One footnote might be useful: It is worth attempting to distinguish between the concepts of *credibility* (of an authority, a witness, or other qualified person), *reliability,* and *consistency.* Reliability (sometimes called validity) refers to the "absolute" question of whether or not the authority is right. That's what we might be able to get from an estimate of prior track record. In the absence of direct evidence of reliability, we tend to fall back on two rather weaker indicators of it. Consistency is one of them. It breaks out into (1) internal consistency, and (2) consistency with others. It's a sign of probable lack of reliability, if there is substantial internal inconsistency. (But some of it can be tolerated, though at the price of not being able to tell what is being said on the specific points on which there is inconsistency.) It's also something of a point against a witness or an authority that there is poor agreement with other alleged authorities. But again, it's not really a fatal objection. It just means that a third party, an observer or listener, isn't able to make a decision: think of all the court arguments between "expert" psychiatric witnesses as to the sanity of the accused. Finally, there is the question of the credibility of the witness, which will likely be assured by evidence of reliability, but might require something more than that. Credibility is a function of the extent to which the audience which we are currently addressing believes the witness; and that may mean that considerations of the extent to which the audience can understand certain technical language that the witness uses, the extent to which the witness appears forthright in manner, meets the eyes of the interrogators, lacks any predisposing personal interests in this case, and so on, may come in, even though they are, strictly speaking, very, very weak and possibly zero indicators of reliability. That is, when we are talking about credibility, we have to talk about what the audience *thinks* indicates reliability, and not just what *does* indicate reliability. This is a serious consideration for lawyers planning which witnesses to call. In the same way, when you are thinking about giving an argument in front of an audience, you have to think about what the audience will understand, not just about what will constitute a valid argument.

The other side of this divergence between reliability and credibility (which is not an ideal state of affairs) is that a ruthless dialectician or debater can often make points illicitly against an opponent by exploiting the extent to which the audience can be persuaded not to believe someone by means which should not actually impugn their reliability. Into this category fall most of the so-called ad hominem moves: attacks on the person rather than the argument. The attempt to disparage testimony by showing that the moral character of the witness is questionable, is sometimes appropriate, but it is often used when it is not appropriate. For example, the sexual life of a plaintiff, including such matters as whether the person is engaged in prostitution, has traditionally been brought in at rape trials, although this is, one might well argue, improper, since it has an effect on the jury that is quite disproportionate to its relevance to the credibility of the witness. Its use is all too often a case of the exploitation of prejudice, and it has no place in sound reasoning or justice.

QUIZ 7-A

1 Suppose that we want to take a poll on the subject of student opinion on arming campus security guards with firearms, and we set ourselves up to interview people at a convenient campus location, let us say near the entrance to the campus cafeteria. Now we interview every tenth person who comes through the door. That looks like a pretty unbiased approach; but is it?

Answer

The population that you wish to generalize about is *all students*. The crucial question is whether a representative sample of all students will come through the campus cafeteria during the time (unspecified) that we sit there. In the first place, the answer is definitely no, since those who bring their own food to campus and eat in offices or classrooms will not show up; and they may well be different from those who use the cafeteria with respect to the question that we're interested in, since they will certainly be different with respect to work habits and socioeconomic status, which are quite likely to correlate with attitudes toward authority. For example, the students who see themselves as important components of the campus social system tend to do a good deal of their socializing in the cafeteria building. These students are more likely to be identified with student government's opinion on campus than those who are relatively more socially isolated and hence likely to be those who eat by themselves without placing the need for human company very high. Similar points may be relevant about those who frequent more expensive eating places than the cafeteria. Again, since the time of our interviewing isn't specified, the extent to which we pick up what may be a substantial population of evening students cannot be determined. And it is well known that evening students tend to come from a different age group, social class, and motivational group from daytime students.

2 Is a Women's Studies department entitled to restrict applicants for its faculty to women?

Answer

No, attractive though the compensatory argument seems (that is, the argument that women have been underrepresented on college faculties for a very long time and should at least be given the chance to have a preeminent position in the line for jobs in "their own" department). The most attractive intellectual type of argument (as opposed to the social-political one just mentioned) is that only women would have the kind of experience that would form an adequate basis for teaching the kind of subjects that are covered in a Women's Studies department. However, that argument is not satisfactory since there are two powerful considerations that suggest the appropriateness of at least some men on the faculty of any such department that aims to provide a reasonably comprehensive view of the kind of topics taught in the department. First, the argument can be made that, at least, "the other side" should be heard from occasionally; that is, it is a characteristic of courses under Women's Studies that they present a rather strong profeminist point of view. It's not unreasonable to require that a total program provide at least some place for a discussion of either the feminist point of view by someone other than a woman, or even a nonfeminist or antifeminist point of view. The second argument is a pedagogical one: At least part of the audience for courses on women will be men, or, at the very least, part of the "audience" with which women will have to interact will be men; a representation of men will therefore have some advantages in making the learning more effective, particularly for men (since they will have at least one role model available), but also for women (who also must deal with men).

You may have chosen one of the other questions. Each has its own special features, and the answer isn't the same in all cases; or at least it's not the same to the same degree. Read the preceding answer carefully for clues to the question which you tackled. (See question 5 in Quiz 7-C.)

3 Comment on Ehrlichman's analogy that was presented toward the end of Section 7-3 (p. 213).

Answer

The direct attack consists here in saying that there's a complete difference in the potential importance of the evidence that would be obtained by the illegal procedure in the two cases. In one case, the information was to be used to denigrate political opponents' criticisms of the government. In the other case, the lives of hundreds of thousands of people would be saved. It is a particularly significant fact that such a difference should have been completely overlooked by Ehrlichman.

The analogy can be turned on itself by arguing that if this kind of analogy is thought to be satisfactory, then doing anything that would further the cause of the political party in power would be justified, since it is clear that this is being identified with the welfare of hundreds of thousands of people, perhaps with the nation as a whole. It would surely then be quite appropriate to imprison vociferous critics of the government in power on the ground that they were causing serious disruption in the society. In short, the standard justification of dictators! (The law is treated as a tool for the party in power, rather than as a protector of all people alike.)

4   How might you explain Uri Geller's "trick" of starting up watches that have stopped running by holding them in his hands in order to "infuse them with psychic energy"—*without* appealing to the supernatural?

Answer

The most usual reason for a wristwatch or pocketwatch to stop running, and still be carried, is that the lubricants have become exhausted or clogged up. (If you drop a watch, you know why it stops running and you don't carry it around from that point on. But watches that stop through lubricant failure do so intermittently, and people commonly carry them around for quite some time in the hope that they'll restart.) The warmth of somebody's hand is often enough to thin the lubricant substantially, so that some of it will flow back to the points that need lubricating and the watch will start running again, though usually only for a short time. Whether or not this is the *actual* explanation of Geller's feat is another question. To settle it, one would have a watchmaker look at the watches prior to their being passed to Uri Geller and thereby test our hypothesis as to the cause of their stopping; and one would also try giving half of them to somebody without any psychic powers but with very hot hands, to see if that person were just as successful.

5   "Professors should not begin a discussion of controversial topics by setting out their 'prejudices,' because this demonstrates professional incompetence" (expanded at some length in the full quotation in Section 7-4, p. 223).

Answer

Although a good point is made here, the line is perhaps a little severe, since one may have general grounds for feeling that one's enthusiasm for certain conclusions slightly exceeds the strength of the evidence, though one hasn't been able to identify a weakness in one's line of argument. In such a situation, it might be argued that one should both recognize that one probably does have a prejudice here and refuse to concede incompetence, since one believes also that the argument possibly is correct; thus one is simply erring on the side of safety and honesty, surely not a bad idea. However, it is hardly a fully scholarly or fully professional response; surely one should have reached the point of being able to identify an adequate argument by the time one is lecturing on it; and if so, one should cut back on one's enthusiasm for a position where the argument does not seem to support the enthusiasm. So the quoted argument seems to be slightly too strong, but not very much so.

Note this is a self-referent argument. What follows from this about the answer I've proposed above?

6 Suppose we discover there's a very much higher incidence of cancer of the uterus among women who are using birth-control pills than among those who are not (that is, we have a high *correlation*). Do we have good grounds for inferring a causal connection? If not, exactly why not, and how could we settle the issue?

Answer

The mere correlation does not give us grounds for inferring a causal connection in general, and in this particular case, it would do so only if no alternative explanations can be thought of. But it's nearly always possible to think of some, which is why the general inference from correlations to causal connections is unsound. In this case, for example, there's a whole string of possibilities. For instance, women using birth-control pills are in a considerably higher economic bracket than those not using them. They will therefore be more likely to be eating certain types of food and engaging in certain types of occupations (particularly in cities) and in different types of sexual activities from those who do not use such pills. So, unless we can rule out all those other alternatives, we cannot begin to make a case for a causal connection. How could we rule out those other alternatives? The easiest way would of course be to use a fully controlled experimental design; almost anything else will only provide weak contributory evidence. Notice that in this case, unlike the smoking case, we can avoid both moral and practical difficulties in the setting up of such a design; we can use volunteers who are willing to be assigned to one of the groups in order to serve the cause of discovering whether these pills do produce cancer.

QUIZ 7-B

1 "Drawing conclusions from information about the mean of a population is just as speculative, or at least probabilistic, as drawing conclusions from data about samples. So what's the point of the distinction between description and inferential statistics?" Analyze as an argument as well as, or in the course of, answering it as a question.

2 Is it statistics, experience, or both that tell you whether a sample of 1,000 or 10,000 citizens is necessary in order to get a good "reading" of attitudes toward the number of children most people want to have?

3 The Texas Bureau of Wild Life Management gets its estimates of desert mammal population by counting the number of carcasses found beside a sample stretch of the desert highway. Discuss the pros and cons of this procedure.

4 Are you ever justified in advertising a job for which you stipulate that only whites should apply?

5 and 6 See last paragraphs of Section 7-4, pp. 224-225.

QUIZ 7-C

1 Do electrons really exist, or are they just a "useful fiction"?

2 To what extent and how (if at all) are reasoning skills involved in the creative part of scientific theorizing?

3 Why is *random* allocation of subjects to the experimental and control groups important if one is trying to design an experiment that will identify a cause?

4 What's a test of the honesty of someone who refuses to employ long-haired hippie types in a restaurant on the ground that their hair might get into the food?

5 Answer one question you have previously not answered in the last paragraph of Section 7-2, p. 210.

6 Find an argument from analogy in an advanced textbook; set it out carefully and assess it.

7 What other way, besides thinking up counterexplanations, can lead to refuting an argument? (See p. 217.)

8 What's the remote possibility that makes the experimental design of the second paragraph of p. 224 not quite watertight? How could you tighten it up? Could you then be confident of the conclusions?

Chapter 8

Extensions and Ramifications

This chapter is just a list of suggestions about directions to go and connections of this subject with others.

8-1 SPEED REASONING

Argument analysis is a laborious business. One scarcely ever gets a good analysis of a serious argument until the third draft. Nevertheless, getting some good points can often be done quickly, and the more practice one has at doing thorough analysis and having it criticized, the faster one becomes at hitting key points swiftly and expressing them clearly and forcefully. For some years I have taught a course called Speed Reasoning at the University of California Extension in San Francisco, assisted at various times by Mary Anne Warren and Bob Ennis. In it, we try to compress a survey of the basic structure of argument analysis and some skill practice into two full days. What remains in most participants' minds from this compression is the outline of the procedure and some ways to do or avoid key moves, plus the conviction that "it can be done," i.e., that quick but reasonably incisive analysis can be achieved *if enough practice is undertaken.* Nobody first watching a film of one of Nadia Comaneci's gymnastic routines on the bars would expect to be able to do it without practice, if then, and intellectual/ verbal skills are no less complex to learn. The extent to which either the physical or the verbal skills depend on some inherent ability is not clear, but most people who work on reasoning skills, even for just two intensive days, show very substantial improvement. Getting a systematic approach and a belief in the possibility of success is half the battle; developing a repertoire of standard traps and counterexamples and the judgment to distinguish be- tween nit-picking and incisive criticism is most of the rest. You have to go for sound basic procedures before you can go for speed; the speed comes with practice, especially practice under time pressure.

One way to improve your skills and your speed is to tape-record some debates or speeches on controversial issues, and then work on them by play- ing back a piece at a time. Gradually, you'll be able to handle each segment of the argument faster, and then you can move to bigger segments, until you can give good replies in the time you would actually have had in real life. Such TV interview shows as "Meet the Press," "Firing Line," or "The Advo- cates" are excellent for this; some of the radio "call-in" shows are, too.

Another practice hint is to make yourself find one example of practical prose to criticize (or praise, for statable reasons) each time you read the daily paper. Even at first, the ads and the letters column will be easy meat. Then you'll progress to the editorials and the columnists and then the news analy- sis features. Do not "do it in your head"! Cut the passage out and tape it to a sheet of paper, mark numbers on it, structure the argument—do the whole thing. Keep a file of these efforts. Look back after a month or so, and you will be amazed at the quality of improvement and at the speed improve- ment.

Doing this with a friend or a group to help is much better. People from the Speed Reasoning course (the Speed Reasoners) have continued to meet in order to sharpen up one another's performance. They started this activity spontaneously and it has proved both durable and enjoyable, as well as effective.

8-2 DECISION STRATEGIES AND REASONING

One of the problems when you get to "the bottom line" of an argument analysis is to decide what action to take. Of course, what risks you take (i.e., how strong an argument you need in order to justify an action) depends on the possible rewards and losses involved. The whole theory of decision mak- ing (and the "theory of games") has developed in the past few decades to assess the kinds of strategies one can adopt in such situations and is a natu- ral extension of the study of reasoning, as well as part of the social sciences.

Within economics, the subject of welfare economics involves the exploration of a number of ways to make a rational subject out of the value-laden private and public policy decisions affecting our economic behavior. Many important distinctions have been developed among types of decision strategy for personal and social decision making. You might want to look up the meaning of "minimax strategy" and "Pareto optimality" in, for example the *International Encyclopedia of the Social Sciences.* Related issues about controlling standards for choices come up in theoretical ethics, and the "categorical imperative" (proposed by Kant) is one example of the attempts to provide general decision strategies there. The Golden Rule is another.

As an exercise, you might see whether you can state the principle of choice that justifies your crossing a city street, knowing that you might be killed by a car running a light, when you could avoid the crossing by walking half a mile further to a footbridge. Does that principle of choice (e.g., "One should ignore very small risks of death entirely") show that the supporters of the speed limit or of the ban on atomic power plants are irrational? (Quiz 8-B, 1) Is it always irrational to buy lottery (sweepstake) tickets? If not, why not? That is, what principle of choice justifies it? Is the same principle inconsistent with the one quoted (in parentheses) in Quiz 8-B, 1? With the one you gave as your answer to 8-B, 1? With refusing to participate in a chain-letter scheme? (Quiz 8-B, 2, all of them)

8-3 BEHAVIOR CONTROL—THE REASONABLE PERSON

The preceding section concerns principles of choice, and is thus still fairly academic compared to practical suggestions, though it's a step in the practical direction since it's at least concerned with choices rather than *beliefs.* But there still remains the problem of translating choices into actions; and in many cases, it's a real problem. One may rationally "choose," that is, "decide" to give up smoking, but one may still be a long way from being able to implement the choice. The true addict is often said to be wholly incapable of implementing that decision.

Just as one can make a study of *decision* strategies, one can also make a study of *implementation* strategies, of how to get the choice or the decision translated into action. And this study is what leads to a number of the expensive services that are now available to assist you in improving your reading or study habits, reducing weight, getting exercise, or giving up smoking, drinking, drugs, or gambling. These "applied behavior modification" approaches are often somewhat more optimistic in their advertising than their results justify, but they are also very often effective—far more often, on the face of the evidence, than most traditional approaches, like psychoanalysis, which are sometimes used to tackle these "behavior problems." It is part of a complete approach to reasoning to look carefully at this area, since it constitutes the slip between the cup and the lip for many decisions. Because that slip so often occurs, people are often motivated to judge reasoning as largely irrelevant to practical action. Of course, it shouldn't be, and it needn't be, provided one follows through all the way to the action level, at every step applying the standards of rationality.

For example, one can rationally analyze the problems of the addict, noticing that the loss of the capacity to act in accordance with reason is extremely localized. Alcoholics are often said to be unable to resist the offer or opportunity of a drink when under stress. (Even more plausibly, they are said not to be able to resist the chance of a second drink after taking one.) But alcoholics have not lost the capacity to pick up a telephone, or any of their other abilities (except in very advanced cases). Hence, it is perfectly possible for an alcoholic to call for help when feeling the temptation to drink is about to become overwhelming. One of the Alcoholics Anonymous strategies is to provide a hot line to an emergency squad who will rush right over and provide diversions and support to prevent a drinking episode from beginning. That's a rational solution to the problem, not a sign that reason is irrelevant to practical problems.

We have often spent time in class on "feasible pathfinding" procedures for coping with irrational behavior of this and other kinds. The first point to convince oneself of is that the conventional "addict" is not very different from you and me, except for a matter of degree. There is no real basis for the idea that addicts are suffering from some physiological hypersensitivity that makes them either "sick" or victims of misfortune and hence not responsible for their situation. There's nothing physiological about gambling, and gambling addicts have just the same general symptoms as other addicts. There's nothing physically special about water or Coke, but there are known cases of addiction to both; the symptoms are grossly excessive consumption or use despite serious adverse side-effects and the wish to "cut down," plus withdrawal symptoms if the supply is eliminated. Start looking at your own behavior: If there's overeating, staying up too late to watch bad TV shows, reading garbage-type escapist literature, playing pool when homework presses, or compulsive buying sprees, you're an addict. Finding your way out of such habits ("addictions") is a matter of finding a behavior pathway through a sequence of those choice points where you can make and carry out the "best" decision, which will eventually lead you to safe territory. Suppose you have to finish a homework assignment; it's important, it's feasible, it's not even all that dull. But you know from previous experience that there's just no way you're going to get it done by just going home and doing it. There are too many alluring alternatives, or even unalluring ones that begin to look alluring. Start looking for ways to commit yourself to some course of action which (1) you can perfectly well do, and (2) will lead to doing the assignment. For example, you can easily decide to spend the evening at the library (public or campus), and that may restrict your goof-off tendencies enough to get the job done. If that isn't tough enough, maybe you have to make a contract with someone in the same situation, with $20 riding on it and whoever doesn't do it paying the other. If $20 won't work, maybe $50 will. Or can you arrange a study date, the deal being three hours' work before going for a late snack? Here your self-respect when under the eyes of someone you value is the lever you use on yourself. And so on—the procedure of pathfinding is analogous to assumption hunting or argument construction in that you're trying to balance off the feasible with the successful, and your imagination can suggest to you a series of pathways to be explored. Very few people, if any, are beyond the possibility of finding their way out of the bad-habit maze, certainly on important occasions and, if it's serious enough, for good. As usual, it helps to make it a joint program with someone else.

Doing this with respect to bad habits of thought as well as bad "social habits" is part of what we expect of a "reasonable person." The phrase connotes a lack of excesses, of prejudices; a commitment to moderation (not meaning passivity or stick-in-the-middle-of-the-road), as well as to rational thought at the preaction level.

8-4 FLOWCHARTS, FORTRAN, FORMALISMS, AND FORWARDS

Where else can you go from here? Perhaps straight on to some professional program, perhaps in the humanities or the arts, in pure science, or in teaching. But there are some little excursions, apart from those already listed, that are worth considering and that carry on the development of your own skills in, and understanding of, reasoning. The obvious ones are the statistics and experimental design courses, which expand on some of the scientific inference discussions we've started here; and the symbolic logic courses, which develop the abstract principles of certain types of formal reasoning into subjects of great interest in their own right. Perhaps less obviously, there are courses in business schools and computer science departments that also tie in. Learning a computer programming language, like FORTRAN, APL, ALGOL, BASIC, or any other, involves an intellectual discipline that deserves more recognition than it has so far received as a branch of practical reasoning. It would be my guess that you would probably be more likely to improve your problem analysis skill (at least) if you pick up a programming language than a formal logic course or two. In any case, it's worth considering, especially because of its tremendous "instrumental utility," that is, because it is so valuable for many other reasons, including research, business, and applied science.

Somewhere or other on a campus, someone is (usually several people are) teaching flow-charting. It may be, and probably is, part of the computer science course, at least in one version. But you may also find it showing up in a management course in the business school, perhaps under the name PERT-charting. The whole subject of analyzing *sequences* of decisions and actions, evaluations and costing, in a way that clarifies responsibilities and lead-times, has been extensively developed in recent years and, if not used obsessively, can be very valuable. It is just an extension of the reasoning approach into a particular area.

Those of you interested in the fiscal dimension of reasoning—for example, cost analysis in various forms, and its ties to management through various management information systems such as PPBS (Program Planning and Budgeting Systems), will find these covered, relatively superficially, in accounting courses, and relatively better in management courses with a strong practical emphasis. The careful working out of the arguments for alternative approaches to the "discount rate of return," for example, will prove fascinating for those of an analytical and inquiring (and practical) turn of mind, though far, far removed from the usual academic company of a logic course.

Somewhere on a big campus, perhaps in the School of Public Policy, perhaps in the School of Education, you'll find a course on *evaluation*, which will pick up and develop the whole procedure of reasoning-to-an-evaluative-conclusion, something we've talked about in connection with the last step of argument analysis where you are evaluating an *argument,* and on a number of other occasions. Evaluation as a discipline is pretty new, or at least has taken on a new form in recent years; you'll find it a very natural extension of what we've been doing here.

And there are other such extensions: operations research is one; some of the courses in applied ethics, in propaganda analysis, and in rhetoric are others; even some courses in historiography. They turn up in many disciplines, whenever someone begins to look hard at the reasoning process.

If you are within range of a law school, you may find someone teaching legal reasoning (the former Attorney General of the United States, Edward Levi, is the author of a brief and highly respected book on that subject). Nobody ties all these together so that you can major in reasoning, but that's an idea worth considering, and, on most campuses today, special interdepartmental majors can be arranged.

If you're not on a campus, it's easy to convert all that I've been saying into a reading program and a library development program of the greatest value to you now and later.

This is one subject which, approached sensibly and seriously, will never be short of credentials at both the academic and the practical end. May it continue to attract you and infuse your thoughts and actions!

QUIZ 8-A

Questions 1 and 2 (several parts) will be found in Section 8-2, paragraph 2.

For Question 3, see if you can select, and justify your selection of, one further course (or solid text) that you will undertake in order to improve your reasoning skills. Make it one you would not have chosen if you had not taken this course (or read this text).

Index

Index